Getting Started in Elementary Music Education

Getting Started in Elementary Music Education

LOIS N. HARRISON

University of Oregon

PRENTICE-HALL, INC., *Englewood Cliffs, New Jersey 07632*

Library of Congress Cataloging in Publication Data

HARRISON, LOIS N.
   Getting started in elementary music education.

   1. School music—Instruction and study.
I. Title.
MT1.H23 1983   372.8'7   82-10222
ISBN   0-13-354852-X

Editorial/production supervision by Dan Mausner
Cover design by Mario Piazza
Cover photo by Harry Houchins,
      University of Oregon photographer
Manufacturing buyer: Raymond Keating

Printed in the United States of America

10 9 8 7 6 5 4 3 2 1

ISBN 0-13-354852-X

PRENTICE-HALL INTERNATIONAL, INC., *London*
PRENTICE-HALL OF AUSTRALIA PTY. LIMITED, *Sydney*
EDITORA PRENTICE-HALL DO BRASIL, LTDA., *Rio de Janeiro*
PRENTICE-HALL CANADA INC., *Toronto*
PRENTICE-HALL OF INDIA PRIVATE LIMITED, *New Delhi*
PRENTICE-HALL OF JAPAN, INC., *Tokyo*
PRENTICE-HALL OF SOUTHEAST ASIA PTE. LTD., *Singapore*
WHITEHALL BOOKS LIMITED, WELLINGTON, *New Zealand*

To my husband, Nelden H. Ward

Contents

Preface

This book is intended for prospective teachers who are enrolled in a methods class and intend to work with elementary school children (grades one through six.) It can be used by both music majors and elementary education majors. A few chapters are designed especially for the elementary classroom teacher, but they may serve the music major as guides for developing in-service training for classroom teachers. This book may also be useful for any teacher who has not taken elementary music methods in college, for the music supervisor to use with beginning teachers, for administrators responsible for supervision of personnel involved in teaching elementary music, or for private and public instrumental teachers studying the instruction their students receive from other teachers or seeking ideas to be used in their own teaching.

This book deals with techniques most needed to implement a comprehensive music program in elementary school. Its use enables students in methods classes to participate in class demonstrations illustrating activities such as those described rather than being tied to note taking. Since college class time is often insufficient to cover the varied subject matters of elementary music teaching, the text attempts to provide insights into areas that may have been omitted during class time.

The ideas presented here are starting points, samples of methods to help the teacher bring music to children. The reader is urged to select the most useful techniques and then to work to improve them. The teacher must use these procedures creatively so that they are most effective for the special group of students in each music class. Chapters will frequently conclude with Recommended Readings treating the topics in greater detail and Suggested Projects involving the prospective teacher in the subject matter.

This text is not intended to teach music fundamentals to the teacher. The following skills are prerequisites for the person who is to use it effectively:

1. Sufficient knowledge of the elements and structure of music to be able to identify and describe musical components from both written scores and aural presentations.
2. Ability to use music notation.
3. Experience in improvisation and creativity with music.
4. Performance skill and accuracy in playing and singing the melody, harmony, and rhythm of materials at the level to be used by elementary school children.

Mastery of music fundamentals and skill in making music are acquired gradually. The prospective teacher is urged to become involved in situations conducive to musical development such as college classes, private lessons, and musical ensembles before studying methods of teaching music to children.

These books, or others like them, can help the teacher if review is needed before enrolling in the music methods course:

MARTIN, GARY M. *Basic Concepts in Music.* Belmont, CA: Wadsworth Publishing Company, 1980. A programed text covering fundamental musical principles.
NYE, ROBERT E., and BJORNAR BERGETHON, *Basic Music.* Englewood Cliffs, NJ: Prentice-Hall, Inc., 1981. An integrated approach to developing musicianship through performing music, including terminology and theory as the need arises.
WACHHAUS, GUSTAV and TERRY LEE KUHN, *Fundamental Classroom Music Skills.* New York: Holt, Rinehart and Winston, 1979. Learning to read music through developing a variety of music performance skills.

It is hoped that this book will help prospective teachers of elementary music to

1. Become confident and competent in teaching musical skills to children.
2. Develop perspective on a variety of possibilities for musical participation by children.
3. Communicate positive attitudes toward music as an integral part of children's lives.

Many people have helped with this book. I am especially grateful to thousands of elementary school children who discovered music through the processes described herein and at the same time helped to create and refine those processes; hundreds of prospective music teachers, both music specialists and classroom teachers who asked the right questions; many colleagues who suggested and shared; Heidi Brennan, who initiated writing schedules with confidence that they would be met; Edmund Soule, an extraordinary editor and teacher; Gloria Hodges, my typist and good friend; and Nelden Ward, without whose help and loving encouragement the book could not have been written!

LOIS N. HARRISON
Eugene, Oregon

1 Music as an Integral Part of the Child's Life

From the moment children are born, certain aspects of music are a natural part of their lives. An adult croons to soothe the baby and rhythmically bounces the small one after feeding is finished. As little children grow, adults entertain them with games, many of which involve rhythmic and melodic components. Self-initiated activities of the young may be described as the beginnings of music. Much of their sound making includes delightful improvisation that develops in a nurturing environment. Music appears as a basic part of human experience. Children become involved in singing, playing, and moving. These musical avenues provide means of expression and enjoyment not available through any other medium. When an environment that nurtures creativity is maintained, the child can be expressive in ways uniquely available through music. As appropriate listening experiences are furnished for the child, more and more possibilities are opened from which the budding student can choose associations with sound that are pertinent and satisfactory.

One of the most important goals of the elementary school is that of equipping each child with skills leading to meaningful musical performance and discriminative listening both in school and in later life. Since student aspirations and capabilities vary widely, music instruction faces the challenge of encompassing in its activities all students, both the slow learner

1

and the talented. The great variety of tastes that the world has developed in music adds an additional challenge: to give students an exposure to a wide selection of music so that their horizons may be broadened beyond their immediate time and culture.

As the teacher works with the children, the primary emphasis should be on music as a worthwhile subject that will contribute much to their lives. It is studied by the children because of its own unique characteristics. No other subject provides aural experiences that can compare to music's evocation of response through rhythm and expression.

Reimer describes the combination of musical perception and musical reaction as musical aesthetic experience. He explains that general education in music

> consists primarily of developing the abilities of every child to have aesthetic experiences for perception and reaction. The "heart of the matter" in music education is to help every child experience the expressiveness of sound as fully as he is capable of doing so.[1]

A secondary emphasis in music education is the role that music plays in support of other areas of learning. Historical figures have viewed music as valuable because of its effect upon varied human attributes such as the moral character of the young (Aristotle), religious beliefs (Luther), and good health (Horace Mann). Contemporary teachers and students realize how much more easily phonics, colors, numbers, seasons, rhymes, and names are learned when they are presented in a musical setting. Music helps to set a mood for the class so that the children are more willing to work. Musical experiences that require cooperation give the children practice in learning to work together. Music can help to enhance the spirit of an entire school when the children sing together. These supportive uses of music as well as others like them help the child to learn through music; still, it should be kept in mind that these are very important *secondary* emphases. The *primary* reason for including music in the curriculum is that every child should learn to build upon the basic, natural relationship to sound through which he or she develops expressive capability. Music education is designed to help the student develop more sophisticated ways of musical expression appropriate to the maturing individual.

Recommended Readings

GLENN, NEAL E., AND EDGAR M. TURRENTINE, *Introduction to Advanced Study in Music Education.* Dubuque, IA: Wm. C. Brown Company, Publishers, 1969. The first part of this book contains excerpts from writings by historically important figures who commented upon music and music education.

---

[1]Bennett Reimer, *A Philosophy of Music Education* (Englewood Cliffs, NJ: Prentice-Hall, Inc., 1970), p. 114.

MOOREHEAD, GLADYS E., AND DONALD POND, *Music of Young Children.* Santa Barbara, CA: Pillsbury Foundation for Advancement of Music Education, 1978. This book consists of reprints of studies which were made from 1937 to 1948 with children from two to six years of age.

REIMER, BENNETT, *A Philosophy of Music Education.* Englewood Cliffs, NJ: Prentice-Hall, Inc., 1970. Discussion of a philosophy of music education based upon the aesthetics of music.

2 Manage the Learning Environment

To teach music, the teacher must maintain a class environment in which learning can take place. The beginning teacher cannot develop the necessary techniques from reading this chapter. It is recommended that the beginning instructor observe teachers who are successful in classroom management, read about discipline and child psychology, participate in workshops, and take college classes that deal with classroom management and related topics. This chapter serves to highlight the importance of skills related to classroom management for every teacher. Among those are skills of consistency, expectation, ignoring, analyzing, prescribing, evaluation, and positive reinforcement.

Consistency. One of the most valuable skills for the teacher to develop is that of consistency. If the children know ahead what is expected of them and if the expectations are maintained consistently, it is easier for them to function. If it is made clear that there is a time for playing instruments and a time for keeping quiet, all the children need to remember is the signal for changing from playing to not playing. It can be as simple as the teacher explaining: "When I am ready to talk to all of you, please keep your instruments quiet." A signal, for example a chord on the piano, tells the children the teacher is ready.

4

Contingencies to help with this understanding will have to be made clear also: "The people who can't keep their instruments quiet will lose them today." While this sounds like a threat, it is only a threat if the teachers uses it like one. When carried out consistently, it becomes an expected part of living in an orderly environment. There is a time for quiet, and there is a time for making music. The quiet time is made so by people remembering the rules. The contingencies are designed to help people who forget or ignore the rules.

If you are the music teacher, the learning environment for which you are responsible will be affected by children entering from many varied classrooms. Unless there has been a concerted effort on the part of the entire faculty, no two homeroom groups will share the same specific expectations or ways of achieving the expectations. What they will all share in music class is the need for an orderly situation in which the children and the teachers can function to the best of their ability. The music teacher is well advised to determine the expectations of each classroom teacher so that procedures followed in each of the other rooms are not contradicted.

Some faculties work together to develop procedures that will help them to maintain consistent behavior not only in the classrooms, but also in the cafeteria, on the playground, in the hallways, and throughout the school. These procedures are communicated to the students and to the parents so that they are aware of them and the contingencies that go with them.

Expectation.   As has been mentioned, expectation is necessary for both the student and the teacher as part of the appropriate environment for the music class. One of the problems associated with the learning of music is that certain activities do not lend themselves to the kind of environment that is absolutely necessary for other musical experiences; creative, independent music making by individuals or small groups of children produces a sound level in the classroom that is far higher than the quiet needed for ear training while listening for variations in timbre, pitch, harmony, form, or the like. Adults who have not been initiated into an experimental working environment sometimes have difficulty with it, especially upon experiencing it for the first time. It is important that the adult become aware of the musical learning that can take place in what may seem to be a noisy room and temper expectations accordingly. There is a difference between noise and the sound of children working at many musical tasks simultaneously. The children do not seem to be bothered because they concentrate upon their own tasks, seemingly oblivious to what else is happening. An orderly classroom may not be a quiet one, but it needs to be one in which children are able to participate in active music making.

The task of the music teacher is to help the children maintain the environment that is needed for experimentation and performance and then to switch the environmental expectation when it is necessary to have quiet in order to be able to concentrate upon listening. A further complication is that the children often need to change swiftly from their production of sound, as when singing together, to a listening posture, as when being given directions. It is not easy for some children to contain themselves so that their responses are appropriate to the immediate activity. Successful teachers need to make clear the expectations for that particular class and then help the children to make the appropriate responses. If most of the class time is to be spent in concentrated listening, the teacher will need to plan times within the lesson in which the students can move, sing, or play to release their normal childhood energies in an appropriate fashion.

Ignoring poor behavior.   Ignoring poor behavior exhibited by some of the children may be the best treatment. Ignoring sometimes extinguishes poor behavior because the child does not get the attention that he or she is demanding. Ignoring may save the teacher from making negative comments. Although negative comments are sometimes necessary, they have more strength if they are exceptions rather than rules.

Analysis.   There is a tendency for teachers to respond immediately to the classroom situation as it arises. The response is sometimes an impulsive one. Unless an emergency is involved, more beneficial long-range results may accrue if the teacher can analyze the behavior of the class over a period of time, trying to identify patterns that may be present before deciding what action to take.

Prescribing.   After having analyzed the classroom situation, the teacher needs to decide on appropriate procedures. Effective teachers sometimes describe the situation to the children and then enlist their help in determining how to handle the situation. This is an ineffective plan if it arises simply because the teacher does not know what else to do. Whether a plan is evolved by the teacher, by teachers throughout the school, or cooperatively by the students and the teacher, the plan must be made clear to everyone and the contingencies defined so that the students will know what is expected of them.

Evaluation.   No matter how successful the procedures are that have been implemented in the classroom, they must be evaluated. Contingencies and procedures may have to be changed to fit more closely the evolving environment of the classroom.

Madsen and Madsen have described a process that uses analysis, prescribing, and evaluation.

1. *Pinpoint:* It is necessary to pinpoint explicitly the behavior that is to be eliminated or established. This takes place at many different levels relating to many differentiated behaviors. It leads to a hierarchical

arrangement of skills and behaviors based on expected specific behavioral goals. Do not deal with intangibles or ideas. If the behavior cannot in some way be both *observed* and *measured*, then you can never know if it has been either established or unlearned.

2. *Record:* List the specified behaviors in time intervals (seconds, minutes, hours, A.M., etc.) and thereby establish a precise record from which to proceed. Keep the record accurate. Do not guess; be scientific. As maladaptive responses are eliminated, or decreased, more time can be devoted to more productive learning.

3. *Consequate:* Set up the external environmental contingencies (including primarily your own personal responses) and proceed with the program. Contingencies include: approval, withdrawal of approval, disapproval, threat of disapproval, and ignoring. Reinforcement techniques can be: words (spoken or written), expressions (facial or bodily), closeness (nearness or touching), activities (social or individual), and things (materials, food, playthings, awards). Remember that when you ignore, behaviors often initially increase (sometimes for long periods) before they are eliminated.

4. *Evaluate:* Be prepared to stay with a program long enough to ascertain its effectiveness. Compare records after consequating with records taken before. Is the behavior increasing, decreasing, or remaining the same? Learn from your mistakes. And: *"If at first you don't succeed..."*— *Well, you know.*[1]

Many of Madsen and Madsen's pinpoint studies describe familiar situations that may occur in music class.

Pinpoint: Unfinished assignments, bothering neighbors, playing (2nd grade, two boys referred by teacher).

Record: Trained observers recorded average of 47% inappropriate behavior.

Consequate: Teacher and class formulated rules. Rules repeated six times per day for two weeks.

Evaluate: Little decrease in inappropriate behavior (average 40%).

Note: Apparently just knowing (being able to repeat rules) is not effective.

Consequate II: Teacher attempted to ignore inappropriate behaviors (teacher not entirely successful). Continued to repeat class rules every day.

Evaluate II: Behavior worsened. Average inappropriate behavior for four observations 69%.

Consequate III: Teacher praised prosocial behavior, repeated classroom rules, ignored inappropriate behavior.

Evaluate III: Inappropriate behavior *decreased* (average of 20%). Combination of procedures effective in reducing inappropriate behavior.

[1]Charles H. Madsen, Jr. and Clifford K. Madsen, *Teaching/Discipline: A Positive Approach for Educational Development,* 3rd edition © 1981 by Allyn & Bacon, Inc., Boston, p. 71. Reprinted with permission. The pinpoint principles were adapted by Madsen and Madsen from the work of O. R. Lindsley, "Teaching Teachers to Teach," a paper presented at the American Psychological Association Convention, New York, September 1966.

Consequate IV: Teacher instructed to act as she had in September. (Observers monitored entire year.)

Evaluate IV: Inappropriate behavior increased same day teacher changed (averaged 38%).

Consequate V: Rules, ignoring, and praise reinstated for remainder of school year.

Evaluate V: Inappropriate behavior again decreased (averaged only 15% for last eight-week period).

Note: Many teachers who believe they use more approval than disapproval do not (monitored by trained observers in classroom). It is necessary to practice delivering responses and to give yourself time cues or cues written on material you are teaching. A mark on every page can remind you to "catch someone being good." It is interesting to note that one boy reported in this study was seen during the entire year by a professional counselor. This boy responded in the same way to consequences as did the other boy who was not seen. It would seem that the teacher is capable of handling many behavioral problems generally referred to counselors, if responses are well developed and applied contingently.[2]

Pinpoint: Disruptive noise (large class).

Record: Absolute cacophony. *No* recording able to take place.

Consequate: Many children removed from class until class size became manageable. Teacher planned specific assignments and scheduled consequences. After small number of children brought under control, one child at a time added to class. Procedure started with limited number of children during special period while others normally out of room— later extended to entire day.

Evaluate: Teachers indicated procedure very effective.

Note: Teachers also stated that initial control of the *entire* group was absolutely impossible.[3]

Positive reinforcement.   In nurturing the learning environment, the teacher can contribute to the attractiveness of the situation by providing lots of positive reinforcement for the children. Although it seems more immediately necessary to shout at a child who is in trouble, complimenting the same child for cooperating has a more positive impact. When using positive reinforcement with the children, be sure that it is accurate and well deserved. To say "You all did a wonderful job on that piece" when three students did nothing at all is not an appropriate teaching procedure. Those three passive students did not deserve to be praised! The observation should have been: "Those of you who sang and played that time were wonderful!" This is a much more accurate statement.

Above all in music class, create a supportive situation in which the

---

[2]Madsen and Madsen, *Teaching/Discipline*, pp. 118–119.
[3]Madsen and Madsen, *Teaching/Discipline*, p. 125.

nonsinger, the child with coordination problems, and the student who needs work in aural discrimination can try to learn. The days when the children were divided into the *crows* and the *canaries* with the former sitting in the corner while the latter gave the program to the parents should have long since disappeared. Find an opportunity to tell each child about progress made so that the young people can feel that they have support in trying to continue to improve. A negative comment from the teacher about one small aspect of incompetence on the part of the child can cause a fear of trying anything musical. Negative feelings formed by the young child are often recalled by adults who do not include music in their lives.

Children learn to make music more expertly by practicing music making. The task of the teacher is to diagnose, to help to encourage the child in creative pursuits, to give ideas when they are needed, and to make it possible for the children to engage in musical activities. The teacher's attitude will be a factor in determining if the child will be an active musician or a nonparticipant.

Even small differences are the cause for celebration through positive reinforcement. Blake's marching with the music for the first time may not seem like much to an adult who has never had any trouble with marching, but to Blake it is a major accomplishment. Susie's first success in matching three pitches in a row seems minimal when considering that she still cannot sing a melodic phrase accurately, but her three matches are wonderful, because this can mean that she is on her way to success. She needs to be told how great her accomplishment is. The entire fifth grade needs to celebrate on the day that they are able to sing in two parts all the way through "I'm Gonna Sing." It's not very sophisticated music and the tonal quality needs improving, but it is the first time that this class has had that kind of success and the children need to feel good about it. Children who do not succeed in music and who do not receive any encouragement not only stop trying but they may turn into severely disruptive members of the class.

The supportive music teacher should have a vocabulary of comments to sustain the spirits of the children in a positive way without being inaccurate musically. When Dale has failed to echo the rhythm pattern again, there is a better chance that he will keep on working if the teacher can say to him: "Not quite right yet, Dale, but you tried harder than you ever have before." When Mary missed her instrumental part, the teacher's comment will help sustain her: "You are such a good sport, Mary. Even when you disappoint yourself, you don't give up."

Perhaps it is because of the artistic nature of music that care must be taken that the students who are involved in its study maintain and develop their positive self-images. The sensitivity of the teacher to the student and the respect that both show for each other are necessary for the creation of a productive environment in the music classroom. The teacher is urged to develop resources and alternatives for nurturing this environment.

Recommended Readings

BECKER, WESLEY C., SIEGFRIED ENGELMANN, AND DON R. THOMAS, *Teaching 1: Classroom Management*. Chicago: Science Research Associates, 1975. This volume is the first of three books that focus on teaching. Its emphasis is upon the use of behavior modification as an aid to effective education.

BELTZ, STEPHEN E., *How to Make Johnny Want to Behave*. Englewood Cliffs, NJ: Prentice-Hall, Inc., 1971. A behavioral approach to child discipline for families.

CANTER, LEE, *Assertive Discipline: Competency Based Resource Materials and Guidelines*. Los Angeles: Canter and Associates, Inc., 1979. A workbook containing materials that can be duplicated to bolster the work described in Canter's book and workshops.

CANTER, LEE AND MARLENE, *Assertive Discipline: A Take-Charge Approach for Today's Educator*. Los Angeles: Canter and Associates, Inc., 1976. A succinct description of a systematic approach to discipline. The author sponsors workshops to acquaint teachers with his work.

DREIKURS, RUDOLF, *Psychology in the Classroom*. New York: Harper & Row, Publishers, Inc., 1968. An alternative approach to behavior modification.

EPSTEIN, CHARLOTTE, *Classroom Management and Teaching: Persistent Problems and Rational Solutions*. Reston, VA: Reston Publishing Co., Inc., 1979. Behavior modification applied to classroom discipline.

KRUMBOLTZ, JOHN D. AND HELEN B., *Changing Children's Behavior*. Englewood Cliffs, NJ: Prentice-Hall, Inc., 1971. Explanation of behavior modification principles and illustrations of their application.

MADSEN, CHARLES H., JR., AND CLIFFORD K., *Teaching/Discipline: a Positive Approach for Educational Development*. Boston: Allyn & Bacon, Inc., 1981. A positive approach for educational development written especially as a guide for the teacher using behavioral principles in the classroom.

STRADLEY, WILLIAM E., AND RICHARD D. ASPINALL, *Discipline in the Junior High/Middle School*. New York: The Center for Applied Research in Education, Inc., 1975. A handbook on discipline for older children that describes specific problems.

WALLEN, CARL J., AND LaDONNA L. WALLEN, *Effective Classroom Management*. Boston: Allyn & Bacon., Inc., 1978. A humanistic look at multidimensional classroom management problems.

Suggested Projects

1. Observe a music classroom and pinpoint behaviors that need attention. Describe the solutions the teacher devises to correct the situations. Evaluate their effectiveness.

2. In teaching your first music lessons, pinpoint potential behavior problems. Apply Madsen and Madsen's four steps to them. Using a cassette tape recorder will help you to analyze class events.

3 *Plan*

THE CURRICULUM

"The curriculum of a school, or a course, or a classroom can be conceived of as a series of planned events that are intended to have educational consequences for one or more students."[1] If the beginning teacher accepts Elliot Eisner's definition as a basis upon which curriculum planning can proceed, the process of working out these events can become an exciting one.

Curriculum guide. A well-written curriculum guide can give a strong sense of security to the beginning teacher by providing direction for learning activities and objectives against which progress can be measured. Every teacher should have goals for the students to achieve by the end of the school year. While masterful plans may have already been written, they cannot apply to every situation because the time allotted to music class and the capabilities of the students vary widely. Furthermore, curriculum guides should be in a constant state of revision. To be effective, they must

[1]Elliot W. Eisner, *The Educational Imagination* (New York: Macmillan Publishing Co., Inc., 1979), p. 39.

be flexible and allow for the yearly changes in class populations. The guide suggests alternatives as the need for them arises. It is a flexible document that contains an abundance of ideas for achieving definite objectives. Many of these objectives can be stated clearly in terms that can be measured.

The curriculum guide should include goals, affective components, activities, content, timing and sequence suggestions, and means of evaluation.

Resources.   The teacher who is developing a curriculum for children in music can turn to many resources for help in getting started.

1. The school system in which the teacher is working may have a curriculum guide. Even though it may be dated, it will give an idea of what has been intended in previous musical work with the children.
2. Music textbooks written for elementary school children are of great influence upon the curriculum. They often have formal scope and sequence charts. If they do not, curriculum information can be found by analyzing the contents of the books themselves. States such as Oregon, California, Arizona, Texas, Oklahoma, and Florida that practice textbook adoption try to identify quality books to be used with children. Although the teacher who is developing a curriculum guide will want to begin with the current texts, it will be interesting and helpful to pay some attention to older books, especially those that are available for use in the school. The teacher should keep informed about new books to be aware of new trends as represented in those books, even though the school may not purchase all of them for the children.
3. Some states publish guidelines that describe desirable curricular practices. They may also publish evaluative materials that help to analyze the effectiveness of their music programs. Oregon's *Self-Evaluation Checklists* are good examples. This kind of publication indicates clearly what should be included in the music curriculum.
4. Experienced teachers are often generous in sharing their observations concerning what children can and will accomplish during the course of a year.
5. The children themselves shape the curriculum through demonstrating their abilities, accomplishments, and enthusiasm. Attention to these student musical processes is vital to the development of a beneficial music curriculum.
6. The teacher's creativity makes it possible to develop a curriculum that will enable students to make music effectively and enthusiastically in most situations. The teacher's musical and pedagogical capability as reflected in both curriculum design and implementation can inspire the children toward high achievement. Conversely, the teacher lacking capability and enthusiasm can hold the children back.

Cooperation.   Classroom teachers sometimes feel apprehensive about teaching music. These teachers need to plan a music curriculum that emphasizes their strengths. Whatever they can do well, they should share freely with the children. If they lack skills, they should work cooperatively with the music teacher to cover neglected areas or, if there is no music teacher, either share the respective talents of other classroom teachers or enlist the aid of interested parents and community members. The enjoyment generated by the classroom teacher when working with music will communicate itself to the students. Any lack of enjoyment will also be felt; therefore, the classroom teacher needs to concentrate on sharing in areas of strongest musical effectiveness. Cooperative planning with other classroom teachers may produce a curriculum guide with less emphasis on certain areas of music one year that will be compensated for in the next year when the students have moved on to work with another teacher.

A curriculum plan that has been produced by someone other than the teacher who is expected to use it may have negligible value. The realities of the children's capabilities, the interests of both the children and the teacher, the time that can be given to the study of music, and the materials and equipment available will all have modifying influence upon the actual content of the curriculum. The beginning teacher is encouraged to become involved in developing a curriculum that adequately reflects the expectations, needs, and realities of the individual students, the school, and the community of which they are a part. If the school district has a music coordinator or supervisor, that person may be interested in revising the existing curriculum plan in cooperation with all the music teachers or in creating an entirely new one. The implication is not that the existing plan is inadequate. It may be excellent for the teachers and children who have been using it, but the arrival of a new teacher in the system brings different talents and perspectives to the music program that will invite re-evaluation of current practices in light of different personnel. Cooperative examination of the curriculum guide can help the new teacher to understand curricular practices of that school system and invite re-examination of the curriculum by the teachers who have been using it.

Whether or not the music teacher has the benefit of working with other music teachers on the curriculum for all the elementary schools, that individual should seek opportunities to work cooperatively with the classroom teachers. This has the advantage of combining the experience of teachers who know the children and the community expectations with the ideas of a person who may bring fresh insight into the contribution of the music program to the children's lives. The classroom teacher can help the music teacher immeasurably in pointing out the potential of the students, in cautioning about their lack of expertise, and in sharing strategies. The music teacher can help the classroom teacher in implementing aspects of the curriculum that need to be included but which the classroom teacher lacks the confidence to handle. Often the music teacher can introduce musical concepts and the classroom teacher can work to strengthen them. They can help each other in being sure that the music curriculum for the children is planned and carried out to the greatest advantage for these young musicians.

The curriculum design with which the music teacher works must be concerned with all grade levels. The classroom teachers are concerned most strongly with one level. Time spent in discussing the total program will give all the teachers a sense of continuity within the program. Smaller group meetings will enable the development of curricular practices for specific age levels.

Goals.   Describing the purposes of the curriculum in general terms is essential to good planning. An overall goal for the music program may be to equip the children to be musicians who can function independently by the end of the sixth grade. Goals that contribute to that overall intent could be

1. to give the children expressive experiences in music.
2. to develop performance skills through singing, playing, and moving.
3. to encourage creativity through using the elements of music.
4. to foster perceptive listening so the student can discuss the elements of music.

Curriculum planners identify the goals that are appropriate for the situations in which they are working. They will also state specific objectives related to each of these goals that will then be used by the teachers as they construct lesson plans.

Objectives related to goal 1:

a. The children will vary tempi and dynamics related to a specific piece of music.
b. The children will read dynamic markings that are indicated on the notation of a specific piece of music.
c. The children will design an orchestration using percussion instruments that enhance their interpretation of a selected piece of music.

Affective aspects.   These may be the most difficult components of the curriculum to describe and certainly among the most difficult to measure. Part of the curriculum guide should speak to these important qualities, which may not be measurable. Enjoyment and appreciation are affective terms often associated with music study. How can they be measured? The study of music would be less than adequate if appreciation and enjoyment were not part of the child's association with music. Perhaps the best solution when developing a music curriculum is to describe aspects of that art that can be measured in behavioral terms as precisely as possible. In addition, affective components that contribute to the planned curricular events should be included consistently as part of the experiential vocabulary that develops aesthetic perceptions and reactions.

At some stages of their lives, a measure of music's value to children may be only that they are involved. Measures of specific musical behavior in a particular situation may be inappropriate when weighed against the fact that the child is participating in a musical experience that has internal meaning and cannot be measured or interpreted by anyone else.

Activities. Music lends itself to interest in curricular events by the nature of the variety of activities in which children can be involved. The music curriculum for the elementary school should include these activities:

1. *Singing* begins with simple unison songs with a relatively limited range and uncomplicated rhythm in the first grade. By sixth grade, the students have progressed to songs that have sophisticated rhythms, at least two-part harmony and ranges that accommodate high voices as well as voices that are beginning to change.
2. *Playing* a note or two on a triangle, some steady beats on a drum, or an elementary ostinato on a pitched percussion instrument are among the first attractive musical experiences for children. By sixth grade, activities should include playing chordal accompaniments on the autoharp, simple chord progressions on the guitar, songs on the recorder, and creative activities on both pitched and unpitched percussion instruments.
3. *Moving* to music allows the student to express creativity and demonstrate conceptualization in the lower grades, while in the upper grades it may be more structured as in dance forms and conducting.
4. *Listening* is a function of all musical involvement. Its contributions can be defined broadly as
    a. Ear training, which in the first grade draws attention to identification of sounds in the environment and pitches to be matched and, by sixth grade, includes identifying salient elements of music and taking simple dictation.
    b. Listening to literature, which gradually exposes the children to music of different styles, periods, and cultures.
5. *Creating* in first grade begins with such activities as making sound effects, singing stories, and playing creative games. By sixth grade, it has progressed to writing songs and musical plays and to combining instruments in creative orchestrations.
6. *Reading* begins in the first grade with readiness activities in which the children's attention is directed to simple visual representations of music. By sixth grade, attention has been given to notation so that the student can realize accurate re-creations of the intended sound.
7. *Writing* music begins with activities as simple as drawing slashes on the chalkboard to represent beats. By sixth grade, the children should be able to notate creative efforts that can be passed onto others.

Content.   The activities just described are the vehicles through which music is experienced. The content of the curriculum is the music. It is made up of elements that can be isolated for the purposes of describing them and for developing skill in performing and identifying them. It is important to remember that music in its most complete expression consists of all the elements interacting with one another.

Constituent elements are those essential components of which music is comprised. *Rhythm* and *melody* are the two most basic elements with which the children begin to work. Melody is the aspect of pitch with which the children have their earliest direct contact. As accompanying instruments and, later, other voices are used, *harmony* is added to the children's experience. The way in which these elements are organized, the phrases and sections of pieces that result from the way they combine, their repetition and contrasts, all contribute to the structure of music, which is known as *form.*

The expressive elements of music generally accessible to children are

Tempo, the speed at which the music is performed.
Dynamics, the degree of volume which is used.
Timbre, the tone color or quality of the voices and instruments.

Timing.   Because of the varying musical capability of each class, one of the most difficult factors in designing musical events for children is the determination of the timing of these experiences. This is especially acute when it becomes evident that some of the children are ready to move into new experiences, when others give little evidence that their musical conceptualization of skill development has readied them for the next step in music making. Some schools attempt to group children homogeneously. These groupings are generally made on the basis of reading or math skills. Unfortunately, these groupings may be inappropriate for music and so do not help in putting children in groups that will enable them to progress together.

Where it is possible, much individualization is to be encouraged within the class. Expectations for the year are to be considered desirable goals, but they should be adapted to meet the particular needs of the current population. Some children learn well when they are working as a class. Other students in certain activities exhibit differences that are so great that they must be grouped into smaller sections or must have a high degree of one-to-one contact with the teacher.

While the curriculum should have clearly described objectives, it should be used with both understanding and flexibility. It is very exciting for the teacher to find at the end of the year that improved attention to student needs has succeeded in bringing the children to approximately the same level of musical achievement this year as the class did last year, even though group ability initially seemed to be much lower and the class was involved in markedly different activities from the previous group.

Sequence. The sequencing of musical concepts can be described generally for the children, but the teacher should be warned that each child does not learn at the same rate as the others or in the same sequence. The spiral curriculum described by Bruner suggests that simple forms of subject matter should be introduced to young children and then reintroduced with greater complexity as the child grows. Ideally, this procedure applied to music enables children with varying capabilities to share the same musical experience with the expectation that they will gain from it the degree of learning that is appropriate for each individual.

A second warning to the beginning teacher is that the acquisition of a concept by a child is strengthened by calling attention to it many times. One lesson dealing with a concept has little chance of seeing it established.

The following listing gives an idea of sequential presentation that is generally appropriate for elementary school children. A new teacher will find it useful to explore the concepts with the children to identify those that have been established and those that should be introduced. It is futile to invite an older child to discriminate between duple and triple meter if no concept of beat has been established.

Rhythm will be established as an element associated with melody and harmony but also as an independent factor expressed through the use of the body and unpitched percussion instruments.

DEVELOPMENT OF RHYTHM CONCEPTS

Beat
Rhythm of the melody
Accented beat
Duration: long and short, even and uneven
Patterns: repeated and contrasting
Duple and triple meter
Division of the beat into equal and unequal parts
Durations longer than the beat
Syncopation
Compound meter
Changing meters

Melody can be used as a vehicle for songs and instrumental pieces, but it is also focused upon as thematic material when listening to music.

DEVELOPMENT OF MELODIC CONCEPTS

Direction: up, down, stays the same
High, low, middle
Steps, skips, stays the same
Patterns: repeated and contrasting
Pentatonic
Major, minor, other
Cadential expectations

Harmony will be created both vocally and instrumentally.

DEVELOPMENT OF HARMONIC CONCEPTS

Single and multiple sounds
Melody with accompaniment
Ostinato
Pentatonic
Descants
Major, minor, other
Chords: I, I-V$_7$, I-IV-V$_7$
Rounds
Partner songs
Two part
Three part
Monophonic, polyphonic, homophonic

Form represents the integration of the other elements into identifiable structure in music.

DEVELOPMENT OF CONCEPTS OF FORM

Phrase
Patterns: repeated and contrasting
Cadence
Sections
Repetition and contrast
Verse and refrain
Two part (A B)
Three Part (A B A)
Introduction, interlude, coda
Rondo
Theme and variations
Free
Sonata allegro
Fugue

Tempo discrimination and application are part of nearly every activity.

DEVELOPMENT OF TEMPO CONCEPTS

Fast and slow
Accelerates and ritards
Changing
Gradations of fast and slow

Dynamics enable the children not only to identify an expressive component but also to participate in using it.

DEVELOPMENT OF DYNAMIC CONCEPTS

Loud and soft
Crescendo and diminuendo
Gradations of loud and soft

Timbre can be personalized in its first presentations through experimentation with voice and body sounds. Creating timbres through construction of new instruments and unusual adaptations of instruments already in use elicits interest on the part of the children.

DEVELOPMENT OF TIMBRE CONCEPTS

Voice sounds
Body sounds
Environmental sounds
Instruments
Electronic sources
Vocal and instrumental ensembles

Evaluation.   This step in the process of developing the music curriculum should be done with consideration of what is transpiring in the schools compared with what the curriculum guide states as the goals of the program. At intervals throughout the year, the teachers must examine the goals in light of the children's progress toward them. The teachers also should discuss the concepts and activities that have been suggested for the children to see if they are appropriate. Each lesson plan (see next section) that has been written should have had some type of evaluation of the experiences that were implemented. The most straightforward types of evaluation are those related to behavioral objectives, because they are written in such a fashion that the assessment of results is clearly indicated. Evaluations of the music lessons will be of great help when discussing the goals and the progress made toward their realization.

Another valuable evaluation measures the music curriculum against expectations that are described as desirable by authorities on music education. The Music Educators National Conference publication *The School Music Program: Description and Standards* is such a resource. Even though state department publications may have been used in designing the music curriculum, they may continue to function as a standard of comparison for the curriculum plan in operation.

Standardized achievement tests can add to the teacher's knowledge about the children. The *Music Achievement Tests* (MAT) by Colwell may be used from third grade on. There is only one form of the test for each musical discrimination.

Test 1:	Pitch Discrimination	Test 3:	Tonal Memory
	Interval Discrimination		Melody Recognition
	Meter Discrimination		Pitch Recognition
Test 2:	Major-Minor Mode		Instrument Recognition
	Discrimination	Test 4:	Musical Style
	Feeling for Tonal Center		Auditory-Visual
	Auditory-Visual		Discrimination
	Discrimination		Chord Recognition
			Cadence Recognition

The *Iowa Tests of Music Literacy* by Gordon include aural perception, reading recognition, and notational understanding for both tonal and rhythmic concepts. The six levels of the test are available on reel-to-reel tapes for use from grade four on.

Since these tests measure achievement, not aptitude, their use on a yearly basis can be one factor in determining the children's progress in concept development.

The grid shown below may be used to determine the balance of the music curriculum as well as to evaluate it. If the events that are planned for the children cluster in one or two areas, the balance of the program may be questioned. A mark is to be placed in the box where one of the elements and an activity have been joined; for example, when the children have listened to contrasting tempos, a mark is put in the box that shows the interaction of Listen and Tempo. If they also moved as part of this experience, another mark is to be placed in the intersecting box for Move and Tempo. When they have created a rhythmic ostinato, a mark is put in the box that is common to Rhythm and Create. A mark will probably be appropriate if placed in the Play-Rhythm box for this activity as well. (Play refers to the playing of instruments, not to other play activities of the children.)

Some of the interactions will naturally occur less frequently, especially at certain grade levels (e.g., first graders will have virtually no Harmony-Read experiences).

ELEMENT-ACTIVITY INTERACTION GRID

ACTIVITIES

CONSTITUENT ELEMENTS	Sing	Play	Listen	Move	Create	Write	Read
Rhythm							
Pitch { Melody							
Pitch { Harmony							
Form							

EXPRESSIVE ELEMENTS

	Sing	Play	Listen	Move	Create	Write	Read
Tempo							
Dynamics							
Timbre							

Broad questions should be asked about the curriculum.

Are the children willing participants in the musical activities?

Do the children elect to be involved in musical activities outside of class time?

Are children developing performance skills?

What evidence can be found that the students are developing as independent musicians?

Is time spent with the children in drawing attention to musical concepts rather than in simply repeating musical events with no attempt to teach concepts?

Do the children have opportunities to engage in creative and expressive musical events?

Are the goals that were part of the curriculum guide being realized?

Teaching skill. The perceptive reader has probably already noted that a negative response to some of the questions just cited may not be related to the curriculum but, rather, to lack of skill in the teacher. The best planned curriculum may fail if taught poorly. The reader is urged not to despair; the rest of this book is intended to help you gain the techniques you need to implement the curriculum guide successfully.

Recommended Readings

AEBISCHER, DELMER W., *Self-Evaluation Checklist for School Music Programs*. Salem: Oregon Department of Education, 1978. The Oregon checklists are available for elementary general music, grades one through six; band and choral music, grades five and six; and kindergarten.

BRUNER, J. S., *Toward a Theory of Instruction*. New York: W. W. Norton & Company, Inc., 1966. Through a description of a social studies curriculum, Bruner set forth his ideas about the spiral curriculum and discovery learning.

COLWELL, RICHARD, *Music Achievement Tests*. Chicago: Follett Educational Corporation, 1969. Further information and test forms are available from the author at 406 W. Michigan, Urbana, Illinois 61801.

EISNER, ELLIOT W., *The Educational Imagination*. New York: Macmillan Publishing Co., Inc., 1979. Perspective on the design and evaluation of school programs from an art teacher is described in terms that apply to broad areas of curriculum planning.

GORDON, EDWIN, *Iowa Tests of Music Literacy*. Iowa City: University of Iowa, 1970.

MUSIC EDUCATORS NATIONAL CONFERENCE, *The School Music Program: Description and Standards*. Reston, VA: Music Educators National Conference, 1974. This publication deals with minimal and desired time and attention to be spent upon public school programs.

Suggested Projects

1. Classroom teachers: Select a grade level in which you are interested. Write a curriculum guide for that grade.

2. Music teachers: Design a curriculum guide in which you concentrate upon one activity interacting with all the elements as shown on the Element-Activity Interaction Grid. Describe how that activity changes from grades one through six.

3. Class: Cooperatively design a curriculum guide that will encompass plans for grades one through six.

LESSON PLANS

Many teacher trainees do not ask *how* to write lesson plans so much as they ask *why* write lesson plans. Sometimes the trainee fails to see the reason for a carefully conceived plan until he or she is standing before a class. Failure to develop a lesson plan can result in a painful experience.

The curriculum guide serves as a map of sorts for leading the children through a school year. The lesson plan is the specific set of directions for learning about the items mentioned in the guide. Although the map has helped the traveler find the town, he will still need assistance from a diagram of the town to get to a particular address.

The lesson plan rarely serves in isolation. One of the most important features of the plan is the evaluation after use. The insight generated with the children in the learning situation, the needs that manifest themselves, and the inspiration for problem solving that the perceptive teacher finds become some of the raw materials of which the next lesson plan is made.

The contents of the plan should vary according to the writer. A music teacher who sees the children for thirty minutes twice a week will probably try to include many musical experiences in the lesson such as the following:

1. Familiar experiences at the beginning and end of the lesson.
2. Review of a recently introduced concept.
3. Introduction of new materials.
4. Presentation of several contrasting activities to support the three types of experiences just mentioned.

A music teacher who sees the children daily, or a classroom teacher who can teach music frequently for varying lengths of time, may develop plans that include only specific activities, such as

1. Teaching a new song.
2. Establishing the environment for a listening experience.
3. Providing opportunities for creative expression.

The wonderful thing about the classroom teacher's schedule is that he or she can interpolate music throughout the day as a subject in its own right, in support of other subjects, and as a mood modifier.

The lesson plan structure to be discussed in the following pages has five parts.

1. Statement of concept(s) to be developed.
2. Behavioral objectives to describe desired observable behaviors.
3. Materials for the lesson.
4. Procedures through which the learning event will be guided.
5. Evaluation after the lesson has been taught.

The format on the following page is useful for methods class assignments.

The lesson plan to be developed as part of this discussion will be implemented in a fifth grade class that has experienced very little part singing. It may be described as a singing-listening-reading lesson.

Concept.   Woolfolk and Nicolich define a concept as "a collection of experiences or ideas that are grouped together based on some common properties."[2] They are abstractions, "sets of attributes or rules for categorizing events, ideas, or objects."[3] In teaching a concept, it must be named, defined, and exemplified to illustrate important features, and its attributes must be identified. In instances where it is difficult to name,

LESSON PLAN

for_____   Name _____
    (type of lesson)   Date_____
                                     For grade_____

Concept(s)

    Concept sentences:

Behavioral objectives

Materials (including name, source, page, record, etc.
       of any music used)

Procedures

Evaluation

define, show examples, and identify attributes, a prototype may be used to capture the concept; for instance, it may be clearer to have the children hear syncopation than to try to talk about it.

In the following lesson, a concept to which the children will be exposed is "descant." Descant may be defined as a harmonic part written above the melody. This is the first descant the class has sung, although individual class members may have sung descants with other groups. In subsequent lessons, the children will play instrumental descants as well as sing them so that they will be exposed to several examples. The attributes they will identify include harmonic and rhythmic compatibility between descant and melody and a comparison of the ranges of the two parts to see which is higher in pitch. Not all the attributes of the descant will be discussed in the first exposure. The formation of the concept of descant will take place over a series of lessons.

To plan adequately, it is suggested that the teacher specify the concept(s) for each lesson and then write a few sentences that children might be expected to say in connection with their concept formation.

Even though the lesson plan specifies the concept(s) to be taught, the children may leave the lesson with many more and perhaps different concepts than were stated in the plan.

The concept for this lesson is descant. The concept sentences from the children may include the following:

> The descant is higher than the melody.
> The harmony produced by the descant and the melody fits together.
> Even though the descant and the melody have different notes, they have the same A A′ A B form.

Behavioral objectives. The behavioral objectives for the lesson are closely related to the concepts. They state behaviors that can be measured by visual or aural observation. The latter is particularly important in teaching music. In writing behavioral objectives, these questions should be answered:

1. Who will be exhibiting the behavior?
2. What will be done?
3. How will it be done?

Who? The behavioral objectives used for music lesson plans will generally identify the child or the children as the subjects.

---

[2]Anita Woolfolk and Lorraine Nicolich, *Educational Psychology for Teachers* (Englewood Cliffs, NJ: Prentice-Hall, Inc., 1980), p. 596.
[3]Woolfolk, *Educational Psychology*, p. 596.

The children will...
The child will...

What? They will

skip jump spin dance step leap strike pluck strum play sing
improvise interpret compose notate dramatize explain compare
discuss select match analyze demonstrate

plus any other musical behavior that can be observed.

Care must be taken when writing the behavioral objectives to use a verb indicating an observable action. To say that the children will listen to music as part of the behavioral objective presents the teacher with a difficult task. Observation of the class to see who is listening is not adequate. Some of the children who seem to be most raptly involved in listening may be thinking about something else. To determine if the children are listening, they must be given another way of demonstrating it. They may be asked to move upon hearing something that has been identified in the music, raise their hands, or click their fingers. Those behaviors are observable. *Appreciate* and *enjoy* are two other verbs that indicate desirable behaviors on the part of the children but are very difficult to observe accurately.

How? asks the manner of behavior. Musical answers may be "accurately," "a tempo," "in proper style," "with suitable phrasing," "in tune." If this seems obvious, the descriptor may be omitted. For example, in regard to this behavioral objective, "The children will sing both the melody and the descant for 'I'm Gonna Sing'," it seems redundant to add the word "accurately" since accuracy is a desirable component of almost every musical experience.

Behavioral objectives for the lesson that follows could be

1. The children will sing both the melody and the descant for "I'm Gonna Sing."
2. They will identify the notation of the descant and the melody by pointing to the correct part when they sing it.

Materials.   Be sure to list the materials necessary for the lesson. The most important material is the music that will be studied. Clear identification of the book and page number will save not only the teacher's time but also the children's valuable class time. With an eye to the future, it is terribly frustrating to return to a good lesson plan a year later only to find that the page numbers, book, or phonograph record sources do not appear on the plan and the teacher must take time to find them again.

If special pieces of equipment are needed for the lesson, note them here also. Anything normally in use in the environment in which the lesson is to be taught need not be singled out (blackboard, chalk, etc.), but if a phonograph is needed, and it is stored in a closet in the back of the room where it is difficult to find, not only note it in this section but also make arrangements for it to be out and available before the lesson begins.

Materials for this lesson are

"I'm Gonna Sing," p. 8, Book 5, *Spectrum of Music,* 1980
Books for students and teacher
6½" by 22" flashcards showing parts of the song

Procedures.   The procedures for the lesson consist of step-by-step accounts of how the teacher will structure the lesson. For the teacher trainee, there is value in noting the details, even to the exact phrasing of each question or comment. The experienced teacher soon learns how to list the salient points of procedure to eliminate detailed writing. Even though it is more than possible that the procedure will not be followed exactly, attention to detail in planning will give the beginning teacher a greater degree of confidence in structuring the lesson. The following lesson plan gives detailed procedures.

Evaluation.   The evaluation is dependent upon what happens during the class in which the lesson is taught; it cannot be done in advance. However, the teacher should think about the evaluation in terms of his or her part in the lesson, asking such questions as

1. Was I prepared?
2. Was my presentation musically accurate?

The teacher will look at the children's responses during the lesson to answer such questions as

1. Was the lesson appropriate for this group of children?
2. Did it take into consideration varying levels of children's abilities?
3. Did it make accommodations for handicapped children?
4. Were the children responsive? If not, why not? If so, how?
5. Were effective procedures of class management carried out?
6. Did it follow the lesson plan? If not, why not?
7. Were the behavioral objectives realized?
8. What needs to be strengthened, changed or supplemented in the next lesson?

The sample lesson that follows was written for a thirty-minute class period.

LESSON PLAN

for <u>singing-listening-reading</u> Name   <u>Lois Harrison</u>
    (type of lesson)   Date <u>September 19, 1983</u>
                                  For grade _____ <u>five</u> _____

Concept(s) DESCANT

Concept sentences:

The descant is higher than the melody.
The harmony produced by the descant and the melody
fits together.
Even though the descant and the melody have
different notes, they have the same A A' A B form.

Behavioral objectives

The children will sing both the melody and the
descant for "I'm Gonna Sing."
They will identify the notation for the descant and
the melody by pointing to the correct part when they
sing it.

Materials

"I'm Gonna Sing," p. 8, Book 5, <u>Spectrum of Music,</u>
1980
Books for students and teacher
6½"×22" flashcards showing parts of the song

Procedures
1. Greet the children with phrases taken from the
   song that they will echo both as a class and individually.
2. Ask the children to find page 8 and place their
   fingers on the parts of the song that they hear.
   The teacher will sing excerpts, the children will
   find them in the music, and their choices will be
   confirmed by looking at the flashcards. The

teacher will move among the children to help them if necessary in finding the correct notation.

3. Ask the children what they think is the purpose of the two lines of music. Show them the double bar lines that join the melody and the descant together. This makes the musician reading the score aware that these two parts will be performed at the same time.

4. Have the children trace the melody line only as the teacher sings it. Have peers help to make sure that this is done accurately by all.

5. Ask the children to sing only the repeated G's of the melody. The teacher will sing the other notes.

6. Elicit from the children the form of the song: A A' A B. Have them discuss the different endings of the A phrases.

7. Have the children sing the entire melody. Correct it if necessary. Ask the children to point to the melody while they sing it.

8. Have the children sing the entire melody while the teacher sings the descant.

9. Elicit from the children their observations on the descant. Is it higher or lower than the melody? Is it sung at the same time as the melody? Is the tune the same as the melody? Are any of the notes of the descant the same as the melody? What is it called when two different notes are sung together? How would you define a descant?

10. What is the form of the descant?

11. Clap the rhythm of the descant.

12. Sing the notes of the G major chord. Show the children where to find the broken chord in the descant.

13. Have the children sing the descant. Correct it if necessary. Ask them to point to the descant while singing.

14. Divide the class in half. Have half sing the melody, the other half sing the descant.

15. Let the halves change parts and sing the song again.

16. Let the children choose the part that seems best for their voices, regroup, and sing the song again.

17. Congratulate the children when the combination is done well.

I'M GONNA SING

Spiritual
Arranged by John Northrup

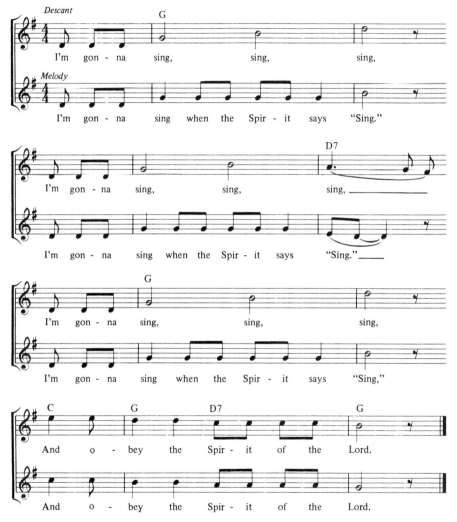

Arrangement from <u>Spectrum of Music</u>, Book 5, by Mary Val Marsh, Carroll Rinehart, and Edith Savage. © 1980 by Macmillan Publishing Co., Inc., New York. Reprinted by permission of the publisher.

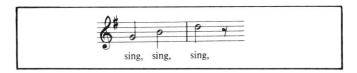

sing, sing, sing,

Spir- it says "Sing,"

I'm gon - na sing,

And o - bey the Spir- it of the Lord.

spir- it says "Sing,"___

sing when the Spir- it says

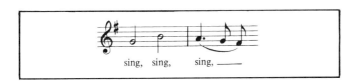

sing, sing, sing, ____

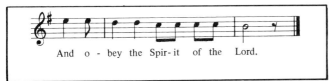

And o - bey the Spir- it of the Lord.

After the lesson is taught prepare an evaluation based upon the attainment of the behavioral objectives, development of concept, effectiveness of procedures, and other questions posed earlier.

Recommended Readings

MAGER, ROBERT F., *Preparing Instructional Objectives*. Belmont, CA: Fearon Publishers, 1962. A programmed text specifically about writing objectives.
WOOLFOLK, ANITA E., AND LORRAINE NICOLICH, *Educational Psychology for Teachers*. Englewood Cliffs, NJ: Prentice-Hall, Inc., 1980. Clear exposition of many aspects of educational psychology, including concept learning.

Suggested Project

For each of the following statements, identify a concept related to the original statement. Write several concept sentences as if the children were saying them. Write one behavioral objective related to the concept. How many of these statements are related to nonmusical concepts?

1. Demonstrate rhythmic and listening skills by participating in simple games and dances. For example, concept: *beat;* concept sentences: *I can move with the music. The music tells me when to move my feet;* behavioral objective: *the children will move their feet with the steady beat of the music.*
2. Relate classroom instrumental experiences to the teaching of harmony.
3. Explore songs that stress learning nonmusical concepts such as the alphabet, colors, numbers, names, and body parts.
4. Identify a repeated rhythmic or melodic pattern and a contrasting pattern.
5. Hear changes in tone color.
6. Establish relationships between written symbolism and sound.
7. Examine words of songs to see what image of our society they reflect.
8. Involve every child, including those with special problems in music.

ORGANIZATION

To the beginning teacher, the value of writing lesson plans in detail is that each aspect of the lesson must be thought out carefully. Vocabulary must be weighed, procedures must be sequenced, and contingencies must be considered. Another value is that, because of the careful planning, the teacher will have a clear idea of how to proceed during the lesson without the use of the actual plan. As valuable as the plan is in getting ready for the lesson, its usefulness diminishes rapidly if it is considered a script to be adhered to during the lesson itself. The carefully written lesson plan can demonstrate its effectiveness if the foundation that it has helped to form results in spontaneous interaction between the students and teacher while still carrying the objectives of the lesson forward effectively.

If the teacher suspects that details of the lesson plan may be difficult to recall during the class, it will be necessary to develop some form of prompt to help retain the lesson's procedure. Whatever form the prompt takes, it must be a simplification of the lesson plan so that it takes little time to consult. Imagine the broken continuity if the new teacher had to stop the lesson periodically to find out the next step in the carefully written plan!

Outline. One of the most obvious forms that the lesson prompt can take is that of a simple outline. An outline for teaching the descant lesson with "I'm Gonna Sing" as written might appear on a small card in this form:

```
DESCANT—"I'M GONNA SING"
A. Excerpts
   1. Echo
   2. Find in notation
B. Notation
   1. Melody
      a. trace
      b. sing repeated notes
      c. form
      d. sing
   2. Descant
      a. T descant, C melody
      b. discuss descant
      c. form
      d. clap rhythm
      e. identify chord notes
      f. C sing
   3. Melody and descant
      a. C divide into two parts
      b. switch parts
      c. choose parts independently
```

List. Some teachers may not wish to write out a formal outline. A list may substitute for the outline. Since the prompt for teaching is not for anyone else except the person who is to use it, there is no need for it to be comprehensible to anyone else.

1. echo
2. find in notation
3. two lines joined
4. trace melody
5. sing repeated notes
6. form
7. sing melody
8. T add descant
9. discuss descant
10. form
11. clap rhythm
12. sing chord
13. sing descant
14. divide and sing
15. switch
16. choose part
17. congratulate!

Score. A musician may find it easier to relate the lesson to the musical score so the prompt may take its main impetus from comments written there.

1. Find patterns
2. Learn melody
3. Learn descant
4. D + M + switch

I'M GONNA SING

Spiritual
Arranged by John Northrup

Arrangement from Spectrum of Music, Book 5, by Mary Val Marsh, Carroll Rinehart, and Edith Savage. © 1980 by Macmillan Publishing Co., Inc., New York. Reprinted by permission of the publisher.

As the teacher gains experience, the lesson prompts may be shorter. Many teachers eventually find no need for prompts during the lessons. Plans also tend to become much briefer. As teaching fluency develops and available time diminishes, detailed lesson planning sometimes becomes unnecessary or even impossible. In spite of mounting time pressures, the new teacher is advised to review lessons frequently; an occasional return to detailed lesson plans may be helpful.

Plan book.   Many teachers use a book that features empty blocks spread across two pages in a way suggesting spaces for the lessons to be taught during a week's time. Although the design of the blocks may not be appropriate for all plans, resourceful teachers adapt it to their own needs. The small size of the blocks is a disadvantage.

Plan books are kept for a variety of reasons.

1. The teacher wants to keep plans in one readily accessible volume and finds it easier to maintain continuity by using this format.
2. The principal wishes to gain an overview of what is being taught and finds information readily available in this format. The principal encourages planning on the part of the teachers by frequently reading the plan books.
3. A substitute teacher can use it to help the classes maintain continuity.

There is a difference between the books written by the classroom teacher and those written by the music specialist. The elementary classroom teacher will make provisions for the musical learning of one class plus many other subject areas for that same class. The music teacher will have up to six grade levels with several classes at each level. The music teacher will probably make a general plan for each grade level and then adapt it to the specific needs of each class at that grade level. The most difficult part of this type of planning is keeping track of what happens during each class. As the children leave the music room, the teacher must take time to note what will be dealt with in their next class session. The music specialist who travels from class to class and is scheduled without a break for record keeping may be able to devise a simple check system that can be used as the class progresses without significantly diminishing teaching time. But the method that the music specialist devises to keep track of many classes in the lesson plan book may make it unique and undecipherable to anyone else.

The question then arises: What about a substitute teacher who may not understand the book? To have the substitute teach a music lesson, the specialist may find it necessary to leave plans especially prepared for the substitute's use. This works well if it is a substitution planned in advance, such as one for attending a professional meeting, and the teacher knows that the substitute can teach music lessons. If the latter does not feel comfortable in handling certain or all aspects of music instruction, the teacher may find it desirable to provide independent study for the students or to schedule a film. In case of emergency absence, music games or filmstrips can be made available with instructions for their use.

As the new teacher becomes involved with lesson plans, lesson prompts, and substitute plans, the concern should be that the child receives the highest quality of instruction possible. Careful planning is a tremendous factor in achieving this quality.

CONCEPT DEVELOPMENT THROUGH A SERIES OF LESSONS

Concepts are rarely formed by children through isolated experiences. Although each lesson is planned with the development of certain concepts in mind, the formulation of a concept may take many exposures over a long period of time. How and when the concept is formed depends upon the readiness of the child for that particular concept, the experience that the child has already had in relationship to the concept, and the stage of the child's cognitive, physical, emotional, and aesthetic development when the concept is introduced.

Music lends itself to concept development in an attractive way: the abstractions that are being developed in the child can be found in a variety of musical examples. Since some of the children in a class may have already established a concept that the rest of the class needs to develop, approaching it through many different selections helps to keep the children who have already developed the concept from being bored.

As the teacher becomes aware of the children who need more help in establishing certain concepts, the lesson should be developed to emphasize these concepts. At the same time, attention should be directed to different concepts for the children who do not need help on those that they have already established. Time should be allowed for review; this is useful to all the children to some extent; some of the children will need it more than others. At least some musical review serves to reinforce and maintain concepts.

The sequencing of experiences needed for concept development takes place over a series of lessons. The ideas discussed in the paragraphs that follow will be incorporated by the teacher into lessons over a long period of time. For each lesson, the beginning teacher will develop a plan in the five-part format.

An important concept for primary school children is that melodic direction can go up, down, or stay the same. First the children will need experiences in singing and listening to music that illustrate that concept. Before talking about melodic direction, activities will be introduced that will help the children to experience it. After they have seen pussy willows in the spring and in the course of learning the song "Pussy Willow", the children will pretend that they are the pussy willows growing. They will move their bodies upward from a squatting position until they get to the top of the scale; then, as the scale goes down near the end they will move their bodies down again until they leap up with the last note.

The children will draw the contour of the melody in the air. If this is too difficult for them to do independently, they will mirror the teacher or students who can do it. The teacher will draw melodic contours on the chalkboard as they sing. As soon as the students get the idea, they will begin to draw the contours.

Pitched percussion instruments can be used by the children to play the melody. They will begin by playing the scale down three measures from the end. Then they can start at the beginning and play one note for each measure as the scale progresses upward. If they have difficulty with this, they can hit the next bar upon a signal from the teacher until they can do it

PUSSY WILLOW

Traditional

* For a contrast in accompanying chords, use either parallel motion with the top chords or contrary motion with the bottom chords.

independently. Next they will repeat each note during a measure, hitting it as the melodic rhythm indicates.

At first the teacher will talk about the melodic direction only as much as is necessary to have the children be involved in the activity. Gradually, the teacher will comment upon melodic direction in greater depth. Then the children will be encouraged to discuss the melodic direction from their aural perception of it. Notation can be introduced and related to the drawing children have been doing both in the air and on the chalkboard. Large-sized notation on newsprint or posterboard that can be seen by the entire class as it is discussed can help to focus the children's attention.

All these activities will be carried out with "Pussy Willow" over a period of time, but to keep the children's interest, they will also be applied to other songs such as "Down Came a Lady."

DOWN CAME A LADY

Virginia Folk Song

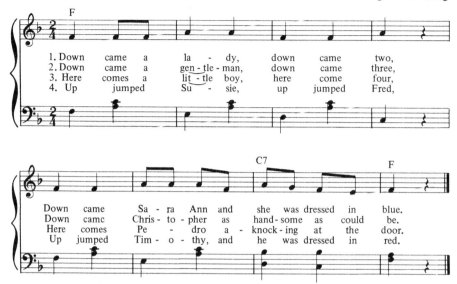

1. Down came a la - dy, down came two,
2. Down came a gen - tle - man, down came three,
3. Here comes a lit - tle boy, here come four,
4. Up jumped Su - sie, up jumped Fred,

Down came Sa - ra Ann and she was dressed in blue.
Down came Chris - to - pher as hand - some as could be.
Here comes Pe - dro a - knock - ing at the door.
Up jumped Tim - o - thy, and he was dressed in red.

From Traditional Ballads of Virginia by Arthur Kyle Davis, Jr. © University Press of Virginia. Reprinted by permis-sion of the publisher.

Space out the following activities in several lessons following a sequence such as this:

Children listen to the music sung on a neutral syllable or played on an instrument. Use arm motions to go with the pitch changes.

React to the words. Encourage the children to do creative rhyming as the teacher leaves words out. What will rhyme with "five"? Or "six" in new verses?

Show melodic direction with body responses. Bending and stretching can be used to show the skips in this song.

Encourage the children to think of other appropriate physical responses.

Have the children place blocks to represent the beginning of the melody:

Play the melody using two bars on a xylophone; then let the children assist in figuring out what other bars are needed.

Before attention begins to wane using "Down Came a Lady," introduce "Can You Dance?" a traditional singing game.

Children will play the game as the teacher sings it in its original version. Next, relate the melody to new words that represent parts of the body: "put your hands on your ankle," "put your hands on your kneecap," "put your hands

CAN YOU DANCE?

Traditional

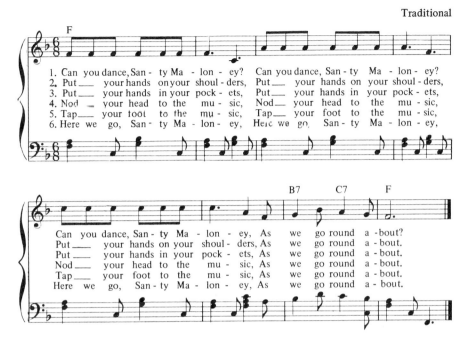

1. Can you dance, San - ty Ma - lon - ey? Can you dance, San - ty Ma - lon - ey?
2. Put___ your hands on your shoul - ders, Put___ your hands on your shoul - ders,
3. Put___ your hands in your pock - ets, Put___ your hands in your pock - ets,
4. Nod ___ your head to the mu - sic, Nod___ your head to the mu - sic,
5. Tap___ your foot to the mu - sic, Tap___ your foot to the mu - sic,
6. Here we go, San - ty Ma - lon - ey, Here we go, San - ty Ma - lon - ey,

Can you dance, San - ty Ma - lon - ey, As we go round a - bout?
Put ___ your hands on your shoul - ders, As we go round a - bout.
Put ___ your hands in your pock - ets, As we go round a - bout.
Nod ___ your head to the mu - sic, As we go round a - bout.
Tap ___ your foot to the mu - sic, As we go round a - bout.
Here we go, San - ty Ma - lon - ey, As we go round a - bout.

on your jawbone, as we go round about." The progression of the children's hands on their bodies corresponds to the melodic direction of the piece.

Make up other verses to give the children the sense of relating the melodic direction to the children's physical environment: "put your hands on your shoelaces," "put your hands on your waistband," "put your hands on your collar, as we go round about."

OR

"Put your hands on the floor," "put your hands on the chair seat," "put your hands on the desktop, as we go round about."

OR

"Tap your foot to the music," "knock your knees to the music," "clap your hands to the music, as we go round about."

Let the children share in the fun of deciding what words and physical dimensions can relate to the notes of this piece. They should see that the melody at first stays the same on F, then dips down before going up to A for several beats, then dips down before going up to C for several beats.

Apply the activities described for "Pussy Willow" and "Down Came a Lady" to "Can You Dance?"

The teacher must be sensitive to the amount of time that the children will use profitably in developing the concept being studied. Ideally, the teacher should allow time for the concept to develop meaning but should also avoid dragging it out so as to produce fatigue or boredom. If a child says, "Do we have to do this again?" the teacher needs to assess the timing of the lesson together with the reactions of the other children. The child may be speaking for others in the class too. There are classes with no vocal leader who will do almost anything the teacher wants them to do, but even these nonprotesting students may resist learning when time spent on a concept has been too long for them. On another day, the children may return eagerly to the concept because it and they are fresh.

At the beginning of the school year, teachers should review the concepts supposedly established during the preceding year with children from second grade through sixth. At that time, they should look at the musical behavior of the children to see if it demonstrates concept understanding. The children can begin their second or third grade music class by moving to and singing "Can You Dance?" If, in response to the request that they show the direction of the melody with their bodies, they can do so, the teacher can see that either they understand that music goes up, down, and/ or stays the same or they remember what they did with that piece the previous year. The teacher next should present the children with a new piece of music to see if they can transfer their concept of melodic direction to another piece of music.

What the teacher is most likely to find at the beginning of the school year is that

> some of the children maintain the musical concept;
> some of them, new to the school, have had no experience with it;
> some of them, students at the school last year, did not form the concept;
> some of the students who were in class last year seem to have partially related to the concept.

With these divergent relationships to the concept in mind, the teacher will attempt to plan activities appropriate for the different levels of learning. In the next approach to conceptualization of melodic direction, Bryan and Gloria may be charting the melody on the chalkboard, Tina is figuring out which bars of the xylophone will be needed for the melody, and the rest of the class is following the teacher in body motion that matches the melodic contour.

This discussion has concentrated upon only one concept in a series of lessons. Working on different concepts with the children will add to the variety of their experiences. The same pieces of music used for melodic direction can also be used for rhythm concepts. Care must be taken by the teacher not to overload the children with too many, or conflicting, experiences.

Two concepts that tend to be confused, probably because of society's use of terminology, are melodic direction and dynamics. Because the family is apt to say, "Turn that stereo down," when the volume is too loud, the child may use body motion in which loud is up and soft is down. The music teacher needs to use precise vocabulary as well as clear examples to help children clarify these conflicting concepts.

The sequence of experiences for the children depends upon their capabilities, learning style, learning speed, and retention. In the examples discussed, asking children who are not discriminating aurally to use notation or who cannot relate what they hear to some kind of spatial reference, be it drawing, body motion, or a similar activity, would be musically meaningless. Asking children who cannot sing in tune to use their voices to show melodic direction may be an exercise in futility. Because music instruction involves much group activity, the teacher may concentrate upon a sequence of instruction that is appropriate for most of the group members. The danger of not making provisions for the sequence of instruction that is needed by individuals is that the child who needs a different type of sequencing can be lost and eventually resentful that he or she is unable to participate in a fashion that is meaningful.

Suggested Projects

1. Write a lesson plan for a fifteen-minute lesson that utilizes one of the suggestions in this section on teaching the concept of melodic direction: music goes up, down, or stays the same.
2. Select another musical concept. Describe how that concept may be developed through a series of lessons.

MATERIALS

Variety. There is a rich variety of music that is appropriate and interesting for children. Music educators have not always been sufficiently inclusive in their choice of literature. A meeting of many professionals at Tanglewood in 1967 produced a declaration that stated, among other things, that music of "all periods, styles, forms and cultures belongs in the curriculum. The musical repertory should be expanded to involve music of our time in its rich variety, including currently popular teen-age music and avant-garde music, American folk music, and the music of other cultures."[4] The declaration spoke for children who looked upon public school music as the "teacher's music" while their own music was that which they enjoyed at home, on the radio, and with friends. The Tanglewood declaration urged educators to select materials to be used in the curriculum from a wide variety of sources.

[4]Robert A. Choate, ed., *Documentary Report of the Tanglewood Symposium* (Washington, D.C.: Music Educators National Conference, 1968), p. 139.

Suitability.   Another primary consideration in choosing the music is that it be suitable for the children who are to use it. Although there are occasions when a difficult piece of music may be done with the children because of its contribution to the total scope of the music with which they are dealing, a steady diet of music that is very hard to learn can produce an atmosphere of drudgery rather than one of spontaneous enjoyment.

The needs of the children help to provide direction in choosing music. Some of those needs will include playing games, experiencing a variety of moods, identifying specific elements of music, building musical skills, and relating to other subject areas in the curriculum.

Even though a second grade child and a sixth-grader may have the same musical needs, the piece of music that is appropriate for the younger child may not be right for the older one. The vocabulary of the text and the subject matter of the song must be scrutinized carefully for suitability. Because of coordination development, older beginners play and move in different ways from the younger beginners. Subject matter and skills that are too advanced for younger children may cause them to flounder and give up music study. With older children, selections that lack an appropriate physical and/or mental challenge may cause these children to avoid musical learning for the rest of their lives. The challenge of selecting appropriate materials for children looms as a large one for the teacher. To find them, the teacher will search music collections, textbooks, octavos, and live sources; he or she will observe successful teachers, talk to specialists, go to workshops, and glean ideas from radio and television.

The children will provide guidance individually and collectively. Each class has its own unique personality whose capabilities and needs will be reflected in the choices of music for them. The individual student's ability to handle the skills connected with the music and the class reactions and preferences will help the teacher to select the music that can be used most effectively with them.

Preferences.   Most children express definite preferences for certain types of music. These preferences are tied to familiarity with that type of music. Experienced teachers have many stories to tell of students who disliked a piece of music when first hearing it and then grew to value it. Teachers who meet with success in expanding student preferences in music are sensitive to the students in many ways. They respect the music that is meaningful to the young people; at the same time, they teach students to respect music that is preferred by others. They help the children to see the diversity that is reflected in music. They expose the children to music of other countries, music of antiquity, avant-garde music, and opera. They broaden the horizons of the students as much as is possible without making them feel that their preferences are unworthy. These teachers teach music concepts through the type of music with which the children are familiar. They identify musical elements that are part of these selections. Then they find the same elements in an unfamiliar piece of music. This process is designed to give the students a wide exposure to many types of music from which they can make informed choices.

When dealing with children's preferences, teachers are deluded if they expect students to express only responses that agree with theirs. The teacher who asks the child, "Did you like that music?" needs to be prepared for a negative, positive, or ambiguous answer and must realize that a negative answer at a crucial point in the lesson may not contribute to the learning process. Children's preferences can be identified without an overt response. Questions directly related to the musical content can help the children to form their preferences by giving them focus on the music and not what other students are saying about their preferences. The teacher can comment fairly about objective answers. When student comments are made about preferences, they need to be treated openly and honestly. When the student contributes these comments spontaneously, not in answer to a question, they tend to be thought out more carefully. Both the students and the teacher have a right to state preferences. The students seem to respond more positively if teachers make it clear that they are stating their own preference and will respect the students' preferences even when there is no argument.

As the teacher becomes acquainted with various age levels of elementary children, it becomes evident that the bulk of the discussion of preferences is centered on the older children. Generally, younger children accept choices that the teacher makes. As the child grows in independence, musical questioning becomes stronger. A contradiction in the development of independent thinking with the older child is that sometimes the peer group takes the place of adult influence, so that many children do not become independent but, rather, substitute one authority for another.

Criteria.   There are many more considerations to be included in the selection of music for elementary school children. The State of Oregon has developed general and specific categories that are used by committees in that state for choosing textbooks. The general criteria cover

1. *Portrayal* of people (in textbooks) shall be fair and lack stereotyping and bias with regard to ethnic and minority groups, age groups, sex roles, and the handicapped.
2. *Readability* (e.g., language, legibility, type size, layout) shall be appropriate to the topic and grade level. Briefs that accompany the texts shall document the readability level.

3. *Content* shall
   a. Be accurate, organized, and clear as to purpose.
   b. Be relevant in terms of learning needs, experiences, and interests.
   c. Involve students in interdisciplinary experiences that draw upon their backgrounds and values and lead to practical skill attainment.
   d. Utilize the metric system where appropriate as a primary system of measurement.
   e. Involve students where appropriate in responsible decision making in the six life roles: individual, learner, producer, citizen, consumer, and family member.
   f. Incorporate where appropriate awareness of safety factors.
   g. Stimulate and encourage critical and analytical thinking.
4. *Format* shall
   a. Be attractive, stimulate student interest, and include illustrative materials that are timely, colorful, creative, and appropriate and serve a definite purpose.
   b. Be of appropriate quality and durability (i.e., covers, bindings, paper, and ink).
   c. Include, when necessary or appropriate, a table of contents, glossary, index, bibliographies, and evaluation materials.
5. *Teacher materials* shall
   a. Describe and encourage the use of effective teaching techniques without limiting the creativity of the teacher.
   b. Be easy to use, durable, and congruent with other program materials as well as include, where necessary or appropriate, reproductions of pages from student text as well as answer keys and other helpful aids.
   c. Include activities for meeting varying pupil interests and abilities such as enrichment and reinforcement materials, individual and class projects, field trips, and evaluative techniques.

All textbooks considered for use in the Oregon public schools are evaluated according to their compliance with the general criteria. A point system is used for each criterion upon which a final rating is established.[5]

Under the leadership of Delmer W. Aebischer, music education specialist for the Oregon Department of Education, specific criteria have been written for music materials. Although these criteria are used in the adoption process for textbooks, a note attached to the document specifies that, wherever the word "textbook" or "text" is used, it may be construed to mean instructional materials as well.

Aebischer has worked with elementary music teachers, college methods teachers, and administrators both in writing the criteria and in their subsequent revisions. They are included here because of the breadth of insight that they bring to bear upon the selection of music materials for elementary school children.

---

[5]Verne A. Duncan, state superintendent of public instruction, *General Criteria Checklist for All Textbooks* (Salem: Oregon Department of Education, 700 Pringle Parkway S.E., 1978).

I. CONTENT should assure that:
   A. *Song Material*
      1. An appropriate system of notation is included for all songs.
      2. All verses are included for songs that are heard on the accompanying recordings.
      3. The songs appeal to both sexes.
      4. Texts include both traditional and contemporary song material in a wide variety of styles from many cultures.
      5. When a foreign language text is used, the phonetic pronunciation is included under the original text. The translation appears nearby.
      6. Seasonal songs, such as Halloween, Thanksgiving, Hanukah, Christmas, Valentine's Day, St. Patrick's Day, and Easter, are included together with selected patriotic songs at each grade level.
      7. Rounds as well as simple to moderately difficult two- and three-part songs are included in editions for grades 4 and 5.
      8. Careful attention is given to voice leading and comfortable vocal range.
      9. Songs are included at each level which are suitable for rote singing, rote to note, note reading, and for fun.
   B. *Creativity, Instruments, History, and Related Activities*
      1. Material is included to provide greater opportunities for creative activities, such as games, simple movements and dramatizations; improvisations on rhythm and melody instruments; creating new verses to familiar songs; creating melodies, introductions, codas, descants, ostinati, rounds, obligatos, and chants through vocal and instrumental media; and pentatonic activities.
      2. There is frequent opportunity to use rhythm instruments with accompanying pictures of the instruments in color, especially in grades K–3.
      3. Autoharp and guitar chords are included, together with several strums, so that a variety of accompaniments can be used. Chord names are included above melody lines.
      4. The series includes a study of the instruments of the orchestra, as well as of folk instruments.
      5. Melodic material that can be played on recorders, especially in grade 4–5 editions, is included.
      6. The song's related activities are illustrated on the page with the songs or on the opposite page.
      7. Creative listening activities in a wide variety of styles, cultures, and historical periods are included.
      8. The musical selections include the works of contemporary as well as traditional composers.
      9. A developmental approach to rhythmic and melodic note writing is included.
      10. Such innovative approaches as the Kodály, Orff, and Manhattanville methods are included, as well as activities involving electronic music.

11. In addition to rhythm, melody, harmony, and form, activities involving the expressive qualities of timbre, tempo, dynamics, and mood are included.
12. Each book will include review materials for the benefit of transfer students or students who have used a different series.
13. Suggestions are included for activities which can be pursued outside of the music class.
14. Provision is made for individualized instruction and/or lab experiences especially at the fourth and fifth grade level.

C. *Other*
1. Background information and word definitions are included in both students' and teachers' editions.
2. The series reflects the interests and maturation levels of the children with special considerations for the needs of the fifth graders (e.g., more lyrics appealing to the preadolescent, and the addition of some independent self-directed activities).
3. People of both sexes, all ages and ethnic groups are portrayed naturally as active participants in music.

II. FORMAT should assure that:
A. *Index*
1. Easy to use alphabetical and subject index is included at each grade level with every page of the text numbered and easy to see.
B. *Illustrations*
1. Illustrations include keyboard, melody bell set correlated with treble staff, 12-bar autoharp chart, and recorder fingering chart.

III. TEACHER MATERIALS should assure that:
A. *Recordings/Cassettes*
1. Supplementary recordings/cassettes are of good quality. Record band "stops" the needle between each selection. Recordings are in stereo (e.g., voices on one track, accompaniment on the other). The recording/cassette is an accurate representation of the material on the printed page.
2. Some recordings make use of traditional folk as well as contemporary instruments and arrangements.
3. In the main, children's voices are used on the accompanying recordings unless song material is particularly suited for adult voices.
B. *Teacher's Edition*
1. The teacher's edition is comprehensive, self-instructive, and suitable for use by both the general classroom teachers and the music specialist.
2. A model class lesson is included at each grade level, listing objectives and activities for achieving them. (This is particularly of value to the classroom teacher who is without the help of a music specialist.)
3. A detailed scope and sequence chart is included for each grade level.
4. The teacher's edition lies flat for use at the piano (e.g., is metal spiral-bound) with clear indication of grade level, and contains an exact duplication of the student's edition, including graphics, color schemes, and reference page numbers.
5. All song verses are contained between the staffs of the teacher's accompaniment rather than in a separate place.

6. Certain songs have a variety of teacher accompaniments; e.g., piano (including a few simplified student accompaniments), guitar, autoharp, tone bells, dulcimer, ukulele, percussion. These accompaniments are simple, musically appropriate, and clearly printed.
C. *Additional Motivational and Enrichment Materials* are included such as
   1. Interdisciplinary correlations.
   2. Listening activities which relate to materials being taught.
   3. Individualized instruction possibilities for grades 4 and 5.

Specific Criteria for Music—Grades 6 8

I. CONTENT should assure that:
   A. *Song Material*
      1. An appropriate system of notation is included for all songs. Layout on the page allows for complete measures to be included on each line of music.
      2. All verses are included for songs that are heard on the accompanying recordings.
      3. The songs appeal to both boys and girls of early adolescence, including contemporary songs relevant to today's society.
      4. Songs representative of various ethnic groups are included.
      5. Songs for the general repertoire are included such as recreational and patriotic songs, hymns, folk music of many countries, and "fun" songs.
      6. When a foreign language text is used, the phonetic pronunciation is included under the original text. The translation appears nearby.
      7. Songs suitable for teaching rote singing and the transition from rote to note are included.
      8. Songs suitable for teaching sightsinging and notational skills are included.
      9. Songs which employ social instruments such as guitar, autoharp, and baritone ukulele for students and teacher are included. Chord names are included above the melody line.
      10. Some songs with easy parts for orchestral and band instruments are included.
      11. Progression is made from rounds to simple three-part songs which meet the various needs of the changing and/or changed voice, including chants and ostinati.
      12. Several songs with the melody in the lowest voice part are included.
      13. Easy-to-sing songs are included with lyrics which are appealing to adolescents.
      14. Songs and thematic material by recognized composers, both past and present, are included.
   B. *Topical Instruction Materials with Creative Involvement in the Following Topics* are included:
      1. Twentieth-century composers, styles, and electronic music.
      2. Jazz, popular, and rock music.
      3. Folk music, including ethnic music.
      4. Social instruments; e.g., recorder, keyboard, guitar, and percussion.

5. Musical structure and design.
6. Historical styles of music since 1600.
7. Interrelationship of the arts, interdisciplinary correlations, and relationship of music to society.
8. Student-directed activities listed in items 1 through 7 assist in implementing individualized instruction.
C. *Other*
1. Each book includes review materials especially for the benefit of transfer students or students who have used a different series.
2. Creative listening activities in a wide variety of styles, cultures, and historical periods are included. The musical selections include the works of contemporary as well as traditional composers.
3. Background information and word definitions are included in both students' and teachers' editions.
4. Suggestions are included for activities which can be pursued outside of the music class.
5. Materials for grades six, seven, and eight may be interchanged. No reference is made to grade levels.
6. People of both sexes, all ages and ethnic groups are portrayed naturally as active participants in music.
II. FORMAT should assure that:
A. *Index*
1. Both an alphabetical and subject index are included for each grade level text with every page of the text numbered and easy to see.
B. *Illustrations*
1. Illustrations such as keyboard, autoharp, recorder, and guitar fingering charts are included on the inside covers or within the text.
III. TEACHER MATERIALS should assure that:
A. *Recordings/Cassettes*
1. Supplementary recordings/cassettes are of good quality. Record band "stops" the needle between each selection. Recordings are in stereo (e.g., voices on one track, accompaniment on the other). The recording/cassette is an accurate representation of the material on the printed page.
2. Some recordings/cassettes make use of traditional folk as well as contemporary instruments and arrangements.
B. *Teacher's Edition*
1. The teacher's edition is self-instructive and comprehensive.
2. The teacher's edition lies flat for use at the piano (e.g., metal spiral-bound) and contains an exact duplication of the student's edition, including graphics, color schemes, and page reference numbers.
3. All song verses are contained between the staffs of the teacher's accompaniment rather than in a separate place.
4. Some songs have a variety of teacher and student accompaniments; e.g., tone bells, piano, guitar, autoharp, dulcimer, percussion. The accompaniments are simple, musically appropriate, and easy to read.
5. Topical instructional material is planned and organized to allow for varying school programs and student interests.

6. Additional motivational and enrichment materials for each unit are included, such as interdisciplinary correlations, listening activities, and individualized instruction possibilities.[6]

Copyright. As teachers search for appropriate materials for the children, they may find valuable selections that are copyrighted and are contained in volumes that are either unavailable or too expensive to give to every child. The teacher is urged to become conversant with the copyright law so that inappropriate decisions are not made concerning the use of the materials. There are many educators who disregard the intentions of the law, and so not only break it, but also set a poor example for the children. Illegal copying of music results in financial gain for the manufacturers of duplicating machines, paper, and other supplies. The creative artist, the composer, and the publisher are not compensated as they should be.

The copyright revision, effective on January 1, 1978, clarified many educational usages. One of the first things the teacher of music must do is to determine if the materials in question are still covered by copyright. If they are not, the law does not apply. These materials can be duplicated, arranged, or adapted at the discretion of the teacher. Materials covered by the copyright law can only be altered or duplicated with permission from the copyright owner.

A short and easily understandable pamphlet called *The United States Copyright Law, A Guide for Music Educators* was issued jointly by the Music Educators National Conference, Music Publishers' Association of the United States, Music Teachers National Association, National Music Publishers' Association, and the National Association of Schools of Music. It is perhaps imprudent to quote interpretations of the law out of context; the student is urged to read the twenty-four-page pamphlet.

These are guidelines related to the 1978 law:

A. Permissible uses:
1. Emergency copying to replace purchased copies which for any reason are not available for an imminent performance provided purchased replacement copies shall be substituted in due course.
2. For academic purposes other than performance, multiple copies of excerpts of works may be made, provided that the excerpts do not comprise a part of the whole which would constitute a performable unit such as a section, movement or aria but in no case more than 10% of the whole work. The number of copies shall not exceed one copy per pupil.
3. Printed copies which have been purchased may be edited OR simplified provided that the fundamental character of the work is not distorted or the lyrics, if any, altered or lyrics added if none exist.

[6]Delmer W. Aebischer, music education specialist, *Criteria for Selection and Adoption of Music Textbooks* (Salem: Oregon Department of Education, 700 Pringle Parkway S.E., 1978).

4. A single copy of recordings of performances by students may be made for evaluation or rehearsal purposes and may be retained by the educational institution or individual teacher.

5. A single copy of a sound recording (such as a tape, disc or cassette) of copyrighted music may be made from sound recordings owned by an educational institution or an individual teacher for the purpose of constructing aural exercises or examinations and may be retained by the educational institution or individual teacher. (This pertains only to the copyright of the music itself and not to any copyright which may exist in the sound recording.)

B. Prohibitions:

1. Copying to create or replace or substitute for anthologies, compilations or collective works.

2. Copying of or from works intended to be "consumable" in the course of study or teaching such as workbooks, exercises, standard tests and answer sheets and like material.

3. Copying for the purpose of performance except as in A-1 above.

4. Copying for the purpose of substituting for the purchase of music except as in A-1 and 2 above.

5. Copying without inclusion of the copyright notice which appears on the printed copy.[7]

Budget.   Some of the most attractive materials for older elementary school children are published in the form of octavo music. These arrangements are appropriate for the child's voice, have attractive lyrics, and often add instrumental parts. Within the last few years, however, prices have risen so that many of these octavos now cost in the neighborhood of 50 to 65 cents each. Since school choruses are popular, membership sometimes ranges from sixty to one hundred voices. Although it is less chaotic if each child has a copy of the piece to use, conserving teachers will often ask the children to share their copies. That still means that the one-hundred-voice chorus will spend at least $50.00 for one piece. If the chorus gives a concert for the public, the children may sing five pieces. The money needed has grown with the addition of each piece, so that it is now at least $250.00.

With insufficient funds, the music teacher is faced with giving up the concert, having the children sing music less suitable for them, or breaking the law. Unfortunately many teachers choose the last option, and the show goes on.

Very few school systems tabulate the cost of copying. That amount comes out of the general office budget. The cost of the inconvenience of loose papers improperly joined together and very hard to read is not measured. Moreover, the music is so hard to read in many cases that the

[7]*The United States Copyright Law, A Guide for Music Educators* (Reston, VA: Music Educators National Conference and others, 1978), pp. 17–18. No copyright is claimed in this booklet. Reproduction is encouraged to assure wide circulation of the information it contains.

students do not try, so the process is reduced to rote teaching at an age when the children should be reading.

Another alternative chosen by some school systems is to teach the material by rote without giving the children the music at all—another undesirable alternative.

As difficult as it is in a time when money is scarce, educators must come to terms with the cost of a music program supported properly and sustained ethically. Buying music for the children results in

1. honesty
2. appropriateness
3. attractiveness
4. clarity

It may come as a shock to beginning teachers that they may be asked to submit their second year's budget during the second week of their first year. To be prepared, beginning teachers should ask the administrator who hires them some practical questions.

When will budget request be due?

Have limitations been placed upon acquisitions?

Is the budget to be submitted with priorities established in case funds are not available for all of the items?

What are the procedures for submitting the budget?

Do bids have to be obtained for items that cost over a certain amount? What is that amount?

With answers to those questions in mind, the next steps will include

Looking at the present inventory.

Determining what items are not in the inventory.

Deciding what needs to be repaired or replaced.

Estimating if requests have to be spread over a period of years rather than be bought in one year.

Consultation with the administrator is vital because budgetary practices vary widely. If it is possible to arrange purchase of music several times during the year, the teacher is advised to do so. What is appropriate for the children at the beginning of the year may not be appropriate halfway through. Their capabilities, interests, and voices may all have changed. Although the music textbook is generally useful for the entire year, supplementary items will help to keep the program fresh and appropriate to the needs of the children.

When submitting items for the budget, each piece of music should be identified by

Name
Composer and arranger if there is one
Place of publication
Publisher
Publisher's item number
Musical components such as voices (SA for soprano-alto, U for unison) and instruments (nonpitched percussion, piano, Orff instruments, etc.)
Number of copies to be ordered
Price

Instruments and other equipment must be described precisely. If a certain brand is better than another, it should be identified so that, when a bid is made, the bid is made only on that brand or its equivalent. If the quality of the alternative is not equivalent, the bid should be rejected. It is helpful if page numbers of catalogues are specified for the convenience of those who will write the purchase orders, and the catalogues accompany the requests.

Recommended Readings

GORDON HARDY, DIRECTOR, *Juilliard Repertory Library*. Cincinnati, OH: Canyon Press, Inc., 1970. A collection of music not generally available for use in grades kindergarten through six. Prerenaissance, renaissance, baroque, classic, romantic, contemporary, and folk music for voices and instruments.

The following books are leading textbooks for elementary music education, grades one through six:
BOARDMAN, EUNICE, AND BARBARA ANDRESS, *The Music Book*. New York: Holt, Rinehart and Winston, 1981.
CHOATE, ROBERT A., RICHARD C. BERG, AND OTHERS, *New Dimensions in Music*. New York: American Book Company, 1980.
CROOK, ELIZABETH, BENNETT REIMER, AND DAVID S. WALKER, *Silver Burdett Music*. Morristown, NJ: Silver Burdett Company, 1978 and 1981.
MARSH, MARY VAL, CARROLL RINEHART, AND EDITH SAVAGE, *Spectrum of Music*. New York: Macmillan Publishing Co., Inc., 1980.

Suggested Projects

1. Apply the Oregon criteria to current elementary school music textbooks.
2. Select ten compositions appropriate for an elementary school chorus (grades five and six). Put pertinent information about each piece on a 3" by 5" card.
3. Select ten compositions that include instruments and are appropriate for general music classes. Put pertinent information about each piece on a 3" by 5" card.

4 *Sing*

Singing has been the most common form of musical experience since the beginning of public school music. In the early years, when Lowell Mason introduced music in the Boston public schools, it was almost the only activity.[1] In recent years, public schools have broadened the scope of general music classes to include instrumental experiences, listening, movement, creating, reading, and writing as well as singing. The amount of time given to any one of these activities varies according to the preferences of the teacher, the reactions of the children, the appropriateness of the activity for the music under study, and the equipment available. Because the children are encouraged to participate in music through these different activities, they develop a wider base from which to make future choices. The fact that singing is considered first in this text does not imply that the approach to children today remains primarily a singing approach; singing is one of many forms of expression children use. Music education is intended to be a musical approach utilizing whatever medium is especially suited to their needs.

[1]Edward B. Birge, *History of Public School Music in the United States* (Reston, VA: Music Educators National Conference, 1966), pp. 66–67.

GETTING THE SINGING STARTED

Singing songs in a group builds a unique *esprit de corps*. It is as if the sound draws a common thread about the participants that makes them feel better about themselves. The child who may not be a strong singer is not reminded of this when singing with a group; the total sound is a wonderfully reinforcing experience. Get the children singing on the first day of school.

Songs can be used for different purposes and may be taught in different ways. Beginning musical experiences based upon singing are easy to plan. The songs need not illustrate any profound musical concept but can be initiated only to provide an enjoyable experience. They should involve everyone actively and can be spaced throughout the school day. They can be used to change moods, to inspire physical activity, or to set the stage for a new endeavor. The children may request the songs because they like music.

Activity-oriented songs are good for starting beginning singers. When the students first hear a song like "Head, Shoulders, Knees and Toes," they may not sing at all. They are so busy trying to touch their head, shoulders, and other body parts as they are mentioned in the song that they can't do anything else. The important thing is that they are involved in a musical activity. They will start to sing when they can. The challenge is learning to sing and move at the same time. The next challenge is speeding up the tempo. Meanwhile, they will have ample opportunity to learn the song sung by the teacher.

HEAD, SHOULDERS, KNEES AND TOES

Unknown

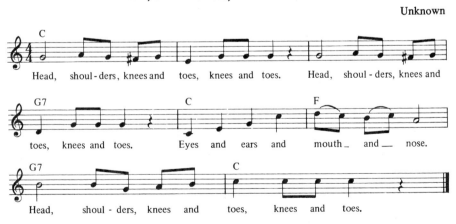

The first time the song is sung, no one should move. The second time through, the children touch their heads but do not sing the word "head." The next time through the head and shoulders are touched, and those words are not sung. Continue in this way, substituting a touch of the body part for the subtracted word. Gradually increase the tempo, so that during the last verse, when there is no singing but there is a great deal of movement, it is very fast.

Some of the easiest songs to use with children are referred to as "call and response" selections. "Bill Grogan's Goat" is sung with the children echoing each phrase after the teacher. As they get to know it, the child volunteer can replace the teacher as the leader. This song lends itself to dramatic interpretation, especially where the goat flags the train, coughs up the shirt, and so on. In time, with the teacher modeling, the children can begin to improvise, especially in harmonizing the cadences.

BILL GROGAN'S GOAT

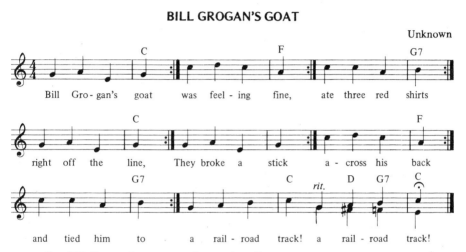

2. Bill Grogan's goat was doomed to die,
   Just as that train came whizzing by,
   He gave a shriek of mortal pain,
   Coughed up those shirts, and flagged that train.

Familiar songs can be changed to make them more interesting to the singers. Adults who have sung "Row, Row, Row Your Boat" many times may not clamor for it to be included in a community sing; still, if it is dressed up a little, it suddenly has new life and provides greater enjoyment for the participants.

Sing the round in unison to ensure that everyone knows this old favorite. It is sometimes surprising to find that what the teacher of music thought was an old favorite is unknown to many of the participants. If the children know it, and if they are singing it accurately, let them sing it as a round. It is highly undesirable to allow children to try a round when they sing it inaccurately in unison, seem uncertain in their performance of it, and wind up holding their hands over their ears so that they won't hear the other parts. The value of a round lies in savoring the harmony that results from an accurate performance.

ROW, ROW, ROW YOUR BOAT
(as is usually sung)

Traditional American

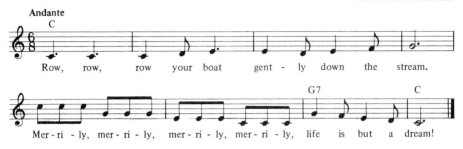

Next comes a marching band version of "Row." Take a faster tempo and sing with a crisper style. In all these variations, have the children sing in unison first and then as a round, if they can do it accurately.

ROW AS YOU MARCH

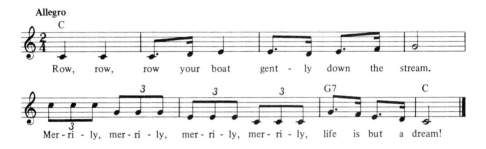

Ask the children to slow down a little, to rest a while after their exertions with the marching band. Conduct this next version in three. The conductor and a few children may even want to waltz to this. Sometimes the children respond well to motions such as rowing the boat, acting out "merrily," going to sleep at the end.

ROW AND WALTZ

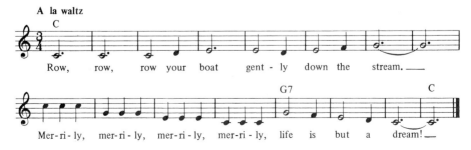

To liven things up again, see if the children can click their fingers on the off beat. Illustrate the jazz version for them. Make sure that they syncopate it and put in the articulation and accents properly.

JAZZ ROW

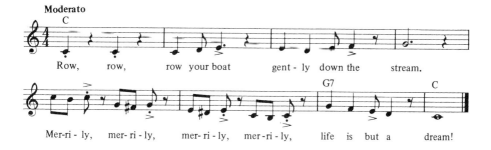

Row, row, row your boat gent - ly down the stream.

Mer-ri - ly, mer-ri - ly, mer- ri - ly, mer-ri-ly, life is but a dream!

Trying a rock version of "Row" will probably find the children getting involved in helping the teacher to make it sound more like rock.

ROCK ROW

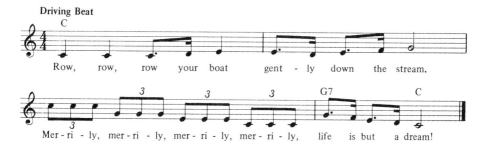

Row, row, row your boat gent - ly down the stream.

Mer - ri - ly, mer-ri - ly, mer - ri - ly, mer - ri - ly, life is but a dream!

Add ostinatos. Add instruments. Encourage the children to describe what the style should be. They may want to add a tambourine at once and improvise freely.

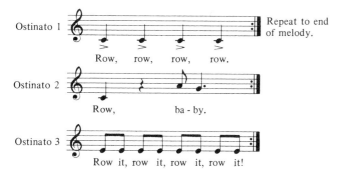

Ostinato 1

Row, row, row, row.

Repeat to end of melody.

Ostinato 2

Row, ba - by.

Ostinato 3

Row it, row it, row it, row it!

Word changes of familiar songs can help the children to develop a closer identity with the music. Be sure to pick ones that are not copyrighted.

Many of the children will know the "Battle Hymn of the Republic." Some will know the words that are sung in church. Some will want to sing with great glee the words that deal with the "burning of the school." Try to blend this diversity into a school song. If the school name is different from ♩. ♪, change the rhythm to suit the syllables you need.

SCHOOL SONG

Howe

As the students get the idea and sing out, start subtracting one word with each subsequent singing. The first word to go will be "well." The next time, the singers will leave out "very well." Next, omit "sing very well," and so on. Never leave out "so lift your voices high." Always sing the chorus completely. You might wish to raise the key for each verse; by all means, speed up the tempo. When the words for the verse have all been omitted, do a verse with no words to see if the students can use their internal hearing to come out together on "So lift your voices high."

Include all-school sings periodically. Strive to give each of the grades some type of involvement. The first-graders can sing the first ostinato for "Rock Row" even if they can't sing all the parts within their own class. Make room occasionally for one grade to sing for the other grades. Then let that group teach a favorite to the others. They can, with help, enter into the teaching process that the teacher had used with them when they were taught the song.

In addition to singing with separate classes of children and with the whole school, expand even further to include adults who may come to an open house or other type of program. Try to find songs that cut across generational gaps, ones that the older people know and the younger people can enjoy. A way to accomplish this is to consult with parents and grandparents who attend school functions about songs that they enjoy singing and then teach them to the children. A wonderful corollary to this experience is the report that comes back to the teacher of music that the family is singing together at home.

Suggested Projects

1. Learn the songs about which you have just read; then use them with a group of children.
2. Collect five other songs that would be easy for you to use to get children started in an enjoyable singing experience.

CONDUCT

The discussion that follows is intended for the student who has had no experience in conducting. Music majors who have had several terms of conducting can skip the section unless they want to review basics of conducting for their work in teaching beginning conductors. Since the fine points of conducting need more extensive study than can be provided here, these materials are intended to give only basic ideas on how to use body signals for initiating and maintaining group music making.

The hands are the primary means for giving conducting signals, but other means are available: facial expressions to give signals of encouragement, posture to show expectancy, and breathing to help the students time their own breathing.

Whether the group is small or large, conducting movements will help to get the music started, maintain the tempo, and show the musicians when to stop. Observation of excellent conductors reveals that these people do not adhere to rigid conducting patterns; they adjust their movements to the spirit and nature of the music. They learned the fundamentals of conducting first; then learned how to adapt these fundamentals to their needs. The person who leads children in singing can do the same thing: learn the conducting patterns and then adapt them so that they are appropriate to the music and the situation.

Give the pitch.   Before conducting the children in a song, always give them the starting pitch!! To keep the song in a singable key, use a pitch reference such as a recorder, pitch pipe, piano, guitar, or bells. The starting pitch must be determined by the teacher in advance to be sure that the song will be in the right range for the children. Research shows that the average range of first-graders is from middle C to the C above. The sixth grade average range is two octaves up from the G below middle C.[2]

The attack on a downbeat.   Songs that begin on the first beat of a measure are said to begin on a downbeat. The conducting motion for the first beat in a measure is always downward. So that the musicians will be able to anticipate that downbeat, there must be a preparatory beat. The preparatory beat is an upward motion that comes at an angle from the right side of the downbeat. Singers take a breath during the preparatory beat. As conductor, you must breathe as you move your hand upward in the preparatory beat so as to give the singers a model for their breathing. Have your hand ready to start the preparatory beat for "America" as you and your singers inhale; the words start on one.

Conduct in three.   The conducting pattern for "America" is in three:

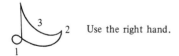

[2]Sylvesta Wassum, "Elementary School Children's Vocal Range," *Journal of Research in Music Education,* Winter 1979, pp. 214–226.

When using conducting patterns, try to have each beat bounce from an imaginary stop in the air. Norvell Church[3] trained his students by having them stop their downbeats with their batons hitting the top of a music stand so that they had a clear definition of the location of that beat. Even though it is desirable to have the exact location of each beat strongly defined, there is a bounce, or reflex at that stopping point that keeps the pattern from becoming rigid. The pattern must show the musical character of the piece being directed.

Get ready to begin conducting "America." Breathe as you show the preparatory beat. Then use the pattern in three to keep the group together.

Indicate the cutoff.   At the end of the piece, show the downbeat for the last note:

Hold the conducting motion at the bottom of the downbeat until the count of the last note has been completed. Then drop the hand slightly as a preparatory signal, raise the hand abruptly, and lower it sharply as if hitting a nail with a hammer. That is the cutoff. The termination of the last note is easier shown than described. The most important component of the cutoff is the anticipatory expression of the conductor. Show the singers that you expect them to hold their last note until you cut them off by holding the note with them. For accuracy in terminating the notes, hold a two-beat note until the beginning of the third beat, a four-beat note until the beginning of the fifth beat. (In $\frac{4}{4}$ this will be the beginning of the first beat of the next measure.)

Conduct in four.   The conducting pattern for "Old Folks at Home" is in four.

Use the right hand.

The attack and cutoff are the same as those described for "America."

---

[3]From conducting class presentation, Norvell Church, professor emeritus at Teachers College, Columbia University.

OLD FOLKS AT HOME

Stephen C. Foster

1. Way down up - on the Swa - nee riv - er, Far, far a - way,
All up and down the whole cre - a -tion, Sad - ly I roam,

There's where my heart is turn-ing ev - er, There's where the old folks_ stay.
Still long - ing for the old plan-ta- ion, And for the old folks at home.

Chorus

All the world is sad and drear - y, Eve - ry where I roam;

Oh, dear ones,how my heart grows wear-y, Far from the old folks at home.

2. All around the little farm I wandered when I was young,
There many happy days I've squandered, there many songs I've sung.
When I was playing with my brother, happy was I,
Oh, take me to my kind old mother, there let me live and die.

3. One little hut among the bushes, one that I love,
Still sadly to my memory rushes, no matter where I rove.
When will I see the bees a-humming all around the comb?
When will I hear the banjo tumming, down in my good old home?

Conduct in two. "Scotland's Burning" is in $\frac{2}{4}$ so the conducting pattern for two will be used with it.

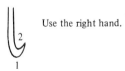

Use the right hand.

The attack is the same as that for "America." The cutoff is different. Use a downbeat for the beginning of the last measure of "Scotland's Burn-ing." Instead of using an upbeat with the word "water," use a second downbeat with the action of a hammer striking a nail as described for a fast cutoff.

SCOTLAND'S BURNING

Traditional British Round

Scot-land's burn - ing, Scot-land's burn - ing, Look out! Look out!

Fire! Fire! Fire! Fire! Pour on wa - ter, Pour on wa - ter.

Conduct in six. "Gipsy Man" is in $\frac{6}{8}$. This is the conducting pattern for six:

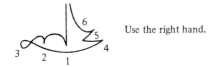

Use the right hand.

GIPSY MAN

Dorothy King

Michael Stevens

Gip - sy man, O gip - sy man, In your yel - low car - a - van,

Up and down the world_ you go, Tell_ me all _ the things_ you know!

Sun and moon and stars_ are bright, Sum - mer's green_ and win - ter's white, And

I'm the gay - est gip - sy man That rides_ in - side _ a car - a - van.

The attack is the same as that for "America," but the cutoff is different. Instead of following the conducting pattern shown in the last measure, start it as shown, then make the fourth beat a downbeat, and hold it for three beats. At the end of the third beat, cut off the note with the hammer-hitting-a-nail motion as described.

The attack on a full beat other than the downbeat.   The pieces used as illustrations so far have all begun on a downbeat. The preparatory beat has been an upbeat. Many songs begin on a full beat other than a downbeat, however. The preparatory beat for these songs will be the beat that precedes the starting beat; for example, if a song begins on the third beat, the preparatory beat will be the second beat.

"Amazing Grace" begins on the third beat. The preparatory beat will be the second beat.

"Sunrise, Sunset" begins on the second beat in $\frac{3}{4}$. Breathe and drop the hand on the first beat of the conducting pattern; start singing on the second beat.

"America the Beautiful" starts on the last beat of $\frac{4}{4}$. The preparation and the breath should be taken on the third beat.

The attack on a divided beat.   If the piece begins on a divided beat, the preparation is the beginning of that beat.

"Dixie" starts on the last half of the second beat. The preparatory beat will be the first part of the second beat.

DIXIE

Words and Music by Dan Emmett

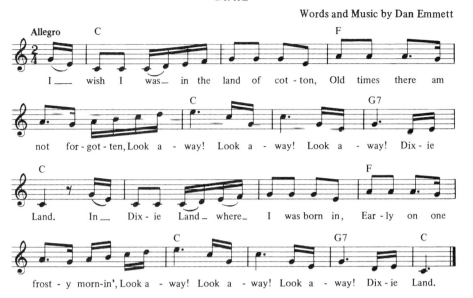

Conductors who feel insecure with this short preparation may wish to count the first part of the measure quietly before moving the hand.

1   2   I   wish

"When the Saints Go Marching In" is in cut time, ₵ , which stands for $\frac{2}{2}$. It begins on the last half of the first beat. The preparation is the first part of the first beat. The preparatory beat must be made in the tempo of the beats that are to follow. The inhalation of the breath takes place as the preparatory beat is given.

Breathe

Oh

Notice the other places in this piece where the phrases enter on the same divided beat as the beginning of the piece.

WHEN THE SAINTS GO MARCHING IN

Spiritual

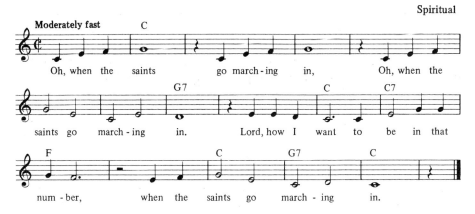

Oh, when the saints go march-ing in, Oh, when the saints go march-ing in. Lord, how I want to be in that num-ber, when the saints go march-ing in.

As soon as you have memorized the conducting patterns, use them whenever you hear music. Apply the patterns to the music you hear on radio and television. The more conducting you do, the more comfortable you will be with your new techniques. The tapes and records that you own will serve you even better than the music that you hear casually because they can be repeated. Since a score will not be available with much of the music that you hear, conducting these pieces requires that you be aurally sensitive to the meter of the selections. Listen for the accented beats; they should be your "one" or downbeat. Then figure out how many beats lie in between the downbeats. Try the pattern that you think is the best. If you are not sure, enlist the aid of a musical friend to determine with which pattern the music will be conducted.

When learning the patterns, practice them as you sing pieces that go with them. Try

in 2: "Ifca's Castle," "I'm Looking Over a Four Leaf Clover," "It's a Small World," "Michael, Row the Boat Ashore," "Hello Dolly," "This Old Man," "Mame."
in 3: "Clementine," "Moon River," "Scarborough Fair," "Daisy," "The Star-Spangled Banner," "Rainbow Connection."
in 4: "America the Beautiful," "I've Been Working on the Railroad," "Tie a Yellow Ribbon," "Raindrops," "Nobody Knows the Trouble I've Seen."
in 6: "Home on the Range," "Greensleeves," "Silent Night," "Drink to Me Only with Thine Eyes."

If the songs listed are unfamiliar, leaf through a songbook to pick out the songs you know, or those you would like to learn, and practice conducting them. If some of them are in more complicated patterns such as five or seven beats per measure, use a combination of a two and a three for five, three and four for seven. Some of the complicated patterns can be simplified. Although "The Impossible Dream" is written in $\frac{9}{8}$, it can be conducted with the three pattern. A common practice is to conduct pieces written in $^6_8$ in two rather than six when their tempo makes it impractical to use the six pattern. Examples of $^6_8$ pieces to be conducted in two are "Over the River and Through the Woods," "Hey, Look Me Over," "When Johnny Comes Marching Home Again," "Here We Come A-wassailing," and "Pop Goes the Weasel."

While the right hand shows the conducting pattern, the left hand is reserved for special effects such as cueing, dynamics, giving special directions, or getting attention. Only with very large groups, or in meeting great problems in keeping musicians together, should both hands be used in the conducting pattern.

When it is necessary to change the tempo of the music, make the conducting pattern get slower or faster. When a ritardando or accelerando is called for in the music, show it with a changing tempo in the conducting pattern. The left hand is useful in calling attention to these changes.

When the dynamic level must be changed, increase the size of the pattern for louder music; decrease its size for softer music. If the changes are abrupt, or if the students do not respond, use the left hand to heighten the feeling of urgency.

The conducting patterns work equally well with instrumental music. Although some instrumentalists such as percussion players need not take the breath, the preparatory motion helps any player sense how the music will go.

Teachers who are oriented verbally may ask, "Why not just tell the students instead of all this hand waving?" Several responses to this question are possible.

1. The verbal directions given in advance cannot always anticipate the needs that arise during the music.
2. If they are given during the music, they probably will detract from the aesthetic experience.
3. If they are given during the music, they may not even be heard.

As you become more and more secure, sophisticated things can be done with the song. Consonants can be cut off precisely. You can show the style of the piece in the way you move your hands. Smooth, legato movement will begin to contrast with choppy, staccato motion. As you gain confidence through experience, you will be able to concentrate on the musical factors instead of the motions to be learned. Practicing in front of a mirror is a good shortcut to acquiring confidence. The struggling conductor can be his or her own best critic.

Recommended Reading

GREEN, ELIZABETH, *The Modern Conductor.* Englewood Cliffs, NJ: Prentice-Hall, Inc., 1981. Comprehensive discussion of conducting for students who wish to study it in depth.

Recommended Resources
(for folk and familiar songs)

DALLIN, LEON AND LYNN, *Heritage Songster.* Dubuque, IA: Wm. C. Brown Company, Publishers, 1980.

LEISY, JAMES, *The Good Times Songbook.* Nashville, TN: Abingdon Press, 1974.

Suggested Projects

1. Practice conducting music in patterns of 2, 3, 4, and 6.
2. Practice attacks and releases in front of the mirror.
3. Select a song to lead while your class sings it. Be sure to choose a comfortable key, use a pitch reference to give the starting pitch, and give a precise cutoff.

LEAD SONGS WHILE PLAYING AN ACCOMPANYING INSTRUMENT

Conducting patterns are valuable tools to use when leading musicial groups. Precision can be achieved by a conductor who can give full attention to the group. However, especially with a small group, the advantage of having an accompaniment may outweigh the absence of a conductor. Even when the teacher plays the accompaniment, the basic components of conducting must still be addressed: the group must be started, it must keep going, and it must be stopped. In addition to implementing those techniques, the teacher must be confident and competent in playing the accompanying instrument.

Choose the chordal instrument you play best. Piano, autoharp, and guitar are good common instruments for accompanying children. Practice the piece you will be playing so that you need minimal reference to the notation. The teacher's security in playing will help to maintain a classroom environment conducive to making music. A teacher floundering with an accompaniment invites disruptions of all kinds. These activities will not be helpful to the children and certainly are destructive to the teacher's morale.

Starting. The teacher should devise a brief introduction to the song to help the students find the starting pitch and establish the tempo. If there is no introduction, the starting pitch must be given before the singing is to begin. If you find that the children cannot find the starting pitch by listening to the introduction, be sure to give it to them before beginning.

Both hands are occupied in playing the accompaniment, so other means must be developed to show the singers when to begin. Use the head, the mouth, facial expressions, and body movement or combine all of them: smile, open your mouth, inhale visibly, tip your head slightly back to show a preparatory beat, and then lower it for the downbeat as you begin singing the words. Guitar players can lift their instruments slightly to show the preparatory beat. The downbeat is shown by the downward movement of the instrument. Even though occupied in playing an instrument, the teacher must show the children when to take a breath and when to begin singing, acting as a role model. Try the starting motions in front of a mirror to see if they are effective and comfortable for you; your judgment of effectiveness is only preliminary. The children's responses will help you to decide whether your movements have achieved results. If the singers do not sing when you expect them to, try another motion or a greater exaggeration of what you are already doing until you and the children start together. Don't give up. The first time you try to lead while playing you may be afraid. Remember, the children can be very supportive if you are well prepared and are trying to do your best. Avoid beginning the song alone hoping that the children will start in some indefinite place. Show them where to start.

Maintaining the tempo.   This can be done by modifying the same sort of gestures employed to get the children started. Move only as much as is needed to indicate the tempo. Show the beat with the body or the head when necessary. Too much shoulder pumping or unnecessary motion will distract from the musical experience. Save body motion to guide the singers if they are not together and to show tempo changes.

Dynamics.   By the use of small body motions for soft music and large movements for loud, the teacher conveys dynamics. These gestures may be unnecessary if the teacher can demonstrate the dynamics through the accompaniment.

Stopping.   If the accompaniment and the singers are to end together, simply stop playing, but keep your mouth open as long as you wish the singers to hold the last note. For the final cutoff, use your head in the same way you used your hand when conducting. Throw your head back *slightly* as a preparation, then emphatically nod it forward for the cutoff.

If the accompaniment is to continue without the singers, use your mouth to indicate that the singers are to hold the last note and your head to show the cutoff while your hands continue to play. You will need practice!

Involving others.   Vary your approach to song leading: sometimes conducting, sometimes accompanying. Try to find other people who can lead the songs when you are accompanying. Find other teachers who can either conduct or play accompaniments. See if the principal or some parents will help. You may have strong skills in leading and accompanying so that it is not necessary to have assistance, but these are good ways in which to involve other adults in the music program. The students will have an opportunity to see that music creates a pleasant way in which to share sound with adults as well as with children.

The best leaders may be some of the students. Teaching them to conduct will strengthen their sense of meter. The response to conducting is particularly strong in the upper grades. Be alert to creating and using instrumental accompaniments that the children can play. The autoharp and the pitched percussion instruments are particularly good for children to use in accompanying. By sixth grade, some of the students may be capable piano and guitar players, too.

Suggested Projects

1. Prepare a song accompaniment on a chordal instrument of your choice. Lead a group in singing the song while you play the accompaniment.
2. Work with a friend as a song leading team. First, you conduct while your friend accompanies the singing; then, reverse roles.

HELP THE BEGINNING SINGER

Looking at the first-graders as they troop into the classroom on the first day of school, it is difficult to generalize about their appearance. First-graders come in contrasting shapes and sizes and various shades of color and make many different sounds. The teacher notices the contrasts between speaking voices first and, then when they sing, finds even more variation in their singing voices. Some of the children sing with a pure, clear sound, having few overtones. Others carry the quality of their speaking voices into song. Some have wide ranges and sing accurately. Some sing close to the pitch, with occasional variations. Others seem to have limited ranges, perhaps of only four or five notes. Still others drone along seeming to be still speaking rather than singing. The last group may also be the loudest of the singers in the group. There seems to be little correlation between accuracy of singing and zealous participation. Although a young musician may complain about someone not singing right, the children seem to accept each other's sounds generally. A few of the shy first-graders participate minimally or not at all.

The first goals for these young singers are to

participate;
feel comfortable about their participation; and
learn accuracy in singing.

They must be encouraged to meet these goals in an atmosphere of acceptance and appreciation of their willingness to be a part of the class activity.

Participation. Some of the children may be reluctant to sing or may not participate at all. The teacher will try to make the experience an inviting one: telling stories about the songs, playing games with the children, adding instruments that are appropriate to the music being used, and encouraging the children to make creative additions to the activities. If some children still do not want to participate, they should not be forced to. Extra attention paid to their unwillingness to participate may reinforce that behavior. They may be too shy to sing, or they may need more observation time before feeling free to participate. Whatever the reason for their reluctance, allow them time to gain confidence in their ability to participate comfortably. Many reluctant participants eventually decide that they will sing along with everybody else.

As the children are drawn into the singing activities, the teacher unobtrusively creates opportunities to hear their individual voices, tracking the voices so as to remember the child who needs work with high-low discrimination, pitch matching, and singing-speaking conflict. A simple checklist is helpful for record keeping.

The teacher uses games to encourage the children to sing alone without fear. The "Yoo Hoo" game encourages independent singing and helps the children and the teacher to learn names.

Yoo hoo, (child's name)

Each person in the class gets a chance to call "yoo hoo" to someone else by name. If the children do not know names, they can call "yoo hoo, blue sweater" or "yoo hoo, red hair." As the children become adept at calling each other's names, they can be challenged to beat the clock, that is, to see how long it takes them to give everyone a chance at singing "you hoo (name)"; then, the next day, try to do it faster. When first playing the game, to help the children remember who hasn't had a turn, let them stand to begin the game, then sit after having a turn. Later, the challenge will be to play with everyone seated to see if they can remember who hasn't had a turn without the aid of people standing. This game can be used with numbers also: either the children call their neighbors by number in consecutive order, or they take numbers out of a hat and call to find who has the next number ("Yoo hoo, number one," "You hoo, number two," etc.). The number variation works only after the first-graders can count up to the number of people in the class.

While the children are playing varying versions of the game, the teacher is identifying those who have difficulty in singing the descending minor third. Games such as these are wonderful for encouraging the children to participate because the teacher isn't asking them to sing a solo; they are just playing.

When the inaccurate singers have been identified, the teacher will plan regular times for helping them. Some of the work should be done in small groups on a tutorial basis. Some of it can be done in music class as long as the children are not labeled as nonsingers or are made to feel inferior. Many of the techniques described in the following paragraphs will benefit the singers without problems because they exercise the voice and stretch the imagination.

Nonsinging exercises.   In helping the children to find their voices, techniques other than singing may be most effective. Include attention to environmental sounds. Encourage the students to listen to what they hear around them. Ask them to imitate these sounds. A child who is nervous about singing may relax when imitating specified sounds in the environment. A child who doesn't pay attention may begin to listen with discrimination. A child who is careless about the sound of his or her voice may be more particular when striving to imitate an environmental sound.

The imitation of sirens is effective in developing flexibility in the child's range. It allows the voice to produce many pitches without demanding accuracy. The children have been exposed to different types of sirens on television programs, so they can demonstrate alternatives to the sound of

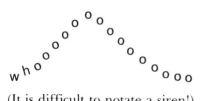

(It is difficult to notate a siren!)

A favorite alternative is

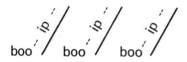

After the children have experimented with the siren sounds, ask them to let their voices go up with the "whooo" sound and then hold at the top. It won't be easy on the teacher's ears, but this technique encourages children to sing high notes. For some, it will be the beginning of range development that they have never experienced previously.

Encourage the children to identify other sounds and try to produce them vocally. They may hear environmental sounds that the teacher has ignored.

Imitation of animal sounds help children to differentiate pitch vocally. They enjoy relating to such stories as *Three Bears* or *Three Billy Goats Gruff.* A variety of sound effects can be added to the story by the children.

One of the effects will be to show how Papa Bear, Mamma Bear, and Baby Bear growl or how the three different-sized goats sound when they converse with the troll who lives under the bridge. Once a first-grader gets the idea of equating size with pitch, the class members can be encouraged to decide on other imitative sounds they can make to show size. Among the things they may want to imitate are rocket ships, their toys, and grown-up sounds.

The imitation of grown-ups is one problem that some boys face in finding their voices. They may be modeling themselves after their fathers' deep voices. Some of them have fathers who either never learned or choose not to sing. The sound that the boys relate to as part of this model is the low-pitched speaking voice. These boys may be responsive to the teacher's explanation that someday they will have voices like their dads, but when they are small, their voices should be much higher. The male music teacher can illustrate the difference for them by using his normal voice and his falsetto.

Singing exercises.   In general, it seems more difficult for children to imitate instruments than to imitate voices. The teacher of music is encouraged to give the children pitch-matching experiences vocally. The male teacher may have to use his falsetto if the children have difficulty in singing the pitches an octave higher than he is singing.

Carrying on conversations with the children using singing rather than speaking encourages them to develop vocal flexibility. In a free conversation, the children can respond with any melodic pattern they choose.

The teacher will develop ear-training experiences in which the children will be asked to repeat the musical phrase that the teacher sings. Either the group or the individual will be asked to echo short melodic phrases. The phrases will be coupled with neutral syllables, sol-fa syllables, words, numbers, parts of a story, or any imaginative addition devised by either the teacher or the children. For example:

Where   are   you   hid - ing?

Lu   lu   lu   lu   Do   re   do

Ghosts   are   fly - ing round.   Where   did   Mar - y   go?

Melodic echoing may be coupled with simple rhythmic devices using body parts.

1. Make this gen-tle sound *(finger snap)*
2.   Make this louder sound (clap)
3.   Make this stamping sound (stamp foot)

More sophisticated echo patterns combine melodic patterns with body sounds.

1.Use your fin - gers, tap like this

The notation ♩ indicates the body sound imitating the teacher on the repeat. The children sing the repeat and use the body part mentioned in the phrase to create the rhythm at the same time.

2.   Use your knees to knock like this.
3.   Use your head to swing like this.
4.   Use your toes to tap like this, etc.

If the teacher observes that the children have difficulty with two concurrent activities, postpone them for a later day.

These are more echoing patterns combining singing and body parts:

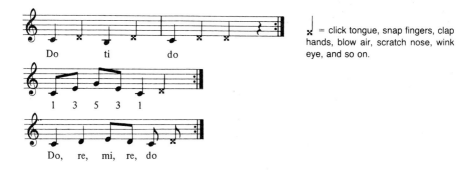

♩ = click tongue, snap fingers, clap hands, blow air, scratch nose, wink eye, and so on.

Do   ti   do

1 3 5 3 1

Do, re, mi, re, do

Body placement.   Children who are having difficulty in finding their singing voices may need to reinforce their concept of high- and low-tone production through physical placement of their bodies. Have the children sit on the floor. While there, use an instrument such as the piano to play low sounds. As the piano plays higher sounds, encourage the children to move their bodies up. When the highest pitch on the instrument is played, the children will be standing as tall as possible with their arms stretched up. As soon as the children get the idea, the teacher should withdraw prompts other than the sound of the piano so the children will respond physically to the pitches alone. Some of the children will have no difficulty in responding. Others who are uncertain will follow them. Even if the uncertain children are not making independent decisions, they will still be coupling physical position with high and low sounds by following accurate leaders. If leaders emerge who are inaccurate, the teacher can give prompts as they are needed.

The activity just described is *ear training.* The children must develop skill in aural perception and learn to transfer their perception of sound to their voices. Encourage them to produce very low sounds while being on or close to the floor. Ask them to move their bodies upward as they make their voices produce higher pitches. Help them to stretch their arms upward while producing the highest sound they can. This activity is hard on the teacher's ears.

If a child still is not using her voice to make high sounds, tell her that her voice can go still higher. (Be sure to do this with only one child at a time.) Help her step on a chair and ask her to let her voice come up with her. The physical sensation of the body being higher helps some children to sing a higher pitch.

Pouring water out of the pitcher is an imaginative exercise that helps some children. Encourage the children to pretend that their voices are like water. As they bend forward abruptly, the water is going to pour out of the pitcher. Admittedly, the image of bending over produces a lower placement of the head, so that logically the pitch might be thought to go down. Practically speaking, perhaps because of the increased support of the diaphragm, this exercise helps many young singers reach higher notes.

Expanding range. Much of the discussion so far has centered on the idea of voices singing high. Actually, it is not so much a case of having children's voices reach an absolute high as it is of showing them that they have a wider range than many of them have been using and that they can sustain tone at different pitches. A problem may be that the child doesn't understand that speaking and singing are two different ways of producing sound. Imitating bumble bees is a good way to learn to produce a continuous tone. Buzzzzz on one pitch, then buzzzzz higher and lower in response to the direction indicated by the teacher's hand.

Matching pitches. Little by little, all these activities move the child toward matching sounds, phrases, and eventually whole pieces. It would be ideal if, by the end of first grade, all the class members can match pitches. Early in second grade, the class should have a good unison sound. If nothing seems to work for certain children, the teacher is urged not to despair! There are a few children who need a little more time to mature. Some of them come back from summer vacation singing accurately when they could not at the end of spring term.

Children new to the school who have not learned to sing can be helped even when they are in the upper grades. Except in rare instances, high school students and adults can learn to sing. Many of them who seem to have problems have never had anyone take the time to help them hear what they sound like. In fact, perception of self gives some nonpitch matchers problems. These children can tell if two phrases are the same or different. They can tell whether or not someone else is singing accurately. They don't seem to pay attention to what is coming out of their own mouths. As soon as attention is drawn to what they hear and what they produce, remarkable improvement can be made. Tape recorders are effective tools in working with some children and their perception of their own pitch production.

Individual attention.   A nonthreatening atmosphere soon makes young children comfortable about singing alone even in front of the class. Older children may find it more difficult to do so. If time can be found, the teacher should try to work alone with these students until they gain confidence and accuracy. In situations that do not allow time for individual work, these inaccurate older singers still can learn to sing well. They may respond to classwork and with an abundance of singing opportunities relax and find their singing voices.

If the children make even a little improvement, celebrate. The children who match pitches today better than yesterday may regress again tomorrow, but because they are better today, they should get lots of encouragement. It is always pleasant to observe the child who makes steady improvement or the one who gets the idea of singing and from that moment on sings well. Even though it is frustrating to work with a child whose progress is limited, the teacher should continue to help her. The concerned teacher may give her the only chance she has to learn to sing. When she finally succeeds, the rewards are great for both student and teacher.

Just as children vary, so do vocal problems and solutions. Some of the problems young children face vocally seem to return when their voices begin to change: the range shortens, a once accurate soprano becomes a very inaccurate cambiata, and last year's confident singer becomes this year's uncertain one. Although the reasons are different, some of the symptoms are similar. (See the section on the changing voice later in this chapter.) In both situations, children need guidance, understanding, and encouragement to help them toward eventual musical achievement.

Suggested Projects

1. Identify a child with pitch-matching problems. Use the techniques described above. Before starting to work, analyze the child's voice as to range, accuracy, and quality. As you work with the child, note progress made, dates and time spent working, questions and problems. Evaluate the effectiveness of the techniques you used.
2. Identify another child who needs pitch-matching help. Follow the procedures described in project 1. Compare the effectiveness of the work done with both children.

TEACH A SONG THROUGH AURAL EXPERIENCE

Songs provide ways for young children to become involved enjoyably and effectively in music. Before singing the songs, the children should have many opportunities to hear them. Some of the children have had a limited aural experience and aural experience is essential if they are to become good music makers. Even if they have sung a lot before first grade, they must still hear new songs enough times so as to form an aural impression before being asked to sing them.

Suzuki[4] calls his method of teaching the Mother Tongue Approach. He consistently exposes the children to good violin sound, maintaining that the natural way in which the children learn to speak their native language by hearing other people speak can be applied to learning to play a stringed instrument. Suzuki's approach is valid for teaching children to sing songs also. The children must have ample opportunity to hear music before being asked to produce it.

Some inexperienced teachers finish a lesson in which they have planned to teach a new song to children with misgivings about the effectiveness of the lesson. They may express discontent with the children, saying that they can't sing, they can't match pitches, or they don't pay attention. While this can be true, it may not necessarily be the children's fault that the song was not learned properly. The teacher must plan the lesson so that the children have many opportunities to hear the song before they are asked to sing it. They must memorize the sound before they are asked to produce it.

Motivation. Another factor in teaching songs to children successfully is motivation. To get and keep the children's attention, the aural experiences must be accompanied by motivations to help them focus. Most children will display little interest if they are told repeatedly just to listen to the song. Their inquisitive minds will respond if they are given reasons for

[4]See Chapter 10.

listening or asked to make some musical response that will accompany the listening experience.

Nonmusical reasons for listening to a song may be related to

1. The season or a holiday.
2. The vocabulary of the text.
3. The story it tells.
4. A lesson it teaches.
5. The mood that it sets.
6. A game that can be played with it.
7. Dramatizations that can be created to go with it.

Musical reasons for listening should include motivations related to concept development such as

1. Identifying characteristics of the melody: high-low notes, contour, steps, skips, repeated notes.
2. Producing a steady beat.
3. Discriminating meter.
4. Moving in an appropriate manner for the song.
5. Finding rhythmic characteristics.
6. Selecting an appropriate tempo.
7. Describing or recommending dynamics.
8. Distinguishing characteristics of form: number of phrases, ones that are similar, dissimilar.
9. Recognizing instruments that are playing or recommending some to be played with the song.
10. Describing the style of accompaniment.

The strength of the motivators will determine the number of hearings the child can handle without becoming bored.

Presenting the song. The presentation of the song to the children depends on the capability of the teacher and the activity involved. The most obvious way is to have the teacher sing the song. A proficient instrumentalist may wish to play it. Accompaniment by a chordal instrument (piano, autoharp, guitar) will add to some of the presentations. When the children need the teacher's immediate presence during an activity connected with the song, the use of a cassette tape will allow the teacher to be free to move close to the children. The teacher or a friend can prerecord the piece with appropriate accompaniments, dynamics, sound effects, or whatever will be most useful in support of the daily activity. It will add to the variety of activities if the music can be recorded in different ways so that a change of tempo, instruments, dynamics, and style can be used to provoke class discussion. Short tapes with the music recorded at the beginning make songs easier to find. A long tape with many pieces on it necessitates constant attention to the tape counter. Frequent fumbling may occur if the classroom cassette player doesn't have a counter. If materials are taken from textbook series, most of them are already on records or tapes that may be purchased with the books.

Materials.   There are many attractive and interesting songs for children. They must be chosen with care as to the suitability of text and the children's musical capability. The manner of teaching the song will vary according to the intrinsic nature of the piece itself. Songs with short repeated motives such as

Hm - hm,   Hm - hm.

in "The Mouse's Courting Song" and

Ee - i - ee - i - o.

in "Old MacDonald" suggest almost immediate involvement through the children learning that short part of the song. They will gradually learn the rest of the song by repeatedly hearing the teacher sing it.

Games and dances involve the children immediately in movement. They learn the song over a period of time in which they are actively involved with the music. After the material has been selected for use with the children, the teacher must study it to determine the most effective way in which to teach it.

Whole-song approach.   If there is ample time, the whole-song approach may be used. Frequent opportunities can be planned for the children to hear the whole song before they are asked to sing it. "Rain Is Falling Down" can be used with first-graders as part of the daily weather report for many days before the children sing it.

At first, the teacher will sing the weather report, gradually including the children in discussing what they know about the weather projection. The teacher will then encourage them to listen for the weather report on radio and television and enlist the aid of the children in determining what to sing about regarding the weather.

RAIN IS FALLING DOWN

Unknown

   1. Rain is fall - ing down.   Rain is fall - ing down.

Pit - ter, pat - ter, pit - ter, pat - ter, Rain is fall - ing down.

  2. Sun is shining bright. Clouds are gone now.
  3. Fog is rolling in. Watch the traffic.
  4. Snow is on its way. Colder weather.

To develop musical concepts in connection with the song, the teacher will have the children show the rain falling down with their hands and draw attention to the contour of the music, which also moves down. The teacher will show the children how the music moves by using his or her hands with the "pitter, patter." The teacher will then ask the children to count the number of times that he or she sings the phrase "Rain is falling down" and ask them to listen to see if the music is the same three times also. The teacher will ask the children to compare the music for "Pitter, patter" with the other phrases. Using vocabulary appropriate for young children, they will discuss the form of the piece. The children may describe the piece by saying it comes down once, then down again, then splashes, and then comes down again. Be cautious about identifying form with letters such as A B A; this may confuse young children.

These activities will take place during short sessions spread over many music lessons. Finally, after repeated exposure to the song, the children will begin to join in singing the weather report. The advantage of approaching the music through the whole-song method is that the children are exposed to the song as a musical experience over a period long enough for them to assimilate it.

"A History of Heat" may be taught to second-graders by the whole-song method in relationship to study of the energy situation.

The children are studying energy. Even though they have just begun school in the fall, the subject is already important to them because a new house near the school has a solar energy system on the roof and the class has discussed how the system works, why it is being installed, and reasons for developing alternate sources of energy. The first time the children hear the song, the teacher has asked them to listen to all of its verses to count the different ways of heating a house that are mentioned in it. A chart is drawn

A HISTORY OF HEAT

Lois N. Harrison

1. When mo - ther's grand - mo - ther was my age, Her
2. My grand - ma had a big iron stove, de -
3. Then mo - ther's fam - i - ly had oil heat, with
4. We have e - lec - tri - cal current in wires, to

house was warmed by wood. She'd hud - dle by the
signed to burn hard coal. To keep the em - bers
radia - tors all a - round. Her house was al - ways
take care of our needs. But what if po - wer

fire - place, right there it felt so good!
glow - ing bright day and night be - came her goal.
ver - y warm for fuel was said to a - bound.
dis - a - pears be - cause we paid no heed?

up to show the ways of heating and the family members who are mentioned with them.

> Mother's grandmother .... Fireplace
> Grandma .... Iron stove
> Mother................................. Radiators
> Me................................ Wires in the wall

To make the song more inclusive, the group is free to change the gender of the words: father's grandfather, mother's grandfather, and so on.

The children will discuss the kind of heat they have in their homes. They will try to recall other heating systems they have observed. Some of the children may not know what heats their homes, so the teacher will ask them to find out.

The next time the teacher sings the song, the children may be asked to stand when the kind of heat that they have in their homes is mentioned. The teacher will see whether anyone failed to stand. Perhaps someone has a kind of heat not mentioned, and verses can be added to the song.

Another hearing of the song can involve the children dramatically. They can pretend that they are doing whatever needs to be done to make the heating system work. If they have not had experience with some of the systems mentioned, it is a good idea to have pictures to help them visualize the heat source. It will be easy for the children to pretend that they are carrying wood for the fireplace, even chopping it. Digging coal may not cause problems either, but dealing with electricity may produce only the action of pushing a button off and on. The dramatization can lead to a discussion of the sources of electricity, with the children's movement expanding to show water falling, turbines turning, and so on.

The song can also be used to develop music concepts. It may appear as part of a melody recognition game. It can be performed for the children without words on the recorder, piano, or melody bells or sung on a neutral syllable. If the children can't recognize it without words, they probably are not yet ready to sing it, because the aural image of the melody has not yet been established.

When the children are working to develop meter recognition, this song can appear as one of the songs that helps them to establish the feeling of three beats per measure. When they are looking for high and low notes, the teacher can help them to find the highest note and the lowest one. As the teacher presents it to them in varying tempos and dynamics, the students can determine which of these expressive elements seem most appropriate for the song. Should the words cause any of these effects to vary from verse to verse?

After many contacts with the song, some groups of children will be more than ready to sing it. Some of the children will not have needed all the experiences for their tonal memory to have captured the song. Other children may need still more listening. For them, the experiences noted can be repeated or other procedures can be developed. A general tendency in teaching songs seems to be to let the students sing the material before they are ready, that is, before the melody has been memorized. As a result, the singing is inaccurate and the children gain an undeserved reputation for singing poorly or for being nonsingers. While children often need special help in tone matching, and in general discrimination between speaking and singing, many problems of the so-called "nonsinger" disappear when the song is presented in such a fashion that he or she knows it thoroughly by sound before starting to sing it.

Find out if the children are ready to sing the whole song by singing it for them, but leave out key parts such as the ending of the phrase so that the singers can fill it in. If some of the students are clearly ready, while others are not, individuals can be selected to fill in when the teacher stops singing. The length and frequency of the missing parts will depend on the readiness of the children. In "A History of Heat," all the verses can be used to challenge the youngsters for the words as well as for the melody. This activity will give the slower musicians still more aural opportunities before being asked to sing the complete song.

In many ways, teaching by the whole-song method is a very musical experience for children. They develop a total feeling for the music instead of a fragmented one. They are not put under pressure to produce a tune accurately almost as soon as they hear it. The song has a chance to become part of their musical vocabulary over a long period of time, which allows for more reflection. They can join in singing the complete piece when they really know it.

Repeated phrases approach. There are times when it is appropriate or necessary for a song to be taught in a short period of time. The procedure described below is for teaching a song during one class period. It can be combined with the whole-song approach, cutting down the total time necessary for that method. It will be described as if the children had never heard the song.

1. Find meaningful motivations for the children to hear the whole song three times.
2. Give them reasons for hearing the first phrase at least three times.
3. Let the children sing the first phrase.
4. If it is inaccurate, give them reasons for listening to the first phrase again, which will help them to make necessary corrections.
5. Let them try singing it again.
6. When the first phrase is accurate, go on.
7. Give the children reasons to hear the second phrase at least three times. If the first and second phrases are the same, help the children to discover this, or find minor differences in either the words or music if they exist.
8. Follow steps 3, 4, 5, 6 as they are applicable to the second phrase.
9. Sing phrases one and two for the children, helping them to discover how the two phrases connect if it is necessary for their singing accuracy.
10. Guide the children to discover if the third phrase is the same as, or different from, phrases one and two.
11. Use steps 2–6 as appropriate.
12. Continue these procedures throughout the song.
13. Sing the song for the children all the way through.
14. Have the children sing the song.

There is nothing magical about the number "three." It recurs in the preceding discussion because it represents the average number of listening times many children need to get an aural impression of the song. This formula for teaching a song in a limited amount of time must be tempered by the needs of the students and its suitability to the song that was chosen. In teaching the lesson, the beginning teacher is urged to listen for the children's accuracy in the music as well as the words.

TEACHING A SONG IN A LIMITED PERIOD OF TIME THROUGH THE REPEATED PHRASES APPROACH[5]

SOLAR ENERGY

Lois N. Harrison

When the children first began discussing the solar energy system of the house near the school, the teacher decided that the energy concepts being discussed could be reinforced by having the class sing about solar

[5]This lesson refers only to teaching the melody of "Solar Energy." The harmony part is included for addition at a later time or for performance by an upper grade.

84

energy immediately. The follow-up lesson included having the children learn the "Solar Energy" song.

"Today, our new song is about something that you were very interested in discussing. Raise your hand as soon as you know what the song is about, but don't tell anyone what you have discovered." TEACHER SINGS COMPLETE SONG.

"It is wonderful to see all those hands go up in the air. You were good about not telling anyone about the song, too." Teacher then picks someone to tell about the song and has the other children add what they heard.

"Will you boys and girls please count this time to see how many things are mentioned in the song that solar energy can do for us? Remember, count only what is mentioned in the song." TEACHER SINGS SONG SECOND TIME.

"How many different things did you find, Sheila? Do you agree with her, Tom? Just to make sure, let's count together with our fingers as you *hear* the song again. Put a finger up each time you hear about the sun doing something for us." TEACHER SINGS SONG THIRD TIME. (If students begin singing before they have been invited to do so, the teacher should stop and remind them that it is their listening time. Although teachers sometimes correctly interpret the students' wish to begin singing as an indication that they are ready, this often means that they are well motivated to sing and wish to do so, but may not yet be ready to sing accurately since they have not had enough aural experience to memorize the melody. The teacher's role in these instances is to maintain the high interest level of the class by giving the students appropriate reasons for listening to the music, while still focusing their attention in ways other than singing. The children generally respond well to giving the teacher his or her turn as long as they know that they will have their turns soon.)

Because the teacher has been raising fingers as each use of the sun has been mentioned in the song and the children have followed, her exclamation should be accurate: "Your fingers are wonderful! They show that you counted three things that the song says that the sun can do for us. What were they?" General discussion.

"Think quietly, now. What was the first thing that the song mentioned that the sun can do for us?" Pause. "As I sing the first two measures of the song, check what you are thinking to see if you really remembered the *first* one." TEACHER SINGS FIRST PHRASE.

"Please smile if you were right." Pause for smiles! "In a little while you are going to sing the first phrase, but before you do, we must discuss something that is tricky in the music. As you listen this time, try to figure out what we have to be very careful of as we sing together. I'll give you a clue: it's not something we sing." TEACHER SINGS FIRST PHRASE SECOND TIME.

The teacher is looking for someone to comment on the rests, or the time in the middle where no singing takes place. If the teacher has looked like a conspirator trying not to give something away during the rests or has covered his or her mouth during the rests, the children will probably comment on the silences. It is necessary to maintain the rhythmic accuracy of the rests even while giving these clues. At this time, the teacher will help the students to discover that there are four beats with rests in the phrase. A third hearing of the first phrase will allow the children to show the beats for the rests by clicking, clapping, or playing steady beats on these rests. TEACHER SINGS FIRST PHRASE THIRD TIME.

"Now, you sing the first phrase. 'You' (sung on pitch), ready, sing (in tempo): 'You mean the sun, . . . '." The teacher's technique of beginning a song or a phrase should be so highly developed that the children experience no hesitation or doubt as to their starting pitch or their starting time. Every time the children sing, they must be given the starting pitch and a clear signal when to begin. (See the earlier section on conducting.)

If the children sing the first phrase inaccurately, the teacher must isolate the errors and help the children to correct them before going on. If it has been sung well, compliment them and say, "Please sing that phrase again but stop after singing it while I sing the second phrase. Tell me after you listen if those two phrases are the same or different." CHILDREN SING THE FIRST PHRASE; THEN TEACHER SINGS SECOND PHRASE FIRST TIME.

"Was this phrase the same as, or different from, the first phrase?" "How was it different?" During this part of the lesson the teacher should respond to what the students heard. If they say that the words were different, the teacher can respond enthusiastically and immediately SING THE SECOND PHRASE A SECOND TIME to reinforce the word difference. If they say the melody was different, the children can draw the melody while the TEACHER SINGS THE SECOND PHRASE THE THIRD TIME. It is appropriate to point out to the children aurally and visually, with their hands in the air, the upward direction of the melody for "water" and the downward direction of "warm my house." If the children hear other differences, or imagined differences, the teacher must be willing to respond to what they are saying. Sometimes the comments of individual students give valuable clues to advanced perceptions they are capable of making or of necessary remedial work.

"Let's sing the second phrase together." If no correction is needed after this singing, then illustrate how the two phrases go together and let the children sing both of them.

"Boys and girls, you have sung half of this new song and you are doing very well. There is something about the last half that is going to make it very easy to learn. What do you suppose it is?" TEACHER SINGS LAST HALF OF SONG.

When the children respond that the phrase is sung twice, challenge them. "Are the words exactly the same?" TEACHER SINGS LAST HALF OF SONG SECOND TIME. When they agree that they are, the teacher then asks them about the music. "Is it repeated exactly?" TEACHER SINGS LAST HALF OF SONG THIRD TIME. If there is any disagreement about the repetition of the melody, draw disconnected lines on the board to show the direction and duration of the notes of the third phrase; then point to these same lines while singing the fourth phrase.

Ask the children to sing the last half of the song. If their singing is accurate, suggest that they close their eyes and listen to the song all together to make sure they have learned the entire piece. TEACHER SINGS SONG.

Have the children sing the song all the way through. If inaccuracies have persisted, help the children with corrections before singing the song again.

When a script is written out for a lesson such as the one just described, it seems lengthy and, for the beginning teacher, may be laborious to write. However, you are urged to do this to assist you in developing the thinking process that must take place in planning music lessons. Experience in working with the children will help you to tailor the procedures to their capabilities and the specific characteristics of the song. Consistent attention to providing aural experience when teaching songs will help you to give them accurate and joyful learning experiences.

Suggested Projects

1. Using the lesson plan form from Chapter 3 as a model, write a plan using the repeated phrases approach for teaching a song.
2. Use the lesson plan to teach the song to a group of children.
3. Plan a series of lessons for teaching a song through the whole-song approach.

INTRODUCE VISUAL REINFORCERS FOR AURAL EXPERIENCES

Teaching music to children through aural experiences is necessary, but when it remains for a long time the only means by which new music can be learned, children tend to remain totally dependent on it. Early in music education, there was great controversy between proponents of music literacy and those educators who wished children to experience music unencumbered by note reading. Those who pushed the reading process seemed sometimes to be encouraging a mechanical, nonmusical approach that drilled the children in a boring fashion. The experiential proponents, on the other hand, taught almost exclusively by rote, allowing the children to attain great heights of musical expression but giving them few techniques or resources on which to draw as independent musicians in the time spent away from the teacher of music.[6]

Ideally, the progress away from exclusively aural learning to reading should take place gradually throughout the students' elementary school years. When first entering school, the children should learn to sing. They should learn a repertoire of songs with which to express themselves as part of their aesthetic involvement. They should perform music that they can learn with help, but that they could not possibly read themselves. They should develop musical memory to help them reproduce accurately the melodies they hear. The development of these skills continues to be important through the first years of school, but as the children grow in their musical capabilities, the exclusively aural procedure should gradually give way to the association of sound with symbol leading to music reading. Since this doesn't happen all at once, the interim activities should combine aural and visual experiences, with the balance being determined by the capabilities of the students.

Reading readiness.   In the early stages of reading, reading-readiness activities should be undertaken. An example is the use of lines drawn on the chalkboard in teaching the second half of "Solar Energy." Reading-readiness activities begin to illustrate visually concepts with which the children are dealing aurally.

As the students progress in reading skill, their musicality will be dependent upon constant listening. Even when they are reading independently, their attention to their own musical sound as well as sounds made by others remains an integral part of their musical development. Instrumental students, such as pianists, when poorly taught, sometimes read in a mechanical fashion where a note indicates a finger to be manipulated, not a sound to be produced. This practice is to be avoided in favor of constant attention to the sound that is represented by the symbol.

SHOWING NOTATION TO THE CHILDREN IN FAMILIAR SONGS

The second-graders had learned the "Hallowe'en Song" in first grade and enjoyed singing it A year later, as they sing it again, they are encouraged to relate the sound to written notation. A large chart of the music notation (no words) is prepared for them.

[6]Birge, *History of Public School Music,* pp. 66–67.

HALLOWE'EN SONG

Unknown

Hal - lo - we'en, Hal - lo we'en, Oh what fun - ny things are seen!

Witch - es hats, coal - black cats, broom stick rid - ers, mice and rats

As they sing the song, the teacher points to the corresponding notes. The children are encouraged to point to them from the distance of their chairs. Volunteers are asked to indicate the notes on the chart as the children sing, with the teacher aiding them if they need help in pointing accurately.

Pictures relating to the words are displayed. The children are asked to determine where the pictures should be placed on the chart. Velcro glued to both the chart and the pictures makes it easy for the children to attach the pictures next to the correct musical phrase.

The children are asked to look for any place in the piece where they see notes that are the same as the first three notes. The teacher shows them the difference between notes in a space and notes on a line. The pictures help them to identify places in the song. This procedure is repeated throughout the song with the children identifying other repeated patterns. The identification process will not be easy for all the children; it can be repeated frequently with other songs so that they learn how to look at notation. Use "Marching to Pretoria" to help the children identify other concepts.

MARCHING TO PRETORIA

English Words by Josef Marais

Dutch Folk Song from South Africa

Ask the children what they can discover about the notes that are above the words "I'm with you and you're with me, And so...". Are there any other places in the music with the same pitches repeated? Are the repeated pitches always eighth notes? What happens to the pitch of the notes that are above the last two words of the song? 5-5-4-3-2-1 or so-so-fa-mi-re-do will be sung for this pattern because it will be talked about and sung in other songs.

CLAP YOUR HANDS

American Folk Song

American Folk Song collected by Ruth Crawford Seeger.

What can the children discover about the rhythm of the lines in "Clap Your Hands"? Are the pitches of those two lines also the same?

There are many musical concepts that the children can be helped to discover in the notation. All the discoveries just described were related to songs the children had been taught through aural experience alone. The discoveries they made coupled the musical involvement with notation after they had learned the song. Since the children experience many music-making activities, they have a treasury of associations that can be made with the printed notes. Above all, the notational coupling must not be dull, overly lengthy, or unrelated to a musical experience!

In addition to having the children look at musical examples in their books or on overhead transparencies, notate the pertinent examples for them on the chalkboard or prepare charts in advance to illustrate the concepts. The value of showing the examples from one large illustration is that it is possible to be very specific about what is being discussed. The children's attention can be focused on one item. The value of prepared charts is that they can be hung in the room for continued student observation and can be used over again when needed.

Textbook series offer a choice between purchasing a first grade book for each child or using a large chart. The advantage of a book in each child's hands is that it can be taken home for work outside the music class. The advantages of the charts are that the class attention can be focused on a central point, the children do not have to concern themselves with finding page numbers, and the chart is kept in the room while the book may be left someplace other than the music class when it is needed. (Bookmarks or ribbon markers may help with the page finding problem.)

Some of the discoveries in notation should be made in songs without words. When we consider that a huge percentage of the child's school time is spent in learning to read words, it is easy to understand that the first thing a child relates to when being presented with a song is the text. Great care should be taken to have the child begin to focus on the musical notation, both alone and in conjunction with the words.

Beginning reading.   As the children become adept at finding concepts in the notation, they will gradually learn to let those symbols help them learn new music. The procedures described have been discoveries after the piece has been learned, so they are not reading experiences. After the children become used to seeing the notation, after they have begun to understand that pitch is indicated by note head placement and that rhythm is shown by the note's shape and color (a difficult concept for some children), they are almost ready to read without the teacher doing everything for them. Caution: Guide these events gradually. To expect children to read before they are ready can be a devastating, frustrating experience that may jeopardize their enjoyment of music.

Despite the stress that has been laid on directing the children's attention to musical notation rather than to the words, attention must be paid to circumstances that may arise in which the text will become the focus of the reading-readiness experiences. Some children have trouble relating to anything on the printed page. These children may be spending extra time working with the reading specialist. They may be even less able to read music notation than words. For these slow readers, a beginning-level approach can use words to find music symbols. Give the children both words and music. Play the song without the words. (If you can't play it well, sing it on a neutral syllable.) Ask them to follow so that when you stop they can tell you which word they were on. By careful selection of readable texts and judicious determination of places to stop, the teacher can help these children learn phrase endings and pinpoint music notation by relating it to the word. Slow learners need extra help. It aids them in their regular reading as well as in music reading readiness.

The following samples indicate ways in which the children can embark upon reading experiences.

HOW CHILDREN GRADUALLY BECOME INVOLVED IN READING SMALL SECTIONS OF PIECES

Refresh the children's memories as to the sight and sound of the first measure of "Hallowe'en." To identify the notes of that measure, there are several alternatives: call the notes mi, re, do; 3, 2, 1; F-sharp, E, D; or use neutral syllables. Have them find the pattern again in the "Hallowe'en" music. Introduce new notation to them. They have not seen this notation previously:

Challenge the children to find the familiar pattern. Have them sing it each time it occurs in the piece with the teacher supplying the new material. They will use whatever means of identification they are used to (syllables, numbers, pitch names, or neutral syllables). Even though the children are not reading a complete song, they are reading a portion of it. Soon the words will be added so that the experience doesn't seem like an exercise. The unfamiliar part of the song will be taught through aural repetition to ensure accuracy. The notation in the third measure will help the children to discover more repeated notes.

HOT CROSS BUNS

Hot cross buns, hot cross buns, one a pen-ny, two a pen-ny, hot cross buns.

If it becomes evident that exposure to the notation of the entire piece is overwhelming or incomprehensible to the children, don't hesitate to show them only as much of the notation as will be helpful to them.

Once the children get the idea of transferring concepts that they have already established to new materials, they can begin to use them in many additional pieces. Look for an opportunity to talk about finding mi-re-do on different notes than those of the first pattern. A necessary concept is that of singing in different places in the students' vocal range or, using musical terminology, in different keys. See how many pieces you and the children can find in which the mi-re-do three-note pattern can be identified. A few samples follow. In each of these pieces, the children can read their familiar patterns. Not only is the mi-re-do pattern in this first song, but there also are good examples of do-re-mi to serve as the next one for the children to read. When changing key, illustrate visually, with notation apart from the song, the appearance of the pattern in the new key.

| Old pattern | Same pattern in new key | Reorganization of original pattern |

COME YE THANKFUL PEOPLE, COME

Henry Alford

George J. Elvey

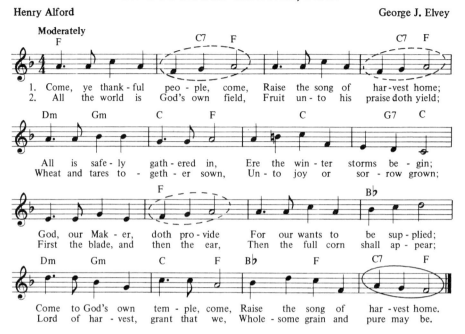

1. Come, ye thank-ful peo-ple, come, Raise the song of har-vest home;
2. All the world is God's own field, Fruit un-to his praise doth yield;

All is safe-ly gath-ered in, Ere the win-ter storms be - gin;
Wheat and tares to - geth-er sown, Un-to joy or sor - row grown;

God, our Mak - er, doth pro-vide For our wants to be sup - plied;
First the blade, and then the ear, Then the full corn shall ap - pear;

Come to God's own tem - ple, come, Raise the song of har-vest home.
Lord of har - vest, grant that we, Whole-some grain and pure may be.

Don't let the different rhythm in the "Seven Joys of Christmas" throw the musical detectives off the track. Will they find the do-re-mi as well as the three mi-re-do's? Can they sing them accurately?

SEVEN JOYS OF CHRISTMAS

United States

1. The first good joy that Christ-mas brings, It is the joy__ of one.__
To buy and wrap the Christ-mas gifts And hide them, ev - 'ry one.__

Refrain

We wish you joy at Christ-mas tide_ And joy through-out the com - ing year; May_

all the world join in our song, The song of Christ - mas cheer.__

Not only is there a mi-re-do in a new key in "Hop Up, My Ladies," but there also are repeated notes and good illustrations of a new concept, the octave.

HOP UP, MY LADIES

United States

Hop up, my la - dies, three in a row, Hop up, my la - dies, three in a row,
Hop up, my la - dies, three in a row, Don't mind the weath-er, so the wind don't blow.

From Spectrum of Music, by Mary Val Marsh, Carroll Rinehart, and Edith Savage, ©1980 by Macmillan Publishing Co., Inc. Reprinted by permission of the publisher.

Review the song "Marching to Pretoria." Then show the notation for a new song as written below without the words. Lead the children to discover the repeated notes in it. Challenge them to sing only the number of repeated notes there are in the notation. (Children find it easy to keep going endlessly with repeated notes!) Help them to discover that some of

these repeated notes are sixteenth notes. Look at the last five pitches of this new piece. How are they similar to the last five notes of "Pretoria"? Are there any do-re-mi or mi-re-do patterns? As the teacher sings the entire song, have the students sing the repeated notes and the last five pitches.

Do not dwell on this experience so long that it becomes dull for the students. Let it flow into complete singing of the song as soon as possible. Be sure that aural procedures are used for the unfamiliar sections, coupled with reference to the notation so that the children will learn the song accurately.

I HAVE LOST THE "DO" ON MY CLARINET

English Text by Alan Mills   French Folk Song

From Chantons un Peu *by Alan Mills.* © *Berandol Music Ltd., Toronto, Ontario, Canada. Used by permission of the publisher.*

Find many examples of the descending five-note pattern (so-fa-mi-re-do or 5-4-3-2-1 as introduced in "Pretoria" and found in "I Have Lost the 'Do' on My Clarinet") for the children to read.

Where is the five-note pattern in these songs?

HANUKAH HAYOM

Today is Hanukah

Hah - noo - kah,   Hah - noo - kah,   Hah - noo - kah   hah - yohm.
Ha - nu - kah,   Ha - nu - kah,   Ha - nu - kah   ha - yom.

A happy day!

Yohm seem - hah,   yohm seem - hah,   Hag hah - Hah - noo - kah!
Yom sim - hah,   yom sim - hah,   Hag ha - Ha - nu - kah!

From *Songs of Childhood*, by Judith Eisenstein and Frieda Prensky. ©*United Synagogue of America*. Used by permission.

Are the syllables in the descending five-note pattern for this song always so-fa-mi-re-do?

MORNING SONG

John Ferguson   Old English Folk Song

The sun is ris - ing out of bed, And in the east the

sky is red; __ Then up and wake each sleep - y head, So

ear - ly in the morn - ing. 'Tis shame to dream the

hours a way, __ When all the world is bright with day, __ And

na - ture calls to work or play, So ear - ly in the morn - ing.

This example of the five-note pattern is in a different key and is not at the end of the song.

ONE MORE RIVER

Spiritual

1. Old No - ah built him - self an ark. One more riv - er to cross. __ He built it out of hick - 'ry bark. One more riv - er to cross. __
2. The an - i - mals came two by two. One more riv - er to cross. __ The li - on and the kan - ga - roo. One more riv - er to cross. __
3. The an - i - mals came three by three. One more riv - er to cross. __ The ba - boon and the chim - pan - zee. One more riv - er to cross. __

Chorus

One more ri - ver, And that wide ri - ver is Jor - dan,

One more ri - ver, There's one more ri - ver to cross. __

Review the rhythm of "Clap Your Hands," p. 91. Ask the children to find the rhythm of the first five notes of that piece in "BINGO." See how many times they can find it. Let them add only that pattern when the teacher claps the entire song.

BINGO

Scotland

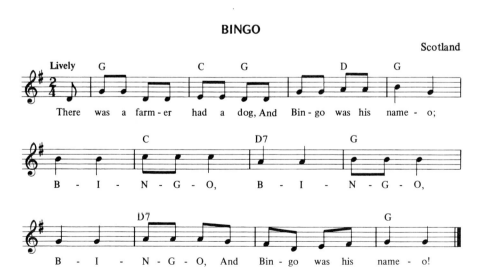

There was a farm - er had a dog, And Bin - go was his name - o;

B - I - N - G - O, B - I - N - G - O,

B - I - N - G - O, And Bin - go was his name - o!

If the children experience difficulty, the teacher may have to point to the notation rhythmically instead of clapping it. Try to find advanced students who can lead. Let them point to the notation, play it on percussion instruments, and help other students. The constant goal of the teacher should be the independence of the students through learning of reading skills.

Some of the experiences described will involve familiar songs that may already have been introduced as part of the whole-song procedure with the aim of making the exposure to the notation easier.

OH, SUSANNA

Words and Music by Stephen Foster

From *Making Music Your Own* by Beatrice Landeck, Elizabeth Crook, and Harold C. Youngberg. © 1964 by Silver Burdett Company. Reprinted by permission of the publisher.

Have the children determine which notes of the first two phrases of "Oh, Susanna" are different. How are they different? In which direction do they go? Are they close together or far apart? Have the children sing the last five notes of the first line slowly with minimal help from the teacher except for the starting pitch. If they are inaccurate, the teacher needs to give assistance. Do the same thing with the last five notes of the second line. When this is quite accurate and the children can do both endings, let them add the ending as the teacher sings the rest of the lines. Repeat this procedure for the rest of the phrases that are alike. Be sure to teach the dissimilar phrase by having the children listen, then sing. Then have them sing the whole song.

Ostinatos provide another good way for children to begin reading notation. They are often part of a song that a child has experienced, or they may be a very easy pattern. To give the children reading experience with ostinatos, the teacher can take a pattern from the song that lends itself to an instrumental accompaniment. Have the children review the song; then read the pattern before using the instruments.

CHARLIE IS MY DARLIN'

An ostinato for "Charlie Is My Darlin'":

Recorder descants provide another source of introductory reading activities. The children need play only five notes in this piece. Even if they are not ready to put the notes in an accurate rhythmic context, they can relate the notes to the words so that they know when to play them.

Children cannot be expected to translate notation into music unless they have had an abundance of prior and concurrent musical experiences. The relationship of the musical sound to the notation must be pointed out, discovered, and transferred to new music. From the first time that the youngster is shown a note until independent reading skill is attained, a

PROSPECTING FOR ENERGY SOURCES

Lois N. Harrison

1. Let's find out what's un - der- ground in pla - ces we can't see.
2. Here's the rich pe - tro - le - um and fields of na - tural gas.

Take a trip be - neath the crust where we can't of - ten be. A
There's the lode of shin - y coal, a huge com - pact - ed mass. Down

la - ser beam will guide us to plac - es we'll ex -
there's an - oth - er lay - er of earth's mys - ter - ious

plore. We'll find the rich re - sourc - es that
core. Our search is get - ting warm - er, we'll

we've been search - ing for. look and find some more!

gradual series of notational experiences must be provided. The teacher should plan to build on the capabilities of each student in the class; they will not all be on the same level. Allow them to help each other; allow them to grow at different rates. Leaders will emerge. Let them help their classmates at the same time you are helping them. Return to these concepts in different music so that the children who didn't get them before will have other opportunities. Provide variety so the children who have established these concepts will find other concepts in the new music and will continue to learn.

While the slow children are rediscovering the reading of ♩ ♩ ♫ ♩ with a percussion ostinato, the children who learn more quickly are reading ♬ ♫ ♬♫.

Because the music specialist often works with children from first through sixth grades, it may be easier to sequence the reading-readiness experiences: to go from exclusively aural learning in the first grade to an emphasis on reading in the sixth grade. It is a highly challenging part of music teaching to fade out the dependent learning while adding just the right amount of independent reading activities. It may not be as easy for the classroom teacher to do this because he or she has not been involved in the long chain of events that have affected the children's musical experiences. This is one of the most crucial areas for cooperation between the music specialist and the classroom teacher. If the school does not have a specialist, it is the responsibility of the classroom teachers to cooperate in teaching the children to read, to determine the sequence of readiness and reading experiences that they should have at each grade level, and to determine the goals for the end of each grade. A worthy goal is the achievement of a high level of reading skill by the end of sixth grade.

Suggested Project

Write a lesson plan concentrating on an aspect of reading readiness appropriate for the grade level you specify.

TEACH THE CHILDREN TO READ

A child has learned to read music when he or she can take a piece of notation and translate it independently into the sound it represents. A child who has learned to read words can pick up a newspaper and find out what the story says. Reading music does not seem to be as easy for children as reading words. Still, if the public schools were to give music reading the same amount of time as literary reading, perhaps it would be as attainable.

The teacher of music must give the children as much help with music reading as possible without neglecting other important musical activities. Regrettably, some of the children will still be musically dependent, even after completing elementary school training. Still more regrettably, some of the students will always be musically dependent. The students who cannot read music, even in mature performing groups, will never feel the joy of independent music making related to notation. A goal of public school music should be to give the students the skills they need to become musically self-sufficient.

Continue the reading-readiness and beginning reading activities described. Increase the sophistication of the activities as the students become more independent. Encourage the children to analyze each piece that they read. Ask them to find out whether the phrases are the same or different. Have them clap or play the rhythm of the piece. Ask them to determine the mood; if the words influence the style of the piece; if any clues are available as to style from the title, dates, or composer of the piece; or if any words or markings on the piece will help with either tempo or dynamics. Ask them to determine the relationship of the first note of the piece to the key; if chords are outlined in the melody; if there are familiar patterns in the melody, repeated notes, skips, or steps; or where the chord changes occur. Have the children read the melody. Accompany them with chord changes if they are needed to help them read more accurately. If the children have developed skill in relating syllables, numbers, or note names for the pitches, encourage them to use those techniques. The Kodály methods of music reading are used successfully by many teachers.[7]

Instruments can be used by the students to aid them in vocal reading. If there are skips that they cannot hear internally so as to be able to produce them vocally, encourage the students to play them on an instrument: recorder, keyboard, or pitched percussion. Let the teacher play difficult passages on the piano as a last resort.

By the time the students have reached the sixth grade, their instrumental music reading may have reached a high level. In addition to the music they study in elementary music classes, instrumentalists may participate in school lessons and ensembles, they may take private lessons, and they may participate in community or church groups. The latter may be vocal as well as instrumental. Children who have developed instrumental reading skill add great contrast to the reading capability of the general music classes. The teacher of music must deal with even greater musical differences than were present in the lower grades and must endeavor to help these advanced instrumental readers apply their knowledge to vocal and classroom instrumental reading. At the same time, the teacher must try to teach students with little background, especially those who have transferred to the school system from an area with different or no musical objectives.

The instruments mentioned in other chapters of this book such as

[7]See Kodály in Chapter 10.

recorders and percussion and chordal instruments offer variety to the advanced students and a chance for them to develop their skills through another musical medium. When students begin their instrumental work, their vocal background is invaluable to them; they can apply their rhythmic and melodic knowledge to the new instrument. Often, children learn to play pieces by ear if they have sung them. As instrumental skill develops, a crossover occurs in which their instrumental reading can now begin to help the children in vocal reading of difficult intervals. When the children are reading a song and have difficulty with part of it, they can teach it to themselves by playing the hard spots on the instrument until their ears have picked up the sound.

A word of caution, appropriate in talking about reading music as it was in earlier reading-related experiences: Be aware of the ability and the interest levels of the children. Tailor the reading event so that the young musicians will succeed and their interest will be maintained.

Children learn to read by trying to read. Arrange for them to be involved in the process of translating notation into sound as often as possible. Provide opportunities for them to read songs as a class. Divide the class into smaller, ability-related groups with materials designed especially for them. Ask the students to read the music in their groups. Circulate in the classroom so that they can get help if they need it. Give the students music to take home. If the reading experience is related to instruments, or if the students need an instrument to help them read, make arrangements for them to have either school time for working alone with the instrument or an opportunity to take the instrument home. Encourage the children to help each other when necessary, but change the groups so that peer dependency is minimized. Maintain an environment in which the children will feel free to perform their music reading for each other and with the class. Gradually reduce your involvement in the reading sessions so the children will become more and more independent.

MUSIC-READING ACTIVITIES
WITH UPPER-GRADE CHILDREN

Help the children to read "Gonna Build a Mountain."

RHYTHM

> Ask the children to locate all the 𝄾 in the song.
> Ask them to comment on ¢ .
> Have them click their fingers for all 𝄾 while counting beats in each measure: click 2, 1, 2; click 2, 1, 2; and so on.
> Was the pattern of rests and counts repeated exactly throughout the piece? Where was the exception?
> What rests other than 𝄾 are in the piece? Click fingers for all rests while counting the meter.

GONNA BUILD A MOUNTAIN

From the musical production *Stop the World - I Want to Get Off*. Words and music by Leslie Bricusse and Anthony Newley. ©1961 TRO Essex Music Ltd., London, England. TRO - Ludlow Music, Inc., New York controls all publication rights for the U.S.A. and Canada. Used by permission.

How many examples of syncopation occur in the piece?

Have the children say the words for the syncopated passages rhythmically.

Are any of the syncopated passages the same?

Have the children click the rests and say the words in rhythm.

Choose students who are clapping accurately to play the rhythm patterns on percussion instruments. Have one percussionist play steady beats only.

MELODY

Ask the students to analyze the melody.

Are any measures the same?

Are any phrases the same?

Are any of the phrases almost the same?

Are both the melody and rhythm different in these phrases?

What is the form of the piece?

Give the students their starting pitch and play a G chord with an added 6th: G B D E. Ask the students to sing the melody.

Give them a chordal accompaniment to help keep them on the right notes. Play a melody note only if it is absolutely necessary.

Encourage the students to identify problem spots. Help them to correct only if they can't do it themselves. Repeat until problems are conquered.

It is unlikely that one lesson could be devoted to all these activities. Focus on the reading of a piece such as "Gonna Build a Mountain" during several lessons, concentrating on rhythm one time, form another, and singing the melody another time. Resist the temptation to sing the song for the students. Have them interpret the notation as completely as they can; help them only to avert disaster or embarrassment.

Obviously the students cannot carry out most of the music-reading activities suggested if they have not had instruction designed to give them prerequisite skills. If the students cannot do the music-reading activities, return to more elementary techniques discussed in previous sections.

The students will perform best when they can look at the time and key signatures; assess the stylistic, dynamic, and tempo characteristics of the music; get their starting pitch; and sing through it. If music classes meet frequently, this may be possible. More realistically, the children will be able to read portions of the music as suggested and then gradually put the piece together. Always try to have reading material available that is within the grasp of the students. Contrast these materials with more difficult literature they cannot read alone but that sparks their interest and gives them a heightened aesthetic perception. If their music reading is weak, let the children read part of a piece and learn the rest by ear. Try to balance plans for the older children so they are not learning most of their music by ear.

Suggested Projects

1. Select one music-reading activity for grade six. Summarize one reading-readiness or beginning reading activity for each grade, one through five, that will prepare the children for this sixth grade activity.
2. Use the form for writing a lesson plan in Chapter 3 to write a plan for a sixth grade music reading experience.

HELP THE CHANGING VOICES

If all the children in the fifth and sixth grade music classes sing enthusiastically and if none of them shows signs of voice change, the beginning teacher can skip this section. But if any of the boys shows a sudden, almost overnight drop in his vocal range, if the boys begin to lose top notes and add bottom ones, if notes disappear at both top and bottom of the range, if their voices are unpredictable, if sudden squawks are produced, and if they begin to lose enthusiasm for singing with no apparent reason, the teacher is urged to consider the effects of the changing voice on the student's participation in music class.

Girls' voices change, too. The change may be less dramatic than the boys' and may be unnoticed by the girl herself or, perhaps more accurately, may be unidentified by the girl herself. Still, the symptoms are there: an insecurity in pitch, frequent missing of notes, development of noticeable registers, and shifting of register breaks. Perhaps she doesn't feel like singing, a very unusual response for her. A girl who has sung soprano with great pleasure may find herself uncomfortable in that part. After a switch to alto, that part may not seem right, so back she goes to soprano. A low voice may switch to soprano and then return again to alto. A girl's changing voice may not settle into a new range as definitely as does the boy's, but the same kinds of changes in growth occur in all children.

As the adolescent begins to grow, hands and feet, head and face, weight and height, and muscles and reproductive organs are enlarging. The larynx or voice box is growing, too. Prior to adolescence, the larynxes of boys and girls are about the same size. As puberty begins, both sexes experience growth there; the boys' vocal cords, however, keep on growing longer than do the girls', so that ultimately their cords, because of their size, are capable of producing lower pitches. The growth spurt may be responsible for the adolescent stoop along with posture problems. Poor breath support and an aspirate vocal quality complicate the development of the voice, so that diagnosis of trouble and suggestions for help do not come easily.

A natural reaction of the children who experience these changes is to give up singing. Many will, if they do not receive encouragement and understanding. If they do terminate vocal music training at a time that can be most productive in terms of developing musicianship, they may not start singing again because they feel they don't know what they are doing and thus will not risk the embarrassment involved in trying to catch up.

Physiologists do not all agree, but the time for the adolescent growth spurt seems to run from about twelve-and-a-half to fifteen for boys and about two years earlier for girls. The period of most rapid change seems to occur at about twelve for girls and fourteen for boys, but there are many exceptions. Because these exceptions may be in the fifth or sixth grade music class, the teacher should be encouraged to be sensitive to the psychological, cognitive, moral, and emotional changes that may be commencing.

The following list of suggestions was written to help choral directors deal with changing voices in choirs. Many of the suggestions apply to general music classes. Even if only a few students seem to have voice changes, the ideas in this list apply to many more who are approaching the age of change.

1. Learn to analyze adolescent problems. What is causing a student's unwillingness to sing? It may be that vocal insecurity is causing what appears to be misbehavior.

2. Establish an environment of acceptance. Encourage students to sympathize with others' vocal problems. Cultivate an atmosphere of understanding of the changing voice so that the singer feels no pressure to sing higher than is comfortable or to force his or her voice down before it is physically ready. Protect the singers from embarrassment that can contribute to guarded use of the voice and eventually complete stoppage.

3. Design the choral group that contains changing voices as a unique entity, neither a continuation of a children's choir nor a miniature high school group.

4. Educate the young people about the physical development of their larynxes, the lengthening of their vocal cords, and the ways in which these changes can affect their singing and speaking. Enjoy the silence of the classroom as these adolescents demonstrate their yearning for information on what is happening to them by giving you their absolute attention as you try to help them understand their patterns of growth.

5. Develop their musicianship to such a level that they can change from part to part as the need arises. Have everyone learn to read in both the bass and treble clefs so that they can read each other's parts. Help the students find their most comfortable range and, if necessary, show them how to switch octaves if all else fails. Help the students to recognize the moment at which they may need to detour from one part to another. Encourage independence so that John can keep right on singing when George finds it necessary to switch to something else. Create with the students new parts that will fit their voices at this particular moment. If literature is not available to meet the needs of the group, use arrangements. If the right arrangements are not available, you or some of your talented young people make your own. (Use proper copyright procedures, of course!) This is a special group and deserves music tailored for them. For example, in the grand finale of a conservation song, perhaps the melody is not comfortable for all the changing voices.

An alto part may solve the problem for some of the voices:

Boys who are developing their lower ranges may need a lower part:

The range of the part above may be too wide; this boy may be able to sing only a few notes:

It would be rare in sixth grade to have a changed voice needing this part, but for that special individual:

Some of the changing voices are developing the upper part of their ranges:

If the example above does not go high enough, add a few more notes:

The total effect is wonderful, and the students are able to sing where they are most comfortable.

6. Encourage the adolescent voices to sound like what they are. They are not the same as children's voices, and they are not the same as adults. The unenthusiastic, breathy, faltering sound could be a result of frustration at unsuccessful imitation rather than of intrinsically bad quality.

7. Try to choose music that appeals to young people. It is remarkable how the choice of music influences the changing voice—or any other voice for that

matter! A piece that is on the students' reject list often will sound bad just because it has been rejected, not because the students can't sing it well. This does not imply a sellout to the latest hit at the top of the charts—although it doesn't necessarily eliminate that piece either; the students need a mixture of styles, periods, and cultures. The secret of producing the appeal? MOTI-VATE! Find reasons that are important to the adolescents for singing something, even if it is brand new to them. Such a reason could be that this song has the potential of involving many chorus members in the accompaniment. It has easy chords that some of the singers can handle on the guitar. There are some interesting percussion effects. The advantages of singing the song from the director's viewpoint may be that, in addition, the melody has a lovely line that will lend itself to a development of sensitive phrasing; the harmonic structure is such that parts for the lower voices can be developed within the students' ranges; and the form is one the singers can analyze to help them learn the music. The positive reaction of the students to the song will often minimize the voice change problems. The boys are so busy enjoying what they are doing that they forget to complain.

8. Help the students to recognize the feeling of strain resulting from improper use of the voices. Be available to them for individual consultation if they need it. Build their confidence in you so that your request that they come in for help is not threatening. Be sure they are aware of problems that hoarseness, laryngitis, or throat infections can produce and when, for physical reasons, they should rest their voices.

9. Be sure that the principles of good vocal production are explained and reinforced positively. Parents will bless you if your attention to posture and good breath control also results in minimizing the adolescent slouch.

10. Allow the students to be a primary resource in structuring the rehearsals, performances, and format of the group. Their nonverbal clues are often just as important as their words. Just as any good detective, you will be looking for them. Smiles and frowns often make words unnecessary.

11. Determine with the students what the primary goal of the group is to be. If they want to perform, fine, but don't necessarily make a performance always the ultimate goal. If they feel the need for a group voice class, provide it. If they just want to have fun singing, that's better than dragging into the rehearsal room for a dull, unmusical time. If they want to have an aesthetic experience that includes developing musicianship along with it, count your blessings and be sure to provide it!

12. Analyze your own voice so that your vocal examples and explanations will help the changing voice. The female teacher should be able to show that a G below middle C is low for her but may be just right for the adolescent. In giving pitches vocally, she may have to sing "This is where the note sounds:"

"but this is where it should be in my voice in relationship to my total range:"

Sometimes it is easier to sing the pitch, ask the students to match it, and then select students who are placing the pitch properly to show students who might not have that concept. Basses sometimes have difficulty in illustrating vocal placement for these young voices because the boy's note may be at the bottom of his range whereas the teacher's may be at the top of his.

13. Encourage the changing voices to maintain the tops of their ranges as much as possible. In their rush to join the world of men, boys often concentrate so much on development of their low tones that the top range is neglected almost completely. (I often wonder how much this contributes to the comparative dearth of tenors in many of our performing groups.)

14. Foster the joy of singing by being as imaginative and creative as you can possibly be. Encourage the students to bring their creativity to bear upon your joint musical ventures.

15. Be judicious in the use of solos. If singing a solo is a potential source of stress for an adolescent but a musical challenge is appropriate for that vocalist, consider including more chamber music in your repertoire. Select duets, trios, quartets, and madrigals that give an opportunity for musical independence while not focusing the spotlight on a lone voice with its potentially disastrous consequences.

16. See that provisions are made for the student who has an early voice change as well as the student who has a delayed one. This means that elementary singing experience should not be awkward for the early changer and that the late changer is not out of place in the high school.

17. Consider the organization of a boys' choir so that their specific vocal problems can be isolated. This is especially helpful in view of the fact that the girls have reached many stages of maturation a year or two before the boys.

18. Contribute your expertise to research dealing with varied aspects of the voice change. It is amazing how little is said in developmental psychology books about the adolescent voice.[8]

Even after trying to carry out these suggestions, the teacher of music may find some students who still don't want to sing. The next best alternative is to encourage these students to find other ways of musical involvement. If they have negative reactions to one musical activity, it does not necessarily mean that they will be adverse to other forms of participation. It is better to let them find satisfactory alternatives than to force them into situations having potential trauma.

Recommended Readings

ADAMS, JAMES F., *Understanding Adolescence*. Boston: Allyn & Bacon, Inc., 1976.
GALLATIN, JUDITH E., *Adolescence and Individuality*. New York: Harper & Row, Publishers, Inc., 1975.
HARRISON, LOIS N., "It's More than Just a Changing Voice," *The Choral Journal*, September 1978, pp. 14–18.
MCKINNEY, JOHN P., AND OTHERS, *Developmental Psychology: The Adolescent and Young Adult*. Homewood, IL: The Dorsey Press, 1977.
MUSS, ROLF E., *Theories of Adolescence*. New York: Random House, Inc., 1975.
RICE, F. PHILIP, *The Adolescent*. Boston: Allyn & Bacon, Inc., 1975.

[8]Lois N. Harrison, "It's More than Just a Changing Voice," *The Choral Journal*, September 1978, pp. 16–18.

TEACH THE CHILDREN TO SING IN HARMONY

Don't try to teach the children to sing in harmony until they sing melodies securely and accurately. Too many children are asked to sing rounds and, while trying, hold their hands over their ears so that the other voices don't throw them off. The idea of singing harmony is to enjoy the complementary sounds rather than fighting to keep from being thrown off the melody. The children must have a concept of harmony before they are asked to produce harmony with their voices.

Chordal accompaniments. Although much of the child's first singing is unaccompanied, harmony can be added to the melody by chordal instruments. The teacher is encouraged to use the autoharp, guitar, piano, or whatever chordal instrument will produce an appropriate accompaniment for the song. Teachers who travel from room to room or who cannot afford a studio upright piano can use a learning module,[9] or suitcase piano. Although the sound of these small electric keyboard instruments is unlike a piano, they are effective alternatives when a piano is not available. Seek other accompanying instruments. One enterprising elementary teacher kept track of the instrumental inventory at the high school and regularly borrowed the celeste for use with the children when the high school students were not using it. It provided another contrasting timbre when adding harmony to the children's songs.

Ear training. As early as first grade, children can begin to make discriminations based upon chord changes. Ask the children to walk around the room in the tempo of the chords the teacher is playing on the piano. Tell them to walk in the direction they have chosen as long as they continue to hear the same chord. When a different chord is played, they should turn around and walk in another direction. It is not necessary to define a chord during this introductory experience; simply have the children listen for changes. To start with, use only the I and V7 chords in root positions. Play several measures of each chord. As the children gain skill in discerning the changes, play the same chord for only a few beats before moving to the next one.

In subsequent lessons, gradually introduce melodies above the chord progressions, still stressing the chords and using only the I and V7. Help the children to discriminate between the melody, which has many different notes, and the ongoing chord, which does not change with each note of the melody. Later, add a IV chord to the progression and suggest a new response, such as hopping, when they hear the IV chord.

[9]Music Learning Module, available from Musitronic Corp., 555 Park Drive, Owattona, MN 55060. Yamaha and Casio have portable keyboards worth investigating also.

Ostinatos. One of the first and most successful ways of having the children add harmony is through an ostinato. This is simply a repeated rhythmic or melodic phrase that complements the main melody. Although the rhythmic ostinato adds no harmony, it does give the children an introduction to the use of an accompanying phrase or to two things happening at once. For example, add this rhythmic ostinato to "Are You Sleeping?":

ARE YOU SLEEPING?

Traditional

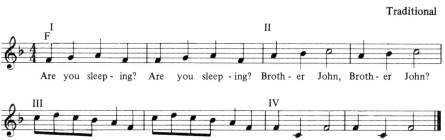

For variety, the children can also sing the French words.

Frère Jacques, frère Jacques, dormez vous? dormez vous?
Sonnez les matines, sonnez les matines, din, din, don, din, din, don.

Before the children are asked to sing a melodic ostinato, they should hear it many times. The teacher can sing it and class members can play it on a pitched percussion instrument. When the children are singing the melody accurately, some of them can sing a melodic ostinato.

As soon as the children feel secure, they can alternate in singing the melody, the pitched ostinato, and chanting the rhythmic ostinato. The number of parts performed at once will be determined by the capability of the children. Additional ostinatos can be invented by the children with the teacher's help at first. Older children should be encouraged to create them independently.

Rounds. Singing rounds provides the children with a polyphonic dimension. The harmony created by the melodic lines sung at the same time can be very satisfactory. Children who have learned "Are You Sleeping" and have added ostinatos to it as described probably know the melody well enough to try it as a round. The teacher should have the children sing without his or her vocal help on a regular basis. When they can sing "Are You Sleeping" without vocal leadership, the teacher can quietly add the second part of the round. If this is successful, the teacher can sing the second part louder and encourage the children to listen to the two parts as they fit together. The next step is to divide the children into two parts, and later three or more parts as long as they continue to sing accurately and independently.

A beginning teacher must understand that not every song is a round. A round can be identified by the identical chord progressions in each phrase. Because the chords change at the same point in each phrase, the melodies contribute to the harmonious sound by the chord progressions they share.

In addition to singing rounds, older children can add ostinatos to the same pieces. "Are You Sleeping" can be sung as a four-part round while all the ostinatos learned previously are added. When the children have gained great skill in independent singing, challenge them to sing all these parts with only one child on each part. In a four-part round, it becomes evident, after the first four children have begun, that later entries duplicate the parts of the first four, but there still is a challenge to the independence of the singers because they are not sitting near each other. Encourage four volunteers to sing the four-part round with no help on any of the parts. Experiences such as these should be reserved for children who have a good chance of succeeding with them. They are not for inexperienced primary children.

Some rounds share complementary chord progressions and can be sung together. "Three Blind Mice," "Are You Sleeping," and "Row, Row, Row Your Boat" present a challenge for the children when they sing these rounds at the same time.

Partner songs. When two songs have chord changes at the same places in the phrase they can be sung together. Usually the words are different in partner songs such as "The Gospel Train" with "She'll Be Comin' Round the Mountain,"[10] or "I've Been Workin' on the Railroad" with "BINGO," or "Four in a Boat" with "When the Saints Go Marching In."[11]

"Swinging Along" has the characteristics of a partner song except that the words of the two songs are the same.

[10]Frederick Beckman, *Partner Songs* (Lexington, MA: Ginn and Company, 1958), pp. 76–81.

[11]Frederick Beckman, *More Partner Songs* (Lexington, MA: Ginn and Company, 1962), pp. 10–16.

SWINGING ALONG

The refrain and verse of "It's a Small World" use the same chord progressions so they can be sung at the same time producing pleasant sounding harmony. A refrain and verse sung together produce another kind of attractive partnership.

IT'S A SMALL WORLD

Words and Music by Richard M. Sherman
and Robert B. Sherman

Harmonized cadences. Another way to add harmony is to suggest a few notes, especially at a final cadence, that will add to the interest of the performance. (Performance is used here to describe music making, not necessarily public performance with an audience.) A harmony such as this can be added to the end of "Rudolph, the Red-Nosed Reindeer":

You'll go down in his - to - ry.

From "Rudolph, The Red-Nosed Reindeer" by Johnny Marks (New York: St. Nicholas Music, Inc.© 1977) Used by permission.

Every time this phrase occurs in "This Land Is Your Land,"[13] a simple harmony can be added:

This land was made for you and me.

From "This Land Is Your Land" by Woody Guthrie (New York: Ludlow Music, Inc., © 1970) Used by permission.

Encourage the children to find chord tones other than the melody for the last word of the song. Older children whose voices are changing may welcome an opportunity to sing in a lower and more comfortable range. A plagal cadence (IV, I) gives the children a structure within which to explore chord tones. Part of the class can hold the common tone

Ah _____

while other singers use their ears to find another chord tone to sing. If the children do not find a chord tone readily, the teacher can devise melodies that will help them. For example:

Find an - o - ther note.   or   Go down for your note.

Adding a scale to "Do-Re-Mi"[12] from *The Sound of Music* gives the children further insight into harmony. While a scale note corresponding to

[12]Richard Rodgers, "Do-Re-Mi" (Rodgers and Hammerstein, © 1977).

the words (do, re, mi, fa) can be held throughout four measures for the first four phrases, the changing chords of the piece beginning with the word "sew" demand that so, la, and ti be held for only two measures. Lead the children to recognize the necessity for cutting the syllables off when they hear the conflict in harmony.

Harmonizing by ear. The campfire-type songs that are easy to harmonize by ear help children to gain a concept of harmonization. The first introduction of the harmony can be by the teacher while the children sing the melody. You can invite a few children who have shown leadership in other harmonizing activities to listen as you sing the harmony while the class sings the melody—and then join you when they can. This harmonization only imitates the teacher; later the children should be encouraged to develop their own ideas. As the fun of harmonizing by ear becomes contagious, it may be difficult to find anyone who wants to sing the melody. Here are a few of the many songs that lend themselves to harmonizing by ear:

ALOUETTE

French - Canadian

Pretty lark, I will pluck your_____.

1. head (la tête)
2. beak (le bec)
3. nose (le nez)
4. back (le dos)
5. feet (les pattes)
6. neck (le cou)

As you sing the song, point to the appropriate part of your body. After singing the additional body part at the beginning of the last line, sing and point to all the parts mentioned previously before finishing the line and going on to the next verse.

KUM BA YA

Africa

1. Kum ba ya, my Lord, Kum ba ya. Kum ba ya, my Lord, Kum ba ya. Kum ba ya, my Lord, Kum ba ya. Oh, Lord, Kum ba ya.

2. Someone's crying, Lord, kum ba ya,...

3. Someone's singing...

4. Someone's praying...

5. Someone's shouting...

6. Someone's hoping...

I'VE BEEN WORKIN' ON THE RAILROAD

United States

I've been work-in' on the rail-road, All the live-long day;

I've been work-in' on the rail-road, Just to pass the time a-way.

Don't you hear the whis-tle blow-in'? Rise up so ear-ly in the morn.

Don't you hear the cap-tain shout-in' "Di-nah, blow your horn."

Di-nah, won't you blow, Di-nah, won't you blow, Di-nah, won't you blow your

horn? ___ Di - nah, won't you blow, Di - nah, won't you blow, Di-nah, won't you blow your horn? Some-one's in the kitch - en with Di - nah, Some-one's in the kitch - en I know. ___ Some-one's in the kitch - en with Di - nah, strum - min' on the old ban - jo. Fee fi fid-dle-ee - i o, Fee fi fid - dle - ee - i o, ___ Fee fi fid - dle - ee - i - o, Strum - min' on the old ban - jo.

Instrumental assistance. Children can learn about chording through their use of the autoharp, guitar, and piano. As their ears are trained to perceive chord changes, they can transfer this perception to harmonization with their voices. At first the singers will be able to sing only one harmony line. They can start singing the chord roots.

DOWN IN THE VALLEY

Kentucky Folk Song

1. Down in the val - ley, the val - ley so low, ___
   Hear the wind blow, love, ___ hear the wind blow, ___

Hang your head o - ver, Hear the wind blow._____
Late in the ev - 'ning, Hear the wind blow._____

I

Later, add another part:

Down in the val - ley, the val - ley so low, _____

Hand your head o - ver, Hear the wind blow. _____

If they have any trouble singing these parts, ask the students to play them on a melody instrument first and then sing them.

Instead of singing the words, show the children how to use the chords as a backup chorus for the melody. Help them learn to sing a simple chord progression like this on "ah" and change the chords appropriately as a soloist sings the melody:

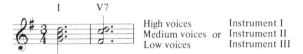

High voices   Instrument I
Medium voices or Instrument II
Low voices   Instrument III

If the children have trouble singing the notes of the chords, encourage them to play them on resonator bells, recorders, or keyboard instruments until they hear them so well that the sound can be made vocally. Add more verses, too. A different soloist can sing each verse.

2. Roses love sunshine,
   Violets love dew,
   Angels in heaven
   Know I love you.
   Know I love you, dear,
   Know I love you,
   Angels in heaven
   Know I love you.

3. Build me a castle
   Forty feet high,
   So I can see him
   As he goes by.
   As he goes by, dear,
   As he goes by.
   So I can see him
   As he goes by.

4. Write me a letter
   Containing three lines,
   Answer my question,
   "Will you be mine?
   Will you be mine, Love,
   Will you be mine?"
   Answer my question,
   "Will you be mine?"

As the children become proficient in vocal chording with one piece, they can learn to transfer the technique to other pieces. In teaching how to make this transfer, the teacher may first have to indicate to them when the chords are to be used. Chord names or numbers can be written on the chalkboard; the teacher can point to them as they are to be sung. Flashcards can be held up to indicate which chord is next. Notation can be used with the melody line to show when the chord changes. If there are a few children in the class who are quick to get the idea of changing chords, let them take the place of the teacher in indicating when the chords are to change. As soon as possible, challenge the singers to change the chords appropriately without anyone showing them where.

Reading harmony.   Even though it may mean little to the children in the beginning, they should see notation as often as possible. Referring to the notation along with or even after the harmony has been learned can help make it relevant.

Music textbooks for the upper elementary grades introduce notation for singing harmony parts. Some of the easiest harmonies to sing include thirds and sixths. Since the harmonizations the children have been singing by ear include these intervals, help them transfer the sounds they have heard to the notation they see. Help them transfer the sound of sixths in "I've Been Working on the Railroad" or "Alouette" to "Walkin' in the Sunshine."

WALKIN' IN THE SUNSHINE

Words and Music by Roger Miller
Arranged by Fred Bock

pa pa pa pa — pa pa, put a smile up-on your face — as if there's noth-in

wrong, pa pa pa pa — pa pa, Think a-bout a good time

had a long time a-go, Think a-bout, — for-get a-bout — your

trou-bles and your woes. Walk-in' in the sun-shine, sing a lit-tle sun-shine

song, La la — la la, la dee oh, — Wheth-er the weath-er be

rain or snow, — Pre-tend-in' can make it real, _____ A

2nd time to *Coda*

Transfer the sound of thirds in the "Battle Hymn" to "Du, Du Liegst Mir Im Herzen" or "Wonderful Copenhagen."

Glo - ry, glo - ry, hal - le - lu - jah, etc.

DU, DU LIEGST MIR IM HERZEN

German Folk Song
Arranged by Mary Val Marsh

WONDERFUL COPENHAGEN
from "Hans Christian Andersen"

Words and Music by Frank Loesser

Co - pen - ha - gen, sal - ty old queen of the sea,_____

Co - pen - ha - gen, sal - ty old queen of the sea,_____ Once I

Sing - ing Co - pen - ha - gen,

sailed a - way, but I'm home to - day, Sing - ing, Co - pen - ha - gen,

won - der - ful, won - der - ful Co - pen - ha - gen for me.____

won - der - ful, won - der - ful Co - pen ha - gen for me.____

When two staves are used for two different voice parts, teach the singers that the black line joining the bars means they are to be performed at the same time. Many textbooks include only the vocal lines to avoid confusion. When the children are exposed to octavo or sheet music, they generally need help in sorting out the voice parts and the accompaniment. Show them that the accompaniment is joined by bars to the voice parts. Help them realize that they all sound at the same time. Be sure that the children singing part I know where to go for their next line. Use arrows or other symbols to show this as in "Who Says I Can't Read Music!" Upper-grade children who have not used notation often give up singing if they have no idea where they are supposed to be.

Arrangements. Some arrangements for children's voices are confined to two parts, but they are very effective in developing musicianship. A typical arrangement may have all the singers joining in the melody at first. In the next section, they may be divided into two parts, with half the children singing an alto harmony. The third verse may find the altos singing the melody again, although in a different key, while the sopranos sing a descant. To develop the sight-reading capability of the children, and to keep them from talking, have all the singers read all the parts. Encourage them simply to leave out notes that may be too high or low for them.

WHO SAYS I CAN'T READ MUSIC

Hank Beebe

Descants are useful because they challenge the children to develop their upper notes and give sopranos a chance to sing parts other than the melody. Note the descant for the last two lines of "Du, Du Liegst Mir Im Herzen," p. 125.

Part singing becomes necessary for older children whose voices are ready to change. The music should be selected with care so that the parts match the capability of the voices. Encourage the singers to develop as much flexibility as possible in spite of their voice changes so they do not think of themselves as always having low or high voices. As often as possible, give them opportunities to sing parts to help develop a wide range. However, be sure to be realistic about the changes that take place in adolescence and provide appropriate experiences as discussed earlier in the changing voice section.

Choir. Some of the children in the upper grades would rather participate in music through activities other than singing. In fact, this preference is a major basis of support for a general music program that includes playing, listening, movement, reading, writing, and creating in addition to singing. To give the children who are very interested in singing continuous experience in doing so, it is strongly recommended that each elementary school have choir for *all* singers who wish to participate. These young musicians may sing for the rest of their lives and should have the benefit of developing expertise without it being forced on others who may find their musical outlets in other ways. Ideally, the choirs should be scheduled during school time so that all who wish to participate may do so. In larger schools, because of the numbers involved, the choirs may have to be designated by grade level (e.g., the Sixth Grade Choir).

In addition to the traditional literature written for children's voices, attractive contemporary songs are available. These pieces may be purchased in sheet music form and enable the singers to produce more sophisticated harmony than that found in many of their textbooks.

The following are examples of appropriate octavo music for children's voices. All are in unison or two parts (grouped alphabetically by publisher).

TITLE	COMPOSER OR ARRANGER	PUBLISHER
"School Days"	Bricusse	Big 3
"You're Never Fully Dressed Without a Smile"	Strouse	Big 3
"The Virgin Mary Had a Baby"	Ehret	Boosey
"Horray! Horray! What a Happy Day"	Thygerson	Choral Concepts
"Alleluia, O Come"	Bach	Chor. Guild
"Al-le-lu"	McNain	Chor. Guild
"Come Go With Me"	Parks	Chor. Guild
"Come, Glad Hearts"	Mozart	Chor. Guild
"Can't Carry a Tune in a Bucket"	Beebe	Hindon
"Who Says I Can't Read Music"	Beebe	Hindon
"Mr. Meter Man"	Ydstie	Jenson
"Take a Little Time"	Myers	Jenson
"Two Horas for Hanukah"	Pellirin	Kendor
"Poor Richard's Almanac"	McAfee	McAfee
"Danny the Drum"	Harte	McAfee
"The Hello Song"	Harte	McAfee
"The Goodby Song"	Harte	McAfee

"Spin Little David"	Emry	Shawnee
"Do Di Li"	Norman	Shawnee
"Little David"	Fleisher	Shawnee
"Old Pharaoh"	Fleisher	Shawnee
"Thanksgiving Calypso"	Eddleman	Shawnee
"Canciones de los Ninos"	Miller	Shawnee
"Carrie Sue from Rocky Fork"	Mason	Somerset
"I Like to Feel Pretty Inside"	Hall	Somerset
"My Music"	Snyder	Studio PR

Suggested Projects

1. Write two ostinatos for a round you would use with sixth grade children.
2. Find five appropriate songs for the first concert of the sixth grade choir.
3. List three songs you can harmonize by ear.
4. Write a lesson plan for introducing the concept of harmony to primary children.

5　*Play*

Children like to play musical instruments. Fortunately, some instruments seem easy to play, so the students find them accessible. The difficult part of instrumental work with young people is helping them to go beyond the immediate fascination with a new instrument to the long-range development of musical playing.

In the elementary music class, instruments provide variety in timbre, help with pitch perception, intensify rhythm, enhance creative activity, inspire expressive action, and assist in learning to read music. This chapter discusses instruments commonly found in elementary music classes: recorders, chordal instruments, and percussion instruments.

RECORDERS

Tonettes, Flutophones, Song-flutes,[1] and recorders were introduced by many teachers in the public schools in the early part of the twentieth century to provide preband experience. Instrumental teachers loaned the instruments to third, fourth, or fifth grade classes, gave the students a

---

[1]These names are capitalized because they are trade names of specific instruments.

series of lessons, and then recommended who should continue in instrumental study. They also recommended the best type of instrument for each child. Since that time, many other uses have been found for these instruments in elementary music. The following discussion centers on the use of the recorder as an asset in developing the child's general musicianship. The approach parallels the preband approach only in the goal of giving the children facility in playing the instrument. It is destined to be part of music instruction over a long period of time; it is not used as a means of determining who should, and who should not, play band instruments, and it is one of many activities taking place in music class, rather than the sole activity of a series of lessons.

The recorder was chosen over the other melody instruments because of its historical tradition, its continuing potential for music students, and its wide chromatic range. The recorder was used extensively in renaissance and baroque music. Delightful literature is available written especially for solo recorder, recorder consort, and recorder in conjunction with other instruments and voices. Although the older instruments were made of wood, plastic recorders are recommended for use with elementary school children. They can be washed so children can share them without sharing germs, and they need less care than do the wooden instruments.

The cost of plastic soprano recorders for a beginning instrumental experience is low. The initial cost and the small size of the soprano make it the best choice for young beginners. Since the soprano written range goes down to middle C, many of the songs the children sing can be played on that instrument.

Musicians of any age who develop an interest in playing the recorder find opportunities to play in small groups. Recorder players who move to a new area where there are no other players frequently start their own groups. These small ensembles need no conductor and no expensive instruments (unless they add a bass) and lend themselves to a musical-social setting including families as well as friends. A typical recorder group, begun in 1973 as part of a church production of Benjamin Britten's *Noye's Fludde*, with its interesting recorder parts, still functions today, playing for weddings, school demonstrations, church services, and social gatherings.

Recorder players who keep on playing generally do not confine themselves to the soprano alone. Gradually they learn to play other members of the family, even adding the more expensive bass recorder. Because of its cost and its size, this instrument is not generally recommended for elementary school children, but one should be available for the exceptional child.

As the child grows, he or she can transfer from the soprano to a larger instrument. This is especially recommended for the child who has an aversive reaction to the high-pitched sound of the soprano. Although the alto is the next instrument in size, because of the different relationship of its fingering to notation, it is more difficult for children. The relationship of the tenor fingerings to notation is exactly the same as the soprano even though the sound produced is an octave higher for the soprano. In making a recommendation that a child play the tenor, the teacher must be sure that the student's fingers can stretch far enough to handle the instrument. Children who are especially interested in recorders can learn the alto readily.

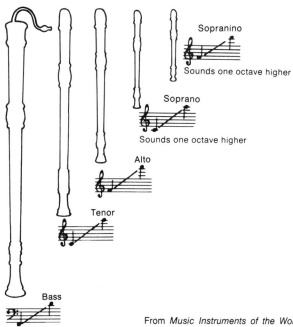

From *Music Instruments of the World,* Ruth Midgley, managing editor, New York and London: Paddington Press Ltd., 1976, p. 29.

The sopranino, alto, and bass recorders are called F recorders. The soprano and tenor are called C instruments. Covering all the holes on the soprano and tenor produces written middle C.

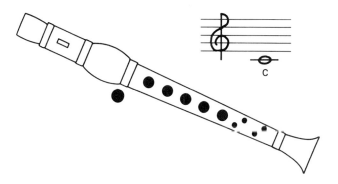

The same fingering for the sopranino, alto, and bass produces written F.

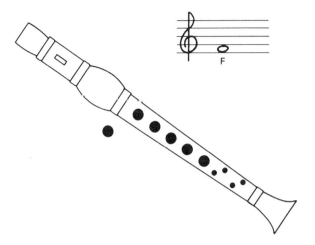

Dedicated recorder players learn the fingering relationships between the recorders readily and have little trouble in switching from one instrument to another. Most children will have difficulty with the differences, so experience on both F and C instruments should be reserved for gifted children who respond to challenges.

The accompanying fingering chart shows the fingerings for both the C and F instruments. Notice that the lowest written note on the F instruments is first space F. The lowest written note on the C instruments is middle C.

(For easy access to the fingering chart, put a paper clip on page 134.)

Recorder in the Primary Grades

It is unrealistic to expect the first grade class to begin recorder lessons, enjoy them, and achieve success with the instrument. There are too many variables in coordination, musical background, and ability to function in the school setting. Group instrumental lessons for young children tend to negate other more significant values for this age level.

Experimentation.   From the time the child enters school, however, instruments such as the recorder should be available. Young children respond well to experimentation. They like to make noises with an instrument such as the recorder. Although this does not create a peaceful learning situation, it is a valuable experience for the children as long as they are taught respect for the instrument and recognize the care that must be given it. These comments apply equally to other instruments to be used by the children.

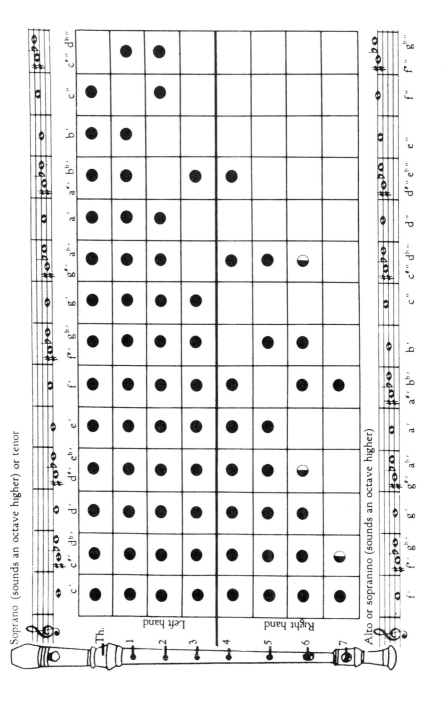

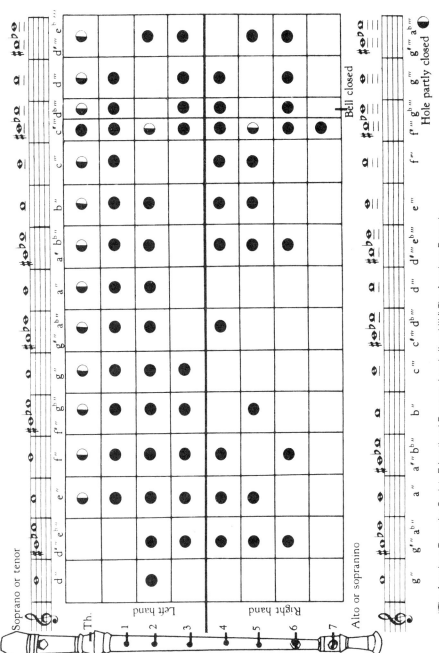

"The American Recorder Society Educational Program, Levels II and III," *The American Recorder*, November, 1980, p. 125. Used by permission of the American Recorder Society.

The teacher is urged to foster the natural curiosity of the child by providing a setting in which that curiosity can develop. Find time during the day when the child can play the recorder alone. Encourage the youngster to blow on it, to take it apart, to see what happens when fingers are used to close the holes. The teacher should spend some time working with an individual on various possibilities for making sound with the instrument and then let that child pass his or her discoveries on to someone else.

Because the sound may be disturbing to the rest of the class, creative thought must be devoted to providing space for the child to carry out the experimentation. Can the child work in the hallway just outside the classroom door? Is there a soundproof area adjacent to the classroom? Is there a room near the principal's office for this work? The teacher must provide for supervision of the students while at the same time giving them opportunities to work with sound. Schedule times for all the children to be involved with music experiments using the recorder as well as many other

TAKE-HOME RECORDER CARD

(Front)

(Back)

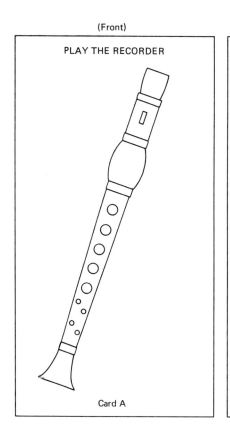

PLAY THE RECORDER

Card A

1. Blow into each recorder hole.

2. Take the recorder apart by twisting it gently. Now what happens when you blow into it?

3. Put it back together again. When you blow into it now, do you hear the same sound or a different one from when you had it apart?

4. Without using the recorder, say "too-too-too." Now use your tongue as if you are beginning to say "too" but don't finish it.

5. Put the part of the recorder that helps you make sound into your mouth and start saying "too-too-too" without finishing the sound.

6. When you bring the recorder back, let your teacher hear the sound you are making with the recorder.

resources. When the entire class is working with sound production, the cacophony that results may be much more disturbing to the teacher than to the children.

Take-home projects. Some schools are so highly structured that no time or place can be provided for such experimentation. Even in an inhospitable situation, the creative teacher should not despair. An attractive take-home bag can be put together. It should contain the recorder and written suggestions for experimentation for a family member and the child to do together. Encourage family participation in take-home projects

The cards shown here are only samples of many projects that can be devised for the children. The best projects attempt to develop continuity so that concept development is made possible. The concept for these lessons is that of pitch production as related to playing techniques.

If no one is available at home to help the young child, put the directions on tape. Add a tape player to the take-home bag if the child does not have one.

FOLLOW-UP TAKE-HOME RECORDER CARD

(Front)

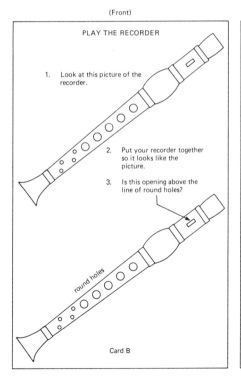

PLAY THE RECORDER

1. Look at this picture of the recorder.

2. Put your recorder together so it looks like the picture.

3. Is this opening above the line of round holes?

round holes

Card B

(Back)

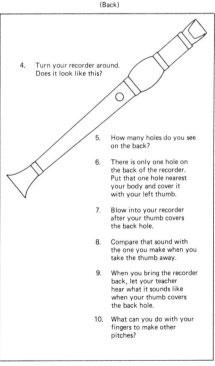

4. Turn your recorder around. Does it look like this?

5. How many holes do you see on the back?

6. There is only one hole on the back of the recorder. Put that one hole nearest your body and cover it with your left thumb.

7. Blow into your recorder after your thumb covers the back hole.

8. Compare that sound with the one you make when you take the thumb away.

9. When you bring the recorder back, let your teacher hear what it sounds like when your thumb covers the back hole.

10. What can you do with your fingers to make other pitches?

Backward recorder. Some children will have trouble when beginning to play the recorder. You can help them have instant success by turning the mouthpiece backward and having the child blow while you finger the melody. Even though it is a partnership, the child is involved in playing the piece through blowing.

In addition to giving the child a sense of shared accomplishment, you can diagnose the reason for the child's problems. Two common ones are overblowing and improper coverage of holes. When you finger, you remove one source of trouble. If the sound is still not right, the problem is probably that of overblowing. If it is, you must show the child how to blow more gently. If the problem is that the child has not placed fingers correctly, the use of the backward technique shows the child the sound that should be produced, and that the instrument is not at fault.

Mirroring. There is little need in the early stages of instrumental experience for the child to couple playing technique with music reading. It is appropriate for them to play by ear. However, children beginning to play instruments often need visual models of how to play the instrument. The mirroring technique helps beginning recorder players to couple their instrumental technique with sounds they wish to produce. In this case, you simply stand before the children who are learning a simple tune and exaggerate the use of the fingers in a rhythmic fashion for the children to follow. You do not have to play; your recorder will be seen more easily if you hold it higher than when playing it normally. Moving the instrument will help you to indicate note values. You must caution the children to keep their fingers close to the holes and not to exaggerate as you do in illustrating.

Beginners should be confined to pieces with only a few notes such as G, A, B, C, as covering many holes may prove frustrating if more notes are used.

PIECES FOR MIRRORING

MARY HAD A LITTLE LAMB

Traditional

"Hot Cross Buns" also offers a good opportunity to work on tonguing.

Mirroring works best if the children have already learned the song so they can anticipate the pitch and rhythm they are to produce. You must adjust the tempos of the songs to the capabilities of the students. Be sure to keep the rhythmic relationships the same even if the tempo of the piece must be slow.

Harmony.   Because of the limited number of notes the primary children usually can play, there are many pieces they cannot play all the way through. However, they can add harmony that uses only those few notes. At first the harmonic additions are learned by ear. Later the children learn them from notation. Descants and ostinatos are satisfactory harmonic additions using only a few notes.

The *ostinato* is a phrase that repeats itself throughout the piece. It may be as simple as this one for "Old Texas:"

OLD TEXAS

Cowboy Song

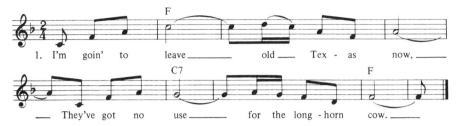

1. I'm goin' to leave ___ old ___ Tex - as now, ___
___ They've got no use ___ for the long - horn cow. ___

2. They've plowed and fenced my cattle range,
   And the people there are all so strange.

3. I'll take my horse, I'll take my rope,
   And hit the trail upon a lope.

4. Say adios to the Alamo,
   And turn my head toward Mexico.

5. I'll make my home on the wide, wide range,
   For the people there are not so strange.

6. The hard, hard ground shall be my bed,
   And my saddle seat shall hold my head.

Begin a second group of singers and players one measure later than the first group for additional harmonic interest.

The *descant* is a harmony part, usually higher than the melody, that does not repeat a pattern throughout. The British call the soprano recorder the descant recorder. This simple descant goes with "Save Electricity!" The children can learn it by mirroring the teacher.

SAVE ELECTRICITY!

Lois N. Harrison

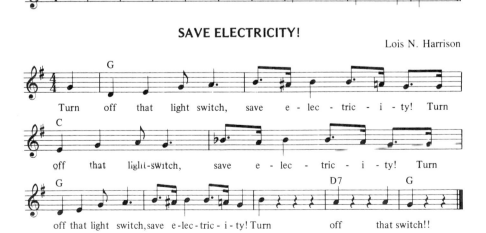

Turn off that light switch, save e - lec - tric - i - ty! Turn
off that light-switch, save e - lec - tric - i - ty! Turn
off that light switch, save e - lec - tric - i - ty! Turn off that switch!!

140

If it's desirable to have either an ostinato or a descant for a piece the children are singing, the teacher can create these harmonic additions using notes of the chordal accompaniment that are easy for the children to play. The ostinato for "Row, Row, Row" can be as simple as for the duration of the piece.

If this is too difficult for the children, divide the players into two groups with half playing

and the other half playing   (notation means to repeat 3 times)

Divided responsibility.   The strategy of dividing the children works well in more difficult compositions. Assign a different note to each child. Use the following piece only if there is a child who can play the low D and the high E. Let each child practice his or her note. Play some games with the children requiring an immediate response when you point to the child to see how quickly each one responds by playing his or her note. Direct the child to hold the note or to cut it short in response to the indications you give. Finally, point to the children in the sequence that will create the melody of "Did You Ever See a Lassie?" Find other pieces like this to enable recorder players to produce melodies together that would be impossible if each had to play all the notes in sequence. This approach is similar to the procedure used by hand bell players. The accuracy of the performance depends on the teacher's ability to give cues and the student's ability to respond to them.

DID YOU EVER SEE A LASSIE?

It may be helpful to both teacher and students who are observing this activity to have the name of the note and its notation pinned on each performer's chest. The children must be arranged in the order in which their notes appear on the keyboard so the teacher can keep track of who is playing what. The labels will help other children who will be asked to select the note they would most like to play. At the end of the piece, the players can choose their replacements and check them to be sure they know how to play the note.

Play by ear.   Encourage the children to play pieces on the recorder by ear. Be available to help them with new fingerings when they need them. Share songs so the children learn to respond to solos as a well-behaved audience. Ask children who have learned songs by ear to teach them to classmates.

Form.   Instrumental activities can help children to understand form in music. Ask a child to create and play a musical phrase on the recorder. Ask another child to play his or her original phrase. Ask the other children to compare the two phrases. Are they the same or different? Ask the children to name a song they have sung with the same form.

Find a child who can remember the musical phrase he plays so that he can play it again accurately. Ask that child to play his phrase, have another child play his original phrase, then have the first child play his phrase again. Relate the ABA form to songs that the children have sung.

Although musicians call these forms A B and A B A, the children may not understand these labels. Let them identify form with any symbols meaningful to them. A B may be a toasted cheese (open-faced) sandwich; A B A may be a hamburger. A B may be cat-dog, while A B A may be mouse-rat-mouse. Ask the children to use their original recorder phrases to make different forms. Their rondo form may be referred to as a "Big Mac."

Ask the children to use their ears in identifying form by having the players stand in the back of the room and play their themes letting the rest of the class identify form by hearing it rather than by seeing who is playing.

Recorder in the Intermediate Grades

The primary children should be encouraged to enjoy many informal experiences with the recorder. Intermediate children can build upon primary experiences and develop more sophisticated skills with the instrument. Even while fostering informal experiences, the teacher should show the children the correct way to hold the recorder (left hand on top!) and how to tongue. Their general music classes will have given the older children some skill in clapping rhythm patterns. They will have had experience with reading and writing elementary rhythm patterns. They will have learned concepts related to pitch such as melodic direction, steps and skips, high or low. They will have looked for patterns in music and identified formal structure of songs. With this background, many of the children will be ready to read music using the recorder.

The teacher may choose to use a recorder method book to teach the children to read or may provide other materials for them to use as part of the regular music classes. Music reading with the recorder should take its place with singing, movement, listening, creating, and writing activities but not dominate the music classes.

Work on imaginative ways in which to involve the children. The method suggested now is a framework on which reading experiences can be developed with the recorder. Each teacher is encouraged to develop his or her own ways of weaving recorder reading into the music class. This series of suggestions is intended to be spread out over many lessons. They are to be incorporated in lesson plans dealing with concept development.

EXPANDING THE READING RANGE OF THE RECORDER PLAYER THROUGH ONE THEMATIC IDEA: PIECES ABOUT DUCKS

Review rhythm patterns with the children. Have them echo these patterns. Ask them to notate some of the patterns on the chalkboard and then clap them. Write patterns on the board for the children to read. Put some of the patterns on posterboard for reference in many lessons.

Ask the children to clap the rhythm on these three posters:

Encourage them to show the duration of the half notes by clasping their hands while moving them to show two beats. The duration of the rest should be shown by a palm-up gesture as if to throw the beat away.

Ask them to find a song hanging somewhere in the room with the same rhythm pattern as one of the posters. (Large posters of all the verses presented here should be made for class use.)

One lit - tle   duck.   Watch out for the   truck!

Ask them to chant the words while clapping the rhythm. Ask them to count the number of different pitches in the piece. Review for them the way the G is played on the recorder and how it looks on the staff by centering their attention on the line running through it. Have each child stamp a picture of the recorder[2] on a piece of paper, then color the holes to be closed with a crayon or felt-tipped marker. Ask the children to play "One Little Duck." Have a chart hanging in the room to remind the children of the recorder fingering and the note it matches.[3]

Ask the children to find a song with the same rhythm as that displayed on another of the three posters.

Ask them to chant the words while clapping the rhythm. Ask them to count the number of different pitches in the piece. Show them the fingering for A, its place on the staff, and the holes to color in on the recorder picture they stamp. Have them play "Two Little Ducklings." Have the children play both verses of their new recorder piece.

Repeat the procedure with "Three Little Ducklings."

The notation ✗ stands for any noise the children can make in the time of one beat.

Prepare posters of the three-note pieces the children learned to play through mirroring: "Mary Had a Little Lamb," "Hot Cross Buns," and "The Angel Band." Focus the children's attention on the notation. Have class members point to the notes as the children play them. Find new three-note pieces in the key of G for them to read.

Add harmony to the pieces, showing the children where to add chords with autoharp, piano or guitar.

[2]Recorder stamp available from Visual Aids for Music, 6665 S.W. Preslynn Dr., Portland, OR 97225.

[3]Charts prepared by Peg Hoenack and Kay Jones show pictures of the recorder and the correct fingering as the child holds it. *Recorder Fingering Charts,* Music for Young Children, 8409 Seven Locks Road, Washington, D.C. 20034, 1974.

Three lit-tle duck-lings stand-ing in a row. Make a noise, Watch them go.

Continue to have children play the melodies on the recorder. Encourage some to sing. Have a few children play the harmony instruments. Add percussion instruments to the orchestration.

Verse 1: All percussion instruments read the rhythm of the melody.
Verse 2:

Encourage the children to create their own percussion parts and their own style of chordal accompaniment. Tell the children they are free to change from recorder playing to singing, to playing another instrument, *or* to stay with one performing medium during the entire lesson (unless problems arise from too many students wishing to use the same instrument).

Four lit-tle duck-lings, read-y for bed.

This piece about ducklings includes a new note and omits words in the second line. Help the children to discover these variations. Explain that you didn't put words for the second line because you had so many choices you couldn't decide. Ask the children to read the words for the first line in rhythm and then listen while you give some of the alternatives for the second line. Ask students to notate the rhythm for

"Brush your teeth, their mother said."
"Mable, Ann and Dick and Ted."
"Dressed in white feathers and a cap of red."

145

Ask the children to find the phrase that uses a different rhythm than the others. Encourage the children to create a rondo chant with "Four little ducklings, ready for bed" as the A phrase. The B, C, D, and E phrases will be ones the children make up. Each pattern will be two measures long and the last word will rhyme with bed. Have the children select their favorite phrase for the second line of the fourth verse. If the children like more than one second line, encourage them to keep as many as they wish. Performance of several verses provides reasons for more playing of the recorders.

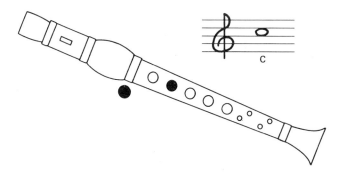

Show a picture of the new note and its fingering. After the children play C, help them locate it in the music and count the number of times it appears. A brief fingering drill of B to C may be necessary before playing the piece.

Play and sing the music as many times as is necessary to allow the children to perform all their original phrases for the second line. Add harmony and rhythm instruments.

Ask the children to find what is new for the recorder in this music:

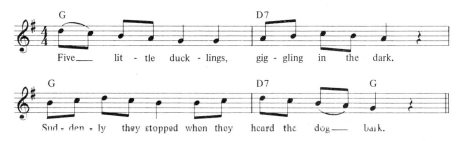

Show the children how to play the new note. Display a chart for fingering and notation.

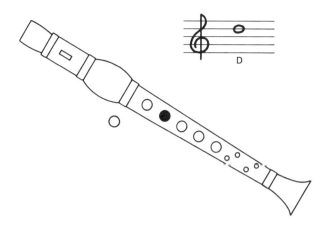

Another fingering drill may be needed:

The children will probably notice the curved line. Introduce the slur. Have them practice slurring drills.

Before the children play "Five Little Ducklings," have them clap the rhythm and say the words with an elongation of the appropriate words showing the location of the slurs. Add harmony and rhythm instruments after they play the melody accurately.

Next present a blank chart to the children and tell them it is intended to be a piece about a duckling.

They will say that you forgot to write something or will wonder what is happening. It is time for the class to write its own piece. The creative process here is based on flexible guidelines, assuming that the children have had little experience in composition.

Suggest that it seems logical to add another note for this piece since the last piece had five notes and the one before that had four. Ask the children to write the five notes they have learned on staff paper, in order, with G as the beginning or lowest pitch. Ask the children to play the notes in this order and identify the sound for them as the beginning of a scale. Ask them to name the sixth note in that scale, E. Show the new note on the recorder; display a picture of the fingering and notation.

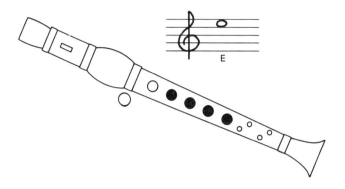

Ask the children to practice playing from D to E.

Get ideas from the children about their wishes concerning content of their composition. Have them chant word-phrases they create about their subject to see if a sense of meter emerges. Let the children choose two phrases having textual sense and the same meter. As they chant them, encourage the class to accent strong beats to find the beginnings of measures. Put the words on the chalkboard and have the children help put bar lines just before the strong beats. Have part of the class count while the other part chants to see if the bar lines are placed correctly and if the meter has been established. Give the class time to decide if they wish to make changes or reorganize the text. Once the children are sure that the words and the meter fit, ask them to notate their rhythm under the words on the board. The teacher can assist in this activity by clapping the notation back to the children as it appears on the board, to help them decide on the accuracy of their writing.

Divide the class into small groups to write melodies with the assistance of their recorders. Tell them their melody must use only the six recorder notes they can play, that it must conform to the rhythmic pattern the class has developed corresponding with the words, and that it must begin and end on one of the notes of the G major chord. An experienced composer may complain that these limitations are too confining, but inexperienced children feel frustration if they have no guidelines. The limitations give them guidelines within which they can work. Have the children play their musical ideas on their recorders as they conceive them. Ask them to notate the melodies they like.

Near the end of the class session, bring the groups together to present their songs to each other. As they share their songs, the teacher's role should be one of encouragement and appreciation rather than critical judgment! If corrections are necessary, make them in constructive ways.

THE MISSING CHILD

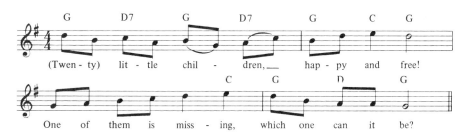

If the teacher has used "The Missing Child" as a game song with the children in the primary grades, the music for the next recorder piece is not new to the players. They have played a game in which the person who is "it" goes into the hall while one of the children hides. The task of "it" is to determine who is missing and to call him or her by name. The game is helpful in the early days of school when class members are trying to learn each other's names. The children like to play it when the music teacher comes to their room, making the teacher find out who is absent. It is a challenge for the teacher who meets three or four hundred students each week. To prompt a faltering memory, the teacher can have the children sing "The Missing Child" song, then call roll by singing the names of the children listed for that class and expect a sung reply from each one. By the time the missing person(s) is found, the other class members have had an opportunity to sing alone. Use this version of the song for the recorder reading:

THE MISSING DUCKLING

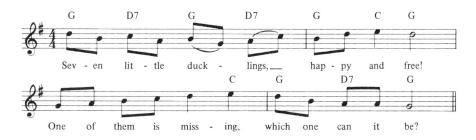

Read the text together. Ask the children which note is missing. Let them play the scale upward from G to E, the last note they learned, and then play the seventh note for them: F♯ . Show the careful finger placement necessary to go from D to E to F♯. There may be disagreement among recorder teachers about which fingering to teach to the children for E. The fingering taught previously was chosen because the children are able to go from D to that particular E fingering with facility. When the need arises, children should be taught alternate fingerings. It is important to encourage them to look for appropriate uses of alternatives as they learn these fingerings.

The fingering for E noted here is an alternative for use when the student plays from E to F♯. Have the students practice playing from E to F♯ using the new E fingering:

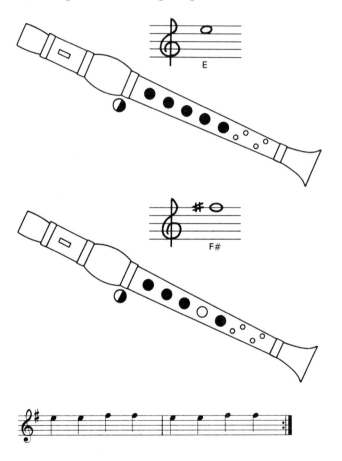

Try the new fingering in these drills also:

Tell the children that, because of the difficulty of the new note, they don't have to play it in the new piece but can add it at the end, after the question is asked. The note will be played instead of giving a verbal answer.

Which one can it be?

Have the children clap the rhythm of the song and say the words rhythmically with the clapping. Ask them to play the melody, adding the F♯ at the end. Another reason for omitting the F♯ in this song was that the singing range is high. Its omission was intentional. With this piece, as with all the previous parts of the recorder reading lessons, singing is to be included as well as playing other instruments.

Add the last note of the complete G scale. Show high G visually and aurally. Discuss vocal and instrumental ranges with the children. There are no words for "The Duck Takes Off!" because instrumental capabilities are different from the vocal capabilities of most singers. Encourage the students to practice exercises such as these to gain skill in note reading and recorder playing.

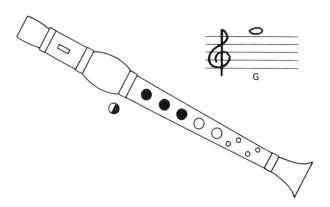

G

THE DUCK TAKES OFF!

Slur four measures, two measures, etc.

* The starred measures are good places to introduce alternate fingering for B.

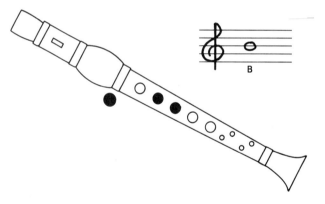

B

Encourage the children to practice the first line of "The Duck Takes Off!" with varying articulations and rhythm patterns. Turn all the quarter notes into two eighth notes:

etc.

Slur all the notes in one measure:

etc.

Slur them all in two measures:

etc.

Slur them all in four measures:

etc.

Change all the quarter notes to a dotted eighth note followed by a sixteenth:

etc.

Have the children make up variations. All the changes should be carried on throughout the entire exercise.

Many recorder methods add low notes to the recorder range much sooner than is done here. The decision was made to proceed with high notes first because they require fewer holes to be covered than the low notes. Children find it difficult to cover all the holes on the instrument. An added problem is that extra fingers must be used to make the low F and F♯ on baroque recorders sound in tune. The beginning student will try to follow the pattern established with B, A, G of simply adding another finger to produce the next lowest note. This works only with German fingered recorders playing F. Explain to the students that one finger alone is not enough to make F and F♯ sound in tune on the baroque recorders. Use the following fingering for F. Add the little finger only if the intonation requires it, or when the instrumentalist can handle it. Urge the students to find a quiet place to hear the difference between using the extra finger and not using it.

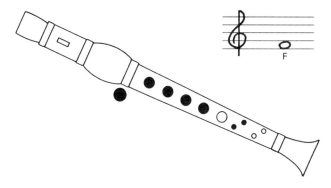

Show them this fingering for F ♯ .

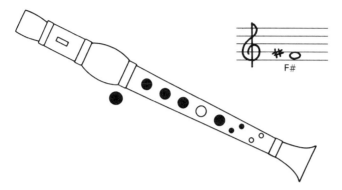

The fingering for the last few notes at the bottom range of the record-er proceeds downward logically. Add a finger for each one to make the sound go lower.

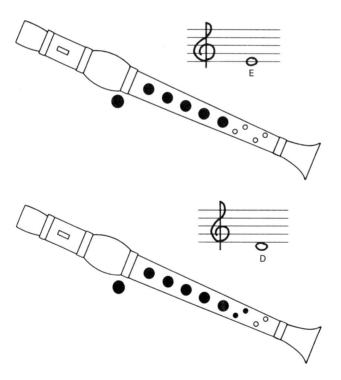

When new notes are introduced, drill is needed to make them part of the student's musical technique. The children will learn them most effec-tively if they are included in pieces they wish to play. The theme about ducks used to teach recorder reading to intermediate children may not be

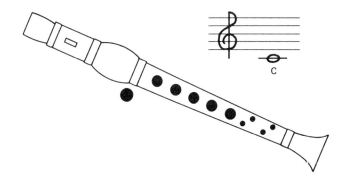

appropriate for some sixth graders. If you suspect that the student will be unresponsive, select materials to which they will respond more readily. You will find many pieces in music textbooks for them to practice reading. Locate special music they will enjoy playing. As each new note is learned, have several pieces for them to read.

Summary

Playing the recorder in elementary music class may be the beginning of a lifetime association with that instrument. It may involve the student in playing chamber music for pleasure. Even if it does not, the instrument can help the children learn to read music and will add to the development of their total musicianship. Caution is needed to ensure that teaching the recorder does not dominate the other facets of the music program. It should be integrated into the total program with flexibility so that students who enjoy the recorder especially can experience it in depth, while those who are more interested in other aspects of music can concentrate on them.

Recommended Resources

BURAKOFF, GERALD AND SONYA., *You Can Play the Recorder.* New York: Music Minus One, 1974. Comes with soprano recorder, record, and book.

BURAKOFF, GERALD, AND WILLY STRICKLAND, *Pine Tree Suite.* Sharon, CT: Consort Music, 1975. Soprano and alto recorder, tuned and untuned percussion, optional voices.

DIETZ, BETTY W., Editor and arranger, "Folk Melodies of the Orient." Sharon, CT: Consort Music, Inc., 1972. Soprano and alto recorder and percussion.

JOHN, ROBERT W., AND CHARLES H. DOUGLAS, *Playing Social and Recreational Instruments,* pp. 31–41. Englewood Cliffs, NJ: Prentice-Hall, Inc., 1972. Good introductory volume for teacher's use.

KATZ, ERICH, *Recorder Playing.* Browns Mills, NJ: Carl Van Roy Publishing Co., Inc., 1951. Excellent resource for learning C and F instruments. Uses literature less commonly known.

KULBACH, JOHANNA E., AND ARTHUR NITKA, *The Recorder Guide.* New York: Oak Publications, 1965. Record and book for soprano and alto.

MARSH, MARY VAL, CARROLL A. RINEHART, AND EDITH J. SAVAGE, *Playing the Recorder*. New York: Macmillan Publishing Co., Inc., 1975. Student's book for group and individual instruction.

Playing the Recorder. Morristown, NJ: Silver Burdett Company, 1974. Student book with illustrations.

SEVUSH, LEO, *Let's Play Recorder*. Winona, MN: Hal Leonard Publishing Corporation, 1973. Learning Unlimited Audio-Visual Series. Includes teacher's manual and cassette tape for class use, child's book for home and class use, and record for home use.

SIMPSON, KENNETH, "Suite on Three Notes." London: Schott and Co., 1957. Imaginative suite for soprano recorder using B, A, G, and piano.

VAUGHN WILLIAMS, RALPH, "March-Past of the Kitchen Utensils," from *The Wasps*. Arranged for recorders (SA) percussion and piano with glockenspiel and xylophone ad lib. by Herbert Hersom, Schott 10995 London.

Suggested Projects

1. Play all the examples in the recorder section.
2. Write a lesson plan for a grade level of your choice using the recorder in the development of a specified concept.

CHORDAL INSTRUMENTS

Chordal instruments support the young singer's emerging sense of harmony, provide alternatives in accompanying instruments for the general music class, and give the young musicians a means of playing accompaniments themselves.

Autoharp

The least difficult of the chordal instruments to play is the autoharp.[4] When a bar with a chord name such as F is pressed, felt-covered blocks fastened to the bottom of the bar dampen all the strings on the instrument except the components of the F chord: F's, A's, and C's. Playing the autoharp requires that the player push the bar at the correct time in the music with the left hand and execute a rhythmic strum with the right hand. Although the instrument can be strummed on both the left and right sides of the bars, it is generally played on the left side, with the strumming right hand crossing over the bar-pressing left hand. To make the lowest strings sound first when playing the chord, begin the strum from the bottom of the instrument to the top. Play the thickest strings first.

Tuning. It is the teacher's responsibility to keep the autoharps in tune. Tune the instruments by chords rather than by matching each note to

---

[4]Autoharp is the registered trademark of Oscar Schmidt International, Inc.; it is used without the capital to describe similar instruments with different brand names.

the notes of the piano. Begin by tuning low F with a pitch pipe or in-tune piano. Tune all the F's to match that one; then tune all the A's; than the C's. It is easier to find them if the tuner depresses the F bar while tuning notes in that chord. Play the chord to see if it sounds in tune. If not, make adjustments until it is in tune. Next tune a closely related chord such as the C chord or the C_7. The C's are already tuned, so tune all of the E's, and so on. Continue until all the strings have been tuned as part of a chord.

Timbre.   Plan lessons on timbre discrimination in which the children determine the appropriate quality for the autoharp accompaniment. Picks used by the guitarist can be used by the autoharp player: plastic, metal, felt. The children should also experiment with items such as pencils (especially the erasers), pens, keys, coins, door stops, and kitchen utensils. The problem with using a pencil eraser is that the metal strings break off parts of the eraser. These parts fall on the board under the strings where it is difficult to clean them out. (Enterprising sixth-graders have used a *slightly* damp cloth on the end of a ruler to reach under the strings. Dampness, like too much heat, is very bad for the instrument, so be sure the cloth is only damp enough to pick up the accumulated dirt.)

Strums.   Other autoharp lessons should be built around the different types of strums. The children should identify appropriate strum styles for lullabies, marches, folk songs, and so on. At first the children observe the teacher's styles in playing the instrument. Later they learn to vary the way they play the instrument according to the requirements of the music.

Technique.   Even in the primary grades the children will ask if they can play the autoharp. They soon discover what happens if they strum it with no bars pushed down. They also discover various ways of producing sound effects with it. Even though Henry Cowell's "Banshee" was written for the piano, it gives the students ideas for alternate ways to play the autoharp.

When the students first express interest in playing the autoharp, they may not be ready to play it independently. The teacher can help by simplifying the techniques for them. At first let the child strum while you change the chords. Then let one student strum while another changes the chords. It is more than likely the child will not know when to change chords. You can help in different ways

1. by pointing to the appropriate bar when it is time to push it.
2. by writing the letter names of the chords on the chalkboard and then pointing to the correct letter when it is time to play it.
3. by showing changes with flash cards.
4. by writing the chord names under the words of the text so that the child who can read can change chords as the corresponding word is sung.

5. by writing the names of the chords under the melody so that the student can relate the chord changes to the written music.
6. by teaching the student to change chords by ear.

Encourage the students to function independently in playing the autoharp. The children who enjoy playing it may volunteer to be class accompanists and will practice pieces in advance if they are given time to work by themselves on the accompaniments.

Ear training.   The autoharp is useful for ear-training exercises. The children can show high and low pitches played on the autoharp with high and low placement of their bodies. They can pluck strings to make high and low sounds. When the class sings a song, a child can tell the teacher when to change chords. When this can be done accurately, the child is ready to play the autoharp and change the chords by ear. Primary-grade children can move to chords played on the autoharp in the same way they do with the piano. When the autoharp chord changes, the children can change the direction in which they are moving.

Choice of keys.   Autoharps do not have chords for all keys, so adjustments must be made when choosing the key for the autoharp accompaniment. A piece written in the key of D can be played in C on an autoharp without chords for the key of D. A piece written in E or E♭ can be sung in F. Remember to keep the songs in suitable ranges for children's voices. Watch the temptation to pitch them low because that is where the teacher may feel most comfortable.

Three of the most popular autoharp keys are C, F, and G. The chords for these keys appear on most instruments. The following chart will help you review the chords for these keys when used with one-, two-, and three-chord accompaniments.

CHORDS MOST OFTEN USED ON AUTOHARPS

I	IV	V7
C	F	G7
F	B♭	C7
G	C	D7

Use I for one-chord pieces.
Use I and V_7 for two-chord pieces.
Use I, IV, and V_7 for three-chord pieces.
Beware of exceptions to these generalizations!

One-chord accompaniments.   The easiest accompaniments for children learning to play the autoharp are those using only one chord. Not having to worry about when to change the chord enables the child to concentrate on rhythm and style as the rest of the class sings. Add one-chord pieces to this brief list as they come to your attention.

SONGS NEEDING ONLY ONE CHORD IN
THE ACCOMPANIMENT (I)

"Are You Sleeping?" (G)
"For Health and Strength" (F)
"Little Tom Tinker" (C)

"Row, Row, Row Your Boat" (C)
"Shalom, Chaverim" (Dm)
"Swing Low" (refrain) (F)

Songs needing more than one chord can sometimes be used in this fashion if the autoharp is not strummed on every beat.

Two-chord accompaniments. Many pieces require only two chords for their accompaniment. Accumulate a list of songs that the children know containing only two chords. These will be easy for the children to accompany provided that the necessary chords are on the autoharp. If the autoharp does not have the bars for the key indicated, consider changing the key of the piece to one that is close. Since autoharps are inconsistent as to number of bars and chords provided, check all the autoharps' chords before using them with children. Pick appropriate songs for the children to play and sing from this brief list.

SONGS NEEDING ONLY TWO CHORDS IN
THE ACCOMPANIMENT (I AND V₇)

"Clementine"
"Did You Ever See a Lassie?"
"Down at the Station"
"Down in the Valley"
"Go in and out the Window"
"Goodby, Old Paint"
"Hail, Hail, the Gang's All Here"
"He's Got the Whole World"
"Irish Washerwoman"
"Joshua Fought the Battle of Jericho" (minor)

"Lightly Row"
"London Bridge"
"Merrily We Roll Along"
"Old Texas"
"Oh Dear, What Can the Matter Be?"
"Polly Wolly Doodle"
"Sandy Land"
"Shoo Fly"
"Three Blind Mice"
"Yellow Rose of Texas"

Three-chord accompaniments. Many more songs require only three chords for their accompaniment. Add songs the children know to this short list.

SONGS NEEDING ONLY THREE CHORDS
IN THE ACCOMPANIMENT (I, IV, V₇)

"Amazing Grace"
"Billy Boy"
"Bluetail Fly"
"Camptown Races"
"Comin' Through the Rye"
"Goodnight Ladies"

"Happy Birthday"
"Hickory Dickory Dock"
"Kum Ba Ya"
"Little Brown Jug"
"Marching to Pretoria"
"Oh, Susanna"

"Old Brass Wagon"	"This Land Is Your Land"
"Old MacDonald"	"When the Saints Go Marching In"
"Red River Valley"	"Yankee Doodle"
"Silent Night"	"You Are My Sunshine"

Special help may be needed by handicapped children in playing the autoharp. Paste brightly colored labels on the bars for easy identification. Put braille markers on the bars for blind children. Anchor the instrument securely to a table of appropriate height for children having coordination difficulties.

Recommended Resources

JOHN, ROBERT W., AND CHARLES H. DOUGLAS, *Playing Social and Recreational Instruments*, pp. 20–30. Englewood Cliffs, NJ: Prentice-Hall, Inc. 1972. Good introductory volume for teacher's use.

NYE, ROBERT E., AND MEG PETERSON, *Teaching Music with the Autoharp*. Northbrook, IL: Music Education Group, 1982. Wealth of information about using the autoharp.

Suggested Projects

1. Tune an autoharp.
2. Prepare two two-chord pieces and two three-chord pieces. Use a different strum for each of the four pieces. Use a different type of pick for each of the four pieces. Play each piece in a different key.
3. Add ten pieces to the two-chord list given. Add ten pieces to the three-chord list.
4. Write an introductory lesson plan for the autoharp for first-graders. Include the concept of high and low pitches in the lesson.

Guitar

The timbre of the guitar is more appropriate for many accompaniments than the autoharp. It is also much easier to tune, having only six strings. The disadvantages to children are (1) it is more difficult to find the chord fingerings than to push the bars of the autoharp, (2) the finger position has little consistency from chord to chord, and (3) the neck of the guitar is too wide for many small hands.

Baritone ukulele.   The baritone ukulele is sometimes used as a substitute for the guitar with intermediate children. The four strings of the baritone uke are the same as the top four strings of the guitar so transfer is possible from one instrument to the other. Its neck is narrower than the guitar's so it is easier for small hands to play. Because the baritone uke is smaller, it does not have the resonance of the guitar.

Holding the guitar.   A handicapped child or one too small to hold the guitar in the conventional way can place it on a table and strum the strings in the same way as strumming the autoharp. A block attached to the table or a rim on the back of the table may be necessary to keep the guitar from sliding away from the player.

Retuning.   Changing conventional pitches for the open strings of the guitar makes it more accessible to young children or those who are handicapped. Rather than tuning it to the usual E A D G B E, retune three strings: D̲ G̲ D G B D̲. Children can strum the guitar with this tuning to play a G chord. If the accompaniment sounds better with the root of the chord as the lowest string, tell the student to strum only the top five strings. If it sounds right to have the fifth of the chord, D, as the lowest sound, tell the student to strum all the strings. Have the children play and sing one-chord songs such as "For Health and Strength," "Are You Sleeping?" and "The Farmer in the Dell."

When the children are ready for two-chord pieces using the altered tuning, they must learn to put a finger flat across the strings (barre). Count seven frets up from the nut (raised piece of wood between the fingerboard and the tuning pegs). Put the index finger across all of the strings. This will produce a V or D chord. If the children cannot do this while holding the guitar in a conventional position, have them lay the instrument on the table, put the left hand across all strings at the seventh fret, and press so all the strings are stopped at that fret. If one child does not have the strength to stop the strings and strum at the same time, divide the activity between two students, one strumming and the other stopping the strings.

Stopping the strings at the fifth fret will produce a IV or C chord. By adding this chord, three-chord pieces can be played.

This activity involving the guitar does little to teach good guitar-playing posture. It is a compromise enabling the students to gain a limited experience in playing the guitar.

Simplifying chords   To play a simple two-chord piece in the key of C with regular guitar tuning, use only the top three strings; put the first finger in the first space on the B string for an inverted C chord. For a G7 move the first finger to the E string. (See chords on p. 162.) Simplifying chords makes the instrument more accessible to the children.

Visual Aids.   The children can use a variety of methods to help them find their places on the guitar fingerboard. Use brightly colored signal markers to show finger placement for chords. Mark all the fingers of one chord with the same color. Put markers on the side of the fingerboard to show the fifth and seventh frets. Even though the children cannot see the markers on the fingerboard when they are holding their instruments in the conventional way, the markers will help refresh their memories before they begin to play.

Conventional fingering.   A guitar fingering chart may be confusing to the beginning guitar player. Make charts using only the chords the student

Simplified C Chord

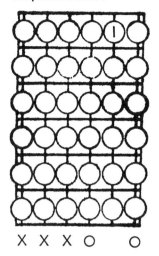

X X X O   O

Simplified G7 Chord

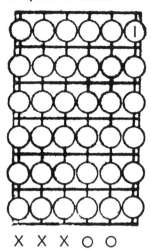

X X X O O

X means "do not play these strings."
O means "do not finger these strings."
The numbers tell which finger to use; 1 is the index finger.
In the key of G, use these simplified chords:

Simplified G Chord

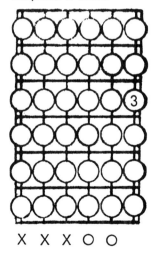

X X X O O

Simplified D7 Chord

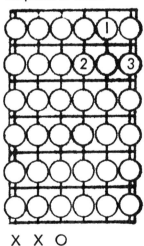

X X O

is to learn. Leave the charts in the classroom for ready reference and make smaller copies for the players to take home with them, especially if they have instruments to use for practice. Use a fingerboard stamp for them to fill in the fingering themselves.[5]

[5]Guitar stamp available from Visual Aids for Music, 6665 S.W. Preslynn Dr., Portland, OR 97225.

Encourage the students to learn chords using the complete resources of the instrument as soon as possible. The introductory activities described here are devices to help the student succeed but not necessarily to give

GUITAR CHORD CHART

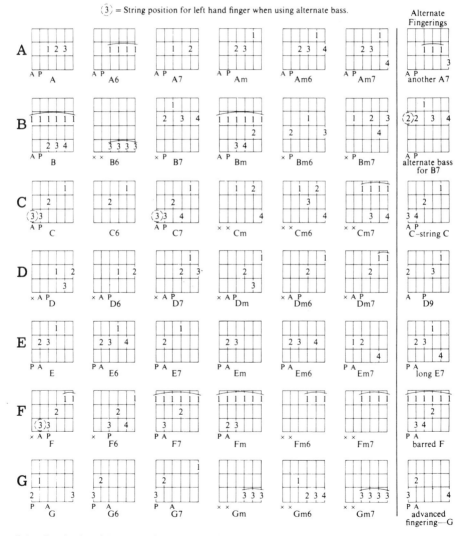

P = Primary bass string (root of the chord)   × = String not to be played.

A = Alternate bass string (fifth of the chord).

⌒ = Barre (1st finger lies flat across several strings).

(3) = String position for left hand finger when using alternate bass.

Guitar Songbook with Instruction by Beverly McKeown, p. 191. copyright © 1975 by Houghton Mifflin Company. Used by permission.

long-range satisfaction. Teach the intermediate guitar players to use the guitar chord chart as soon as possible.

(For easy access to the fingering chart, put a paper clip on page 162.)

Guitar class.   Since guitars may not be available for every student, and since learning to play the guitar requires more instruction time than may be available in general music classes, special sessions should be scheduled for children who wish to play it. After they gain proficiency, opportunities should be made for them to play along with their singing classmates in class and in concerts. Guitar playing provides another desirable opportunity for children to diversify their musical experiences. Guitar classes should have access to instruments owned by the school so children will not be deprived of the opportunity to play if their families cannot afford an instrument.

UNICEF Photo by Jacques Danois

Ear training.   The teacher can use the guitar to give the same kind of ear training suggested for the autoharp.

Recommended Resources

GARCIA, SALLY YOUNG, AND VICKI TJARKS SCHRAMM,   *Guitar.* Morristown, NJ: Silver Burdett Company, 1976. More difficult than *Playing the Guitar.* Coordinated with songs in *Silver Burdett Music* 7 and 8.

JOHN, ROBERT W., AND CHARLES H. DOUGLAS,   *Playing Social and Recreational Instruments,* pp. 1–19. Englewood Cliffs, NJ: Prentice-Hall, Inc., 1972. For teachers' use.

MARSH, MARY VAL, CARROLL A. RINEHART, AND EDITH SAVAGE, *Playing the Guitar and String Bass.* New York: Macmillan Publishing Co., Inc., 1975. For teacher's or advanced student's use.

McKEOWN, BEVERLY, *Guitar Songbook with Instruction.* Boston: Houghton Mifflin Company, 1975. Includes suggestions for using guitar in the classroom.

Playing the Guitar. Morristown, NJ: Silver Burdett Company, 1974. A satellite for independent study coordinated with *Silver Burdett Music.*

Suggested Projects

1. Practice retuning the guitar and playing pieces with the G, C, and D chords, simplified chords in keys of C and G, and conventional chords in two keys of your choice.

2. Write a lesson plan for primary-grade children using the guitar to develop the concept of high and low pitches.

Ukulele

The soprano ukulele is easier for children to play than the guitar. It is smaller, lighter, requires less strength to finger, and has only four strings. The disadvantages of the instrument are its limited resonance and its unique fingering pattern, which does not transfer to either the baritone uke or the guitar.

Tuning. The chords shown in the following chart are based on a tuning of A D F♯ B. Children may tune their instruments by singing "My dog has fleas," which is fine, as long as they are singing the notes accurately.

To give the soprano ukulele more depth, an alternative is to replace the normal A string with a guitar string and tune it an octave lower than shown above.

Sometimes the instrument is tuned G C E A:

Rather than learning two sets of fingerings for the two different tunings, teach the students to finger the chords for the first tuning and then retune the ukulele and use the same fingering if lower keys are required. The children should be told when the instruments are retuned so their sense of relative pitch is not jeopardized. Understanding the effects of retuning will help the children to add other instruments in keys matching the ukulele key and will help them to develop the concept of transposition.

UKULELE CHORD CHART

Major Chords

C

F

B♭

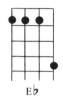

E♭

A♭

G

D

A

E

B

Dominant Seventh Chords

G7

C7

F7

B♭7

E♭7

D7

A7

E7

B7

F♯7

Minor Chords

a

d

g

c

f

e

b

f♯

c♯

g♯

Instruments tuned to

will use the fingerings shown in this chart.

Suggested Projects

1. Write a lesson plan dealing with concepts of timbre and pitch using the ukulele, baritone ukulele, and guitar to help illustrate the concepts. Be sure to differentiate between pitch and timbre.
2. Prepare soprano ukulele accompaniments for four pieces in different keys, styles, and tempos.

Piano

Children rarely have an opportunity to hear a grand piano in elementary school. If a grand is not available, the school should have at least one good piano centrally located in the school so the children have access to it. This piano, like all keyboard instruments used with children, should be kept in tune and at concert pitch (A = 440). The music teacher must be concerned with the pitch of the instrument so that the children sing in suitable keys, their relative pitch is developed, students with absolute pitch are reinforced accurately, other instruments can be tuned with the piano, and fixed-pitch instruments (such as pitched percussion) will be compatible with the piano when they are used together.

Studio upright. The studio upright piano was developed for school use. Its size makes it easier to move from one classroom to another than a larger piano. Its construction helps it to stay in tune even when used heavily. Special attention must be paid to any piano that is moved frequently. Broken or unstable wheels may result in a piano overturning, with the possibility of grave consequences to the children. A reputable piano technician should be consulted for safety recommendations. No child should ever move a piano unsupervised.

Portable pianos. Although portable pianos (suitcase pianos, keyboard modules) often do not sound like pianos, they offer convenient and inexpensive access to a keyboard instrument. The classroom teacher whose school does not have a large enough budget to buy a conventional piano for the classroom may find sufficient funds for the smaller instrument. Students can play these electronic instruments in the classroom without disturbing other students; as soon as the earphones are plugged in, the external sound stops. The music teacher who carries equipment from room to room on a cart will find the small electronic piano more convenient than a heavy upright or more desirable than doing without a keyboard. If a school has several portable pianos, children can gather them from homerooms on the way to music class for a group lesson with the music teacher.

Visual help for music theory.   An advantage of working with a keyboard instrument is that it is easier for the children to visualize note relationships, scales, chords, and so on than with other chordal instruments. Encourage the children to use the keyboard to help make theoretical aspects of music meaningful. Elementary music classes need experience with music making much more than they need theory lessons; keep this to a minimum.

Improvisation.   When orienting the children to the keyboard, the teacher should show them the black-note sets of two and three. The perception of the location of the black notes can be heightened by giving the children opportunities to improvise on them.

The black notes form a pentatonic scale. Have the children sing pen-.atonic songs. Most of the current music textbooks list pentatonic songs in their classified indexes. Encourage the children to show the mood of the song, the meaning of the words, and the rhythm and meter in their improvisations. The following songs lend themselves to contrasting accompaniments to be improvised by the children on the black keys. Give the singers the starting pitch of F♯ so they are in the same mode as the black-key improvisation. The songs are written in easier keys in case the teacher wishes to play the melodies on recorder or piano before teaching them to the children.

TURN THE GLASSES OVER

American Singing Game

turn the glass-es o-ver. Sail-ing east, sail-ing west,

Sail-ing o-ver the o-cean, Bet-ter watch out when the

boat be-gins to rock, or you'll lose your girl in the o-cean.

The singers will start this song on F♯ when performing it with a black-key improvisation.

NIGHT HERDING SONG

Cowboy Song

1. Go slow, lit-tle do-gies, stop mill-in' a-round; I'm
2. Lay down, lit-tle do-gies, and when you've laid down; Just

tired of your rov-in' all o-ver the ground. There's
stretch your-selves out for there's plen-ty of ground. Stay

grass where you're stand-in', so feed kind of slow; You
put, lit-tle do-gies, for I'm aw-ful tired; If

don't have for-ev-er to be on the go. Move
you get a-way I am sure to be fired. Lay

slow, lit-tle do-gies, move slow,— Hi-o, hi-o,— hi-o.—
down, lit-tle do-gies, lay down,—

The singers will start this song on B♭

TROT, PONY, TROT

Maryette Lum   Chinese Folk Song

Trot,   trot,   Po-ny, trot!

Trot to Grand-ma's gate   way.   She comes out and   calls the dog, And

then we'll ride on   jog-a-jog,   Trot, trot,   Po-ny, trot!

From Spectrum of Music, Book 1, *by Mary Val Marsh, Carroll Rinehart, and Edith Savage.* © 1980 by Macmillan Publishing Co., Inc. *Reprinted by permission of the publisher.*

Accompaniments.   The children can learn simple accompaniments for songs. Several children can work together playing chords. They can play on a steady beat while the class sings "Row, Row, Row Your Boat" or "Little Tom Tinker."

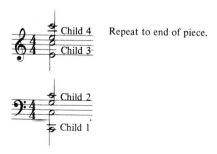

Child 4   Repeat to end of piece.
Child 3
Child 2
Child 1

Show children notes for the G chord to accompany "Are You Sleeping" or "Reveille." Find other one-chord pieces for similar accompaniments.

Give each of the children one note to play for the accompaniment to "Trot, Pony, Trot."

 Repeat to end of piece.

Tonal pictures. In addition to accompanying songs, encourage the children to experiment with tonal pictures using the piano. Ask them to create a mood or make sound effects for a story. Many children can lose themselves completely in exploring the sounds of the keyboard.

Note names. When it is time for the children to learn the names of the keys, let them use the black keys as guides. Ask the children to find a set of two black keys, then play the white note to the left of the set. Tell them that note is C and the note to the left of any set of two black keys is a C. Have them find all the C's on the keyboard. Relate other notes to the C's and the sets of two and three black notes. Rather than teaching all the note names at once, introduce them a few at a time.

Changing chords. As the children get used to the keyboard and they begin to discriminate, assign chords to individuals. Help them play the appropriate chord when required by the music. Although the voice leading is not good, give them chords in different octaves so they don't get in each other's way. At first, the teacher should help them to play at the appropriate time. Later, the children should be challenged to play their chords at the right time with no help. When teachers help, they can point to the students when they should play or to chord names on the board; they can use flashcards, chord names with the text, or music in the manner described in the section on autoharps.

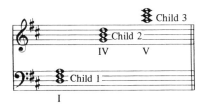

If more than one piano is available, the children should play their chords in closer proximity to each other.

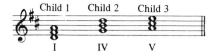

Using the chords in root positions as illustrated helps children under-stand how chords are built. When they are ready to play more than one chord, the teacher should show them how the fingers move to play chords in inversions. This skill may not be grasped by the whole class; a few moments with an individual may be of greater benefit. Challenges like this may be designed for the gifted child:

Playing melodies.   Simple melodies can be given to the children for them to pick out on the piano. With some encouragement they will do this by ear. With more encouragement they will try to play with notation as an additional reference. Older children, especially boys whose voices are changing, should have opportunities to explore music reading through using the bass clef. Even though their voices cannot sing that low yet, let them read in bass clef on the piano.

Recommended Reading

PACE, ROBERT, *Music for the Classroom.* New York: G. Schirmer, Inc., 1967. Teacher's manual and student's book showing useful techniques for giving children keyboard experiences in the classroom.

Suggested Projects

1. Practice keyboard techniques.
    a. Improvise accompaniments to the three songs shown.
    b. Play chords on a steady beat for one-chord songs.
    c. Play a broken chord accompaniment.
    d. Create a tonal picture appropriate for Hallowe'en.
    e. Create sound effects for a story you will tell to the children.
    f. Play the I, IV, and V_7 chords in three different keys.
    g. Pick out the melody to a familiar song by ear.
    h. Read the melodies to two new songs from notation.
2. Write a lesson plan dealing with the concepts of beat, dynamics, and tempo in which the children create appropriate black-note accompaniments to a pentatonic song.

PERCUSSION INSTRUMENTS

Children like to play percussion instruments. These instruments, perhaps more than any others, suffer if the children look upon them as noise producers rather than as musical instruments. From the first time the instruments are introduced to the children, instruction should be given in proper ways to take care of them. Attention must be paid, too, to the quality of sound unique to each instrument when proper playing techniques are used.

Harry Houchins, University of Oregon photographer.

Pitched Percussion

The pitched percussion instruments commonly used in elementary classrooms are xylophones, glockenspiels, metallophones, and resonator bells. Many schools have chromatic bell sets. The disadvantage of the chromatic bell sets is that the bars are permanently fixed whereas the other instruments are flexible. The xylophones, glockenspiels, and metallophones have removable bars. By determining in advance the notes needed for the music, distracting bars can be removed. The bars to be played are left in place on the instrument to take advantage of its resonance. The bars of the resonator bells have separate resonator chambers,

Soprano, alto, and bass xylophones (wooden bars); soprano, alto, and bass metallophones (metal bars); soprano and alto glockenspiels (metal bars, front row, second and third instruments from the left). *STUDIO 49 Orff Instruments. Courtesy of Magnamusic-Baton, St. Louis, MO 63132, U.S. Agents.*

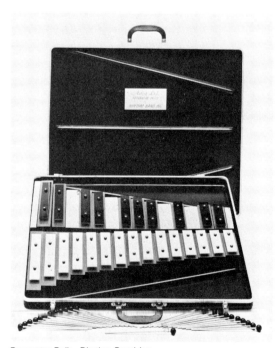

Resonator Bells. *Rhythm Band Inc.*

Chromatic Bell Set. *Rhythm Band Inc.*

so that the notes needed can be held by the children or placed on desks without losing their sonority.

The popularity of the pitched percussion instruments for elementary music education is related to the contributions of Carl Orff.[6] To give depth to the instrumentation, Orff recommended soprano, alto, and bass metallophones and xylophones plus soprano and alto glockenspiels.

Pentatonic creativity. It is easy for children to develop melodic ostinatos to accompany melodies based on the pentatonic scale. The simplest way to build a pentatonic scale is to subtract the fourth and seventh degrees of a major scale, thus eliminating the semitones and the dissonances they produce. Classified indexes of many music textbooks list pentatonic songs. If you are not sure if the song is in the pentatonic mode, count the pitches used in the melody to see if there are five or fewer different pitches used. Next check the key signature. If the piece does not use the fourth or seventh degree of the scale, it is probably pentatonic. The mode most often used in elementary school music has the same tonal relationship as do the black keys of the piano. It does not seem to matter whether the set of two black keys begin the scale or the set of three black keys. The pentatonic pattern can be transferred to any combination of white and black notes as long as they have the same relationship to each other as the black keys.

When children begin to work with the pentatonic scale, prepare their instruments in advance. Take all the bars off the instrument except the notes for the pentatonic scale of the piece to be played. Many schools do not purchase chromatic instruments with removable bars because the extra F♯'s and B♭'s that come with the diatonic instruments give as many choices of keys as are necessary.

[6]See Chapter 10.

PITCHED PERCUSSION INSTRUMENT USED WITH
PENTATONIC SONGS AND CHILD-CREATED OSTINATOS

Teach "Ringing Bells" to the children.

RINGING BELLS

English words by Trudi Eichenlaub   Folk Song from Germany

1. Sounds of bells are in the air: Ding, ding, dong, ding, ding, dong.
2. Time to wake up, morn-ing's here: Ding, ding, dong, ding, ding, dong.

From Sing Mit. ©1975, by R. Oldenbourg Verlag. Reprinted by permission of the publisher.

Prepare the pitched percussion instruments by taking off all the bars except G, A, B, D, E, the G pentatonic scale. If resonator bells are to be used, take only those notes out of the case.

Experience with ostinatos is a prerequisite to this activity. Be sure the children have played repeated patterns taught to them by the teacher on a variety of instruments before asking them to create their own. Ostinatos consisting of repeated melodic patterns create an appropriate accompaniment for "Ringing Bells." Other songs are best supported by the addition of repeated rhythmic patterns using nonpitched percussion instruments or a combination of melodic and rhythmic ostinatos.

Begin a discussion with the children regarding appropriate kinds of instruments to use with "Ringing Bells." They will probably decide on metallophones and glockenspiels or resonator bells—the pitched percussion instruments with metal bars. Give the children time to develop ostinatos on the instruments they have chosen. Let each instrumentalist play his or her ostinato alone. Ask the children to sing the song while the instrumentalists accompany with their ostinatos. Try more than one ostinato with the song. Discuss whether or not all the instruments should play at once. Encourage the children to choose their style of accompaniment. When they decide upon instrumentation, the number of ostinatos to be played at one time, and the sequence in which the ostinatos will be played, they are beginning to arrange music. If they disagree on the arrangements, try alternatives. Is there only one "correct" accompaniment for this song?

Prepare the instruments for another piece by removing all the bars except those of the C pentatonic scale: C, D, E, G, A. Ask the children to talk about lullabies. What are they? How are they used? When singing a lullaby, what dynamics are appropriate? What tempo?

176

Sing "Birthday Presents" for the children.[7] When the children are improvising, do not use the piano accompaniment. Its major modality distracts from the pentatonic mode in which the instruments have been prepared.

BIRTHDAY PRESENTS

Translation by Willis Lamott
Paraphrase by Edith Lovell Thomas

Japan

4. Here's another present, Jesus,
When you want some fun:
On his back the Colt will take you
Riding in the sun.

From The Whole World Singing *by Edith Lovell Thomas.* ©1950 *by Friendship Press, Inc. Used by permission.*

[7]If the religious text is inappropriate for public school use, consider singing "little baby" instead of "Baby Jesus."

Ask the children if that song sounded like a lullaby. What were its dynamics? Its tempo? Teach the song to the class. Group the children into pitched percussion sections using wood or metal bars. Ask them to create ostinatos in character with the song. Give the children a common tempo for all to use. After the children have developed their ostinatos, ask them to begin playing in response to conductor cues. You will then conduct them so that the instruments build a pyramid of instrumental sound beginning with the bass metallophone and then adding the higher metallophones one at a time. You will next cue the xylophones, followed by the glockenspiels. When all the instruments have joined the ensemble, bring in the singers. When the song has been sung with the instrumental accompaniment, gradually stop the ostinatos in reverse order from the way in which they were added to the ensemble, ending with the bass metallophone.

If the school has only chromatic bell sets with nonremovable bars, show the children how to stay within the pentatonic framework by using only the specified notes for the scale. Write the names of the notes on the chalkboard. Since the bars of the bell sets are marked with letter names, the children should be able to play the correct notes. If they have difficulty in remembering which notes to play while they are creating, mark the bars with either washable felt-tipped markers or signal dots.[8] Color code the marks (e.g., yellow for notes of the C pentatonic, green for G pentatonic).

The more the children become involved in using pitched percussion instruments, the more responsibility they should be given. Teach them to prepare their instruments for different pieces. Encourage them to make distinctions about the kind of mallets to be used for contrasting timbres in differing pieces.

Other pentatonic songs are

"Amazing Grace"	"Lonesome Valley"
"Get on Board"	"Mister Rabbit"
"Good Bye, Old Paint"	"The Old Brass Wagon"
"Go Tell It on the Mountain"	"Old MacDonald"
"I'd Like to Teach the World	"Old Texas"
to Sing" (refrain)	"Shortnin' Bread"

Some songs lend themselves to pentatonic accompaniment only partially: "Oh Susanna" inspires the children to engage in spirited improvisation during its A phrases. The B phrase is not in F pentatonic (F, G, A, C, D), so accompaniment on the prepared instruments will not sound right. The children may decide to use a nonpitched percussion accompaniment for that phrase; they may decide to have no accompaniment there. Whatever their decision, dealing with this particular problem heightens their perception of the modality and the form of the piece.

---

[8]Signal dots are small, brightly colored, round pieces of paper with adhesive on the back. They are available at stationery stores.

STUDIO 49 Orff Instruments. Courtesy of Magnamusic-Baton, St. Louis, MO 63132, U. S. Agents.

Form.　Using instruments in composition helps in leading the children to understand form. If the children are given guidelines for composition that expand as the children's capability grows, they can be successful. If the children are given too broad an assignment, the experience may be frustrating and generally counterproductive.

Make both pitched and nonpitched percussion instruments available to the students. Divide them into small groups asking each group to produce an A B A composition in $\frac{4}{4}$ time with each section consisting of four measures. Prerequisite to this assignment are experiences in identifying form, discriminating phrases, exploring instrumental timbres and capabilities, and constructing measures with accuracy in rhythm. The teacher must be available to help the students as needed. When the compositions have been completed, the students should share them with the other small groups. Future assignments can be varied according to the instrumental resources available, the form designated, the meter, and the length. As the students become more skilled, they can begin to determine the specifications. Individuals may elect to create compositions without being involved in a group. The children may decide that, rather than using real instruments, they wish to create music using other sound sources such as kitchen utensils, classroom objects, and playground resources.

The work just described is appropriate for older children. Similar work with younger children can begin with large-group experience and be largely teacher directed. Teach the xylophone players to play a phrase. Teach the glockenspiels a contrasting phrase. Have them play in this order: xylophones-glockenspiels-xylophones. This demonstrates three-part form, or A B A. Call it A B A only if that label has meaning for the children. On another day, the three-part form can be triangle-drum-triangle or pitched percussion-nonpitched percussion-pitched percussion. Other forms such as A B and rondo can be used as well.

Writing music. To share the compositions, add the musical skill of notating them. Challenge the groups to devise some means of writing their work down so it can be passed to another group to see if they can perform it exactly with no instruction except the written communication. Guidelines can be suggested for these experiences. On one day, the students may be asked to use any means of writing the composition down that they wish. On another day, they should be asked to use only conventional music notation. On yet another day, they may be asked to devise their own form of communication, excluding musical notation and language directions.

Direct the children's attention to the music produced in response to the notation. Was the reproduction the same as the original? Did the style of notation change the character of the composition? Which type of notation was most precise in showing the new group how to duplicate the work of the composers? Which style of notation was most difficult for the players to interpret?

Melodies. Resonator bells can be used like hand bells to play melodies. When playing a melody, young children can each contribute one pitch toward the sound. The teacher points to the child who is to play next. Begin with easy melodies that all the children know. Next, use unfamiliar material, perhaps songs the children will be learning. To show the pitch each child is playing, pin a letter name and staff notation on each participant. Arrange the children in musical order similar to the keyboard. Through this coupling of notation with playing and pointing to the proper pitch, you are moving the children toward the use of the staff. Next try pointing to the notes on the staff rather than directly at the children to see if they are ready to respond to the notation rather than to the teacher's direct clue. Finally, see if the children can play the melody without anyone pointing to either them or the notation.

If resonator bells are not available, bottles can be tuned and used in the same way except that they lose resonance if held by the children. Try to collect matching bottles; then tune them with varying levels of water to obtain the desired pitch. Other pitched percussion instruments can be adapted also, especially for easy songs requiring few notes. The bars of the xylophone can be spread out so the children, each with one mallet, can reach their assigned notes.

Encourage the children to play and read melodies by themselves on the pitched percussion instruments. Give them time and privacy to use the instruments without distractions. After having learned to play a melody independently, ask the child to play it for the class.

Reading.   The teacher should constantly place musical symbols before the children. Large charts of musical materials under study such as melodies and instrumental scores should be displayed frequently in both the music classroom and the regular classroom. As a special reward for classes that do well in music, have the chart used for the day's lesson sent back to their classroom until the next music session. Children should see notation, not just words for songs.

Harmony.   Bars from the resonator bell set can be put in chord trays or holders and played with spray mallets to make accompanying chords. The other pitched percussion instruments can be used to play chords also. The techniques described for chordal instruments can be used with these instruments. First, indicate the proper chord to be used; later, encourage the children to respond independently when the chords are to be changed.

Recommended Resource

BRADFORD, LOUISE LARKINS,   *Sing It Yourself.* Sherman Oaks, CA: Alfred Publishing Co., Inc., 1978. A collection of 220 pentatonic American folk songs.

Suggested Projects

1.   Select three pentatonic songs. Create two appropriate ostinatos for each song.
2.   Write a lesson plan for the grade level of your choice using a pitched percussion instrument to teach the concept of ostinato.

Nonpitched percussion

The nonpitched members of the percussion family are those that produce indefinite pitches. They include tambourines, wood blocks, maracas, claves, drums, finger cymbals, jingle bells, cow bells, triangles, cymbals, gongs, sand blocks, castanets, temple blocks, and guiros. Their use heightens rhythmic experiences and produces interesting timbre effects. Children can create spontaneously with these instruments when other means seem to fail.

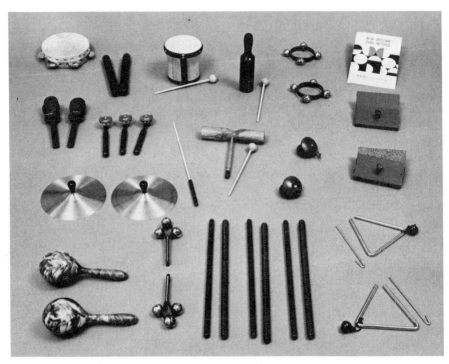

Assorted non-pitched percussion instruments. *Rhythm Band Inc.*

Discipline. When instruments are played by children, guidelines must be established so the lessons do not turn into chaos. A basic guideline is that the children do not play instruments when the teacher asks for their attention. If the children choose to do so, they choose to give up their instruments. Set time aside for them to use the instruments freely so they can explore the potential of the various instruments. Another basic guideline is that the instruments must be treated with care so they will have them to use in the future.

Basic rhythm. Experiences for children learning rhythm are: playing the steady beat, echoing, engaging in question and answer activities, pattern reading, and ostinato playing. Many of these activities are initiated by the children clapping responses. Too much clapping tends to tire their hands and leads to boredom. All the experiences are enhanced by using instruments.

The children can use their instruments to show the *steady beat.* When they are proficient at this, they can use the louder instruments to show the accented beat and the softer instruments to show the other beats in determining the meter of the music. The steady beat and the accented beat can be played with many different types of music, live and recorded.

Give the children instruments for *echoing patterns.* Have a variety of the instruments available, but do not use them all at once. Seek to vary the echo sound from lesson to lesson by changing the timbre. Be careful to give all the children chances to play the echo responses. Practice clapping the pattern and indicating the time of their entrances to the children, so there is a rhythmic interaction between teacher and student. Echoing helps the children to develop rhythm skill by imitating an accurate model.

Question-and-answer activities ask the child to respond to the teacher's pattern with a pattern of equal length rather than echoing it. The answer will begin like the teacher's but will come to a more definite conclusion.

The teacher's question using the tambourine:

A possible student's answer using the jingle bells:

A possible student's answer using the jingle bells:

The teacher's question using the claves:

A possible student's answer using the temple blocks:

If the children have difficulty determining the length of their answers, ask the class to help by counting the number of beats in the teacher's pattern and then counting again with the student. If the patterns written below are too difficult, they should be simplified to match the capabilities of the students:

Ask the children to *read* patterns from the chalkboard or a chart. Give an instrument to the child who claps a pattern accurately. Ask four children to play a percussion ensemble using the patterns they have clapped accurately.

If they cannot play four independent lines, let them try two. If that is still too hard, let the class help by clapping along with the soloist. To let each child have a chance to play an instrument, the teacher must notate some very easy patterns and save them for the child with limited rhythmic reading ability. The triangle part shown is for this child. The tambourine part with syncopation is for the gifted child who needs to be challenged.

Patterns can also be played that become *ostinatos* for the songs. The patterns can be some of the ones they read, or they can be some of the ones they echo. Aural presentation of ostinato patterns will be necessary when more complicated rhythms are to be used than the children can read. This ostinato for "Tinga Layo" adds to the interest of the song, but it would be too difficult for many children to read.

Here is an easier ostinato, though it, also, may be too difficult for some children to read.

TINGA LAYO

Calypso Song From
the West Indies

Copyright 1943, M. Baron Co. Reprinted by permission.

Timbre. As the children become adept at rhythmic discrimination, couple their activities with timbre discrimination. Discuss the construction of the instruments with the children. Ask them to categorize them according to the materials that produce the sound: wood, skin, metal. Encourage them to make decisions based upon what they hear, especially with instruments having more than one timbre capability. Help them to realize that, when the tambourine is struck on its head by a mallet, it is closer to a drum sound than when it is shaken and produces a sound made from metal.

Ask the children to play the echo only if the sound they hear is produced in the same way their instrument sounds. This is like an instrumental "Simon Says." The drums should only echo if they hear the pattern produced by a drum. The triangles should echo only if the pattern is produced by a metallic sound source. In the preliminary stages of timbre discrimination, let the children see the instruments the teacher uses to play the patterns so that their visual observations can help them make the classifications. Later, play the instruments out of the children's sight (in the back of the room, or behind a shield) so their responses are made only on the basis of what they hear.

Another way of using timbre classification and rhythm patterns is to give out only three instruments: one wood, one skin, one metal. After you play a pattern on the cymbal, the child with a metal instrument should echo it. You should play the next pattern on a different instrument. The child who just finished echoing will pass his or her instrument to another child.

Creative activities. Plan many opportunities for nonpitched instruments to add sound effects to experiences in which the children are involved. Stories, made up by the children, told by someone else, or read aloud, will be more interesting when creative sounds are added. Surprise, a storm, something breaking, a snake, crossing a bridge, plus dozens of other effects can be created by imaginative use of the instruments.

They can be used creatively in setting a mood. The mood may be caused by reaction to a song or in response to words or a drama. The children can plan ways their instruments will show excitement, haste, tension, fear, peace, celebration, and so on. They may decide that the non-pitched instruments are not sufficient to do the job alone, that they need to incorporate the pitched percussion instruments and a variety of body sounds. When the children become involved in creative activity, it is not surprising that they find objects around the classroom for additional sounds. Many wastepaper baskets produce useful loud sounds. A handicapped child who has difficulty in holding a drum stick may experience no difficulty in dropping paper clips on a hand drum to simulate the sound of a hail storm. Devise ways in which to include children who have unique problems.

The creative teacher will explore many more ways in which instruments can add to the quality and variety of music experiences of the chil-

Harry Houchins, University of Oregon photographer

dren. Be alert for ideas from them. They will probably be most creative in their use of instruments to color the compositions they perform. Whether the music is a piece they have learned, or one they have made up, the sonorities they develop through instrumental additions can help make it a special experience.

Recommended Resources

Let's Play Percussion. Milwaukee: Learning Unlimited, Hal Leonard Publishing Co., 1971. Tape and book for independent instruction.

RINEHART, CARROLL, MAX T. ERVIN, AND GEORGE DEGREGORI, *Sounds for Success, Percussion*. Tucson: Sounds for Success, 1963. Record and score included. Students hear, then play, rhythm patterns with help of score and accompaniment.

Suggested Projects

1. Select an appropriate song for a grade of your choice. Arrange the song by adding at least three nonpitched percussion instruments to the song.
2. Write a lesson plan for sixth grade in which the children write two rhythm ostinatos to go with a song they know.
3. Play pieces on the instrument of your choice while the children are finding the steady beat. Be sure the pieces vary in tempo so the children realize that the steady beat is not always performed at the same speed.

Conclusion

In addition to all the instruments discussed, the beginning teacher should be encouraged to include still more instruments in music classes. Borrow instruments originating in cultures all over the world from travelers, museums, and music stores. Ask children if their families have instruments at home that they could bring to show the other children. Use these to create a global awareness of kinds of music differing from the students' immediate experience. If a musician is not available who can play the instrument, find recordings of it. Help the children to transfer their skill on their present instruments to new ones. More important, arouse their curiosity about the many ways in which sound can be produced and inspire them with respect for the immensity of human musical expression.

6 Move

Rhythmic movement is a basic human response to music; foot tapping and hand clapping seem to be universal. Children should have opportunities to develop large-body responses in addition to rhythmic use of hands and feet. If body response to rhythm is not encouraged, it may disappear by the time the child reaches the upper elementary school grades. In some sections of the country, community attitudes toward expression through movement, especially if it is called dancing, may be negative. The music teacher can help to educate these communities through effective inclusion of movement in the music curriculum.

The movement activities described here are designed to increase the child's musical involvement. There are many more in addition to these. In planning lessons, the teacher should be sensitive to ways in which movement can help the children to become musical by providing expressive experiences using the body. It is the rhythmic movement of the most sophisticated instrumentalist's finger that enables him or her to carry out the composer's intention in the music.

Concept development. Movement adds another activity useful for helping children to develop musical concepts. They can

Use their bodies to show high and low pitch.

Draw in the air or use the whole body to show melodic direction.

Show interval distances through body response.

Move in one direction until the end of a phrase and reverse direction for the next phrase.

Show form through contrasting movements.

Show repetition and contrast through repeated or varying movement.

Show contrasting dynamics and tempos through bodily response.

Use movement to illustrate the steady beat.

Move to match regular and irregular rhythm patterns

Show accented beats.

Identify chord changes through physical reactions such as moving only when the tonic chord (I) is heard.

Respond only to certain motives heard in the music.

Create body rhythm patterns.

Create body ostinatos and rounds.

Show theme and variations with movement.

Respond physically to timbre differences.

Imagination. The children's imagination should be encouraged. If they seem uncreative, suggest different imaginative settings to which they can respond with movement.

1. Today, we are at the zoo. Will you be yourself or one of the animals?
2. Our spaceship is in the Milky Way; sometimes it is moving along peacefully; sometimes flying objects come dangerously close.
3. Today is your birthday; you are very sad because no one has wished you a "Happy Birthday." Move through your day with the music to see if anyone remembers or surprises you.
4. Enlist the children's assistance in inventing other situations.

The children can respond to these situations with or without music, at first. When music is added to them, it can be pieces chosen to match the situations or improvisations played by the teacher.

Improvisation. Develop improvisational skills through which you can provide musical variations to which the children will react. The piano is ideal for this; a drum can be used if your pianistic skill is limited. Pitched percussion instruments or the autoharp can be used also. Simply ask the children to do what the music tells them to do. Play slowly, then accelerate; play fast, then ritard and stop. A familiar song can be used to do this.

When the music stops, the children should stop. Teach this rule to prevent chaos before any movement activities are initiated. Two other useful movement rules are (1) avoid touching anyone else and (2) don't talk when moving.

Improvise a variable combination of dynamics and tempos so that the children can demonstrate loud-slow movements as well as fast-soft ones. Avoid the temptation to consistently couple loud with fast and soft with slow. Use a hand drum for this improvisation.

Improvise on the black keys for the spaceship flight suggested. Try adding glissandos. (Let your fingernails brush backward across the keys.)

Movement responses to creative instrumental work can be part of almost every musical contact the teacher has with young children. These movement experiences are especially valuable if the students show lack of interest in another part of the lesson. The classroom teacher should save these activities to help change moods after intense periods of concentration spent on another subject.

Note values.   The children can express the steady beat with their bodies in many ways. One way is to march with music with a strongly defined beat. In teaching them the differences between symbols standing for note values, call the steady beats they are marching to quarter notes. Give a picture of a quarter note to the leader of the marchers. Use the name of the note and the picture so often that the label and the image are associated by the children with the movement they are making.

Next, play a series of chords held for two beats. Ask the children to move with the chords. If they have trouble keeping still for two beats, have them chant "Hold it, hold it" to help them know how long to remain in one position. Contrast the quarter note movement to the new movement that is the half note. Give the new card to a leader who can demonstrate that duration easily.

Illustrate eighth notes in music next for the children. Show them how to move their feet to the shorter notes. Give the picture of the eighth note to a capable leader. Continue to have the children move like quarter and half notes as well and to associate the pictures with the notes.

The most difficult notes for the children to show with their bodies are the whole notes. Demonstrate whole notes in music. It can be a series of whole-note chords played by the teacher. If the children have difficulty in keeping still for this long note, ask them to chant "Hold it longer!" keeping their feet in place for the duration of the note. Give the picture of the whole note to a decisive leader.

Help them associate movement with the note pictures and their names during many lessons. Change leaders frequently. As they become sure of the musical directions the pictures are giving them, play less obvious clues for them to respond to. Divide the class into two, then three, and finally four groups so two different ♩ ♩, then three ♪ ♩ ♩, and, finally, four ♪ ♩ ♩ 𝅝 kinds of movement can be done concurrently.

Form. In developing listening lessons, especially in pieces with marked contrasts in form, use movement to help illustrate the structure of the composition. A listening lesson built upon "Circus Music" from the *Red Pony Suite* by Aaron Copland is described in Chapter 7. A creative activity associated with that composition involves having the children decide what movement they would like to do in the A section. They may decide to be circus animals. Let them do the movement they chose with the music for section A. Ask them to listen to part of the B section to determine if the music there indicates a change in movement. Is the music of B faster or slower than the music in the A section? Is it louder or softer? Does it tell you to move differently?

Let the children respond to the B section with their bodies. After the B section, ask them what the music tells them to do. Ask them if they have heard music like that before. These activities are not necessarily to be done all in one session. Observe the children's involvement. Have they been overstimulated by too much activity? Are they tired of moving? Are they still involved constructively? Adjust the length of the lessons and the movement of the children according to their reactions.

Ken Karp.

Creative instrumentation.   Movement activities combine readily with the creative instrumental activities described in Chapter 5. At the time the children are producing instrumental compositions, they can be devising movements related to the sounds being produced. This is a good way to involve students when the number of available instruments is limited. The instruments creating the A section can have counterparts who will move according to their interpretation of the A sound. The movement counterparts of the instruments in B will move differently because the sound they hear is different.

Ostinatos. Movement ostinatos can be devised to correspond to the melodic or rhythmic sound of the repeated pattern. The movement for the do-sol ostinato will be different from the movement for the sol-mi-sol-la one.

Limitations. For some movement assignments, ask the children to use only their feet. Another day, ask them to use only their bodies from the waist up. Sometimes ask them to use movement that adds sound to the composition such as thigh slapping, finger clicking, and chest thumping. Contrast this to movement using no sound.

Dramatization. Creative dramatization is an activity that combines many aspects of music, including movement. It is probably easier to begin with a previously written composition or story, although eventually the children should plan their own dramatizations. The movement included in dramatizations can be quite different from rhythmic movement.

CREATIVE DRAMATIZATION STIMULATED BY A SONG STORY

Before beginning to dramatize "The Mouse's Courting Song," sing it to the children as many times as they need to become familiar with the story. They should be able to add the "Hm-hm's" whenever they come in the song. Ask all the children to respond appropriately to each verse.

1. Please show how a mouse who was rough and tough like Buffalo Bill would move.

THE MOUSE'S COURTING SONG

Pennsylvania Folk Song

There was a lit-tle mouse who lived on a hill, Hm - hm, Hm - hm, There was a lit-tle mouse who lived on a hill, He was rough and tough like Buf-fa-lo Bill, Hm - hm, Hm - hm.

2.   Pretend that you are now riding your horse with your two six-shooters on.

  One day he 'cided to take a ride,
      Hm—hm, Hm—hm,
  One day he 'cided to take a ride,
  With two six-shooters by his side,
      Hm—hm, hm—hm.

3.   What do you do when you see the house of Minnie Mouse?

  Then Mickey rode till he came to a house,
  And in this house was Minnie Mouse.

4.   If you were the mouse, would you really do what the words for this verse say?
     Show what you would do.

  He strutted right up to the kitchen door,
  And bowed and scraped his head on the floor.

5.   Pretend that you are asking Minnie to marry you—or if you don't want to be
     Mickey, pretend that you are Minnie being asked by Mickey to marry him.

  O Minnie, Minnie, Minnie, will you marry me?
  Away down yonder in the orchard tree!

6.   Now show how Minnie answers.

  Without my Uncle Rat's consent
  I would not marry the Pres-eye-dent!

7.   Choose whether you want to be Uncle Rat saying that she can marry Mickey
     or the Weasel writing the public announcement that the wedding will take
     place.

  Her Uncle Rat gave his consent,
  The Weasel wrote the publishment.

8.   How can you show the wedding feast and what is being eaten?

  Oh, what you gwina have for the wedding feast?
  Black-eyed peas and hogshead cheese.

9.   Now you're going to be the guests at the wedding. First show how Uncle Rat
     comes in the door.

  The first one came was Uncle Rat,
  Head as long as a baseball bat.

10. Can you show Mr. Snake?

    Second one came was Mr. Snake
    He wrapped himself 'round the marble cake.

11. The little moth may be easy for you to show.

    The next one came was a little moth,
    To spread on the tablecloth.

12. How can a big black bug carry a little brown jug?

    The next one came was a big black bug,
    Carrying 'round a little brown jug.

13. Can you still fly if you are a bumblebee with a broken wing and a crooked knee?

    The next one came was a bumblebee,
    With a broken wing and a crooked knee.

14. How does a nimble flea move? Can he dance?

    The next one came was a nimble flea,
    Saying, Minnie, Minnie Mouse, will you
        dance with me?

15. Mr. Cow (Can a cow be a Mr.?) says he can't dance. What does he do?

    The next one came was Mr. Cow,
    He wanted to dance but he didn't know how.

16. Can you look mean just before you eat Uncle Rat?

    Last one came was Mr. Cat,
    He ruffled and tuffled and ate Uncle Rat.

17. What was everyone doing at the end of the wedding feast?

    And that was the end of the wedding feast,
    Black-eyed peas and hogshead cheese.

Use your judgment in deciding whether or not to do all the verses in one lesson. If the children are responding well, dramatize all of them; if not, save some for another day.

In a follow-up lesson, seek volunteers to act only one of the roles. If there is an unpopular character none of the children will volunteer to be, save that role for yourself. The children who did not volunteer for special parts will still be involved as "Hm" singers and as members of a well-behaved audience. The teacher's appreciative remarks to children who show respect for others' contributions should be a consistent part of music class. Developing good audience behavior is a component of music education. Its success in classroom experiences such as creative dramatizations should spread to school assemblies and concerts with the help of all the teachers.

To encourage the children, the teacher should make comments such as, "Ann, you were such a good listener just now. Could you use the coconut shells to make the sound of Mickey's horse?" "Bill, you paid close attention. What instrument can you find to help Mr. Cow dance?"

Ask for volunteers to create instrumental effects to help in dramatizing "The Mouse's Courting Song." If instruments are not available to make the sound of the bee, might some voices do it? In addition to sound effects, create simple ostinatos to go with the piece. It is in F pentatonic (F G A C D).

The song can be sung many times, each time with a different cast and different instrumentalists. As the children hear the song over and over, they will eventually be able to sing it also.

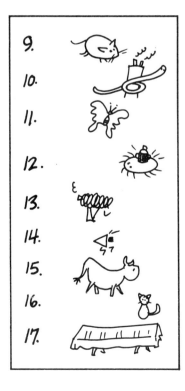

Even after the song has become fairly familiar, a visual will be useful to help everyone, including the teacher, remember what comes next. If you are not a talented artist, ask for help, especially from the children. In anticipation of this help, make a visual aid with slots for the pictures. Use those made by the children whenever possible.

Rather than beginning with a story, the dramatic movement may stem from a piece of music. Let the children listen to an unfamiliar composition such as "Anitra's Dance" from the *Peer Gynt Suite* by Grieg. Ask them to talk about some of the musical characteristics of the composition. Does it begin with low-pitched instruments or high ones? Does the instrumentation change during the piece? What happens to the tempo? Is there dynamic variety? Could body movement show what happens in the music? Are there repeated rhythmic or melodic phrases in the piece? Could a few non-pitched percussion instrumentalists join in playing the rhythm pattern?

Games and activity songs. Many children's game songs encourage movement. "The Farmer in the Dell," "Ring Around a Rosie," "London Bridge," and the like may be known to the children before they begin school. Whether or not the children have learned them, they are worth reintroducing to the children for both their musical and movement values.

AN ACTIVITY SONG FOR INVOLVING YOUNG CHILDREN

THE HOKEY POKEY

American Folk Song

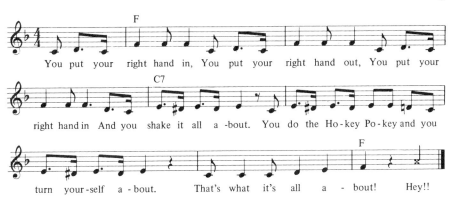

"The Hokey Pokey" is a circle activity song. The directions are contained in the song: various parts of the body are thrust toward the inside of the circle and then moved out. Doing the "Hokey Pokey" unleashes any creative movement the participant wants to do as he or she turns around. Almost any part of the body can be put in and out of the circle. The children delight in suggesting the part to be sung about next. The song helps very young children to learn names for parts of the body. It also helps them to distinguish between the right and left sides of the body.

Folk dances.   These are enjoyed by older children once they get over the idea of having a partner of the opposite sex. If you are well prepared before the lesson, having even laid out the sets for the dances with the children's names listed, considerable time will be saved in deciding on partners. You can give them the option of choosing their own partners if they come in the door of the classroom with selections already made rather than taking class time to make them. Movement activities in conjunction with the physical education classes have the double advantage of involving two cooperating teachers in the project and of using the gymnasium with enough space to carry on the activity.

Hand jives.   A type of rhythmic ostinato, hand jives, may be used with rock or other pieces selected by the children. Show a pattern of movement for the children to duplicate and repeat such as two claps, two clicks, two stamps, two shoulder taps. These movements are done on the steady beat at first. For variety, the movements should be changed during the piece. Later, more complicated hand jives can be created.

Choose two student leaders. Assign half the class to each leader. Ask the leaders to begin with the same pattern, then gradually change parts of it. Ask the leaders to keep going, but tell the class to switch to the leader they have not been following.

Common steps.   Show the children how music influences the performance of basic dance steps. Have them practice this pattern with their feet very slowly: right-left-right, left-right-left, and so on. Ask them to keep the pattern going, but vary the size of the steps. In place of right-left-right, left-right-left use big-small-small, big-small-small. Add the appropriate music, and the children are doing a waltz.

Begin with the same pattern: right-left-right, left-right-left. This time, move the feet with this rhythm: ♪♩ ♪♩. Add the proper music, and the children are doing a polka.

Use the same pattern right-left-right, left-right-left. Now add a hop on the end of the pattern with the same foot just used: right-left-right-right hop, left-right-left-left hop. Add the right music, and the children are doing a schottische.

The same foot pattern in this rhythm produces a foxtrot.

R L R – | L R L –
♩ ♩ ♩ 𝄾 | ♩ ♩ ♩ 𝄾

Disco.   If the children enjoy movement activities consistently throughout their school years, they are more likely to enjoy dancing as they grow older. In a supportive environment, the older children may be happy learning disco dancing. If you are not aware of current dance steps, seek advice from children and adults who are knowledgable. Guest dance instructors can be of great benefit to the music program.

Recommended Resources

DOLL, EDNA, AND MARY JARMAN NELSON,   *Rhythms Today.* Morristown, NJ: Silver Burdett Company, 1965.
JENKINS, ELLA,   *Song, Rhythms and Chants for the Dance.* New York: Folkways, 1977. Records of songs for dancing and interviews with people in occupations related to dancing.
KAY, BOB,   *Children's Body Awareness and Movement Exercises.* New York: Think Stallman Productions Ltd., 1974. Record of songs to help the child with movement.
STATON, BARBARA,   *Music 1 ... 2 ... 3.* New York: Columbia, 1977. Recordings of songs and accompanying booklet with song words and directions for moving.
TANNER, VIRGINIA,   *Come Dance with Me.* Waldwick, NJ: Dance Records, 1964. Teaching booklet and record with music and narration for creative dance.

Suggested Projects

1. Write a lesson plan for the grade level of your choice using movement to establish a steady beat.
2. Select three movement activities described in this chapter and do them.
3. Practice improvisation on an instrument of your choice. Write a lesson plan using your improvisation skill to teach the children tempo concepts: fast, slow, ritardando, accelerando.

7 *Listen*

All musical experiences should be based on listening. Unfortunately, children are sometimes taught to engage in mechanical responses such as pressing keys, responding to teacher direction, or answering questions with no reference to sound. The development of auditory discrimination is necessary when a child learns a melody, changes harmony, responds rhythmically, identifies form, and perceives the expressive uses of tempo, dynamics, and timbre. Singing, playing, moving, creating, reading, and writing are meaningful in their relationship to music only if the children are encouraged to develop awareness of both the sound coming from other sources and the sound they are producing.

Teaching students to identify the components of music is often called *ear training*. Many of the experiences described throughout this book show examples of it. The ear is being trained as the child is asked to identify syncopation, or theme and variations, or an octave. The heightening of musical perception should be a consistent part of all music lessons.

LISTENING LESSONS

Types of listening experiences not discussed previously are those based upon music more difficult than the children can perform. In these lessons, ear training is still very important, but the main focus is upon the music, with listening experiences designed to help the child's perception of what is being heard.

To help the children hear what is in the music, you must be confident of your ability to analyze it. If, after reading about music for presentation to children and listening to it, you cannot hear what is being described, it is better not to use that selection. Seek examples easy for analysis and, especially, ones that you enjoy.

Older children will often volunteer to share their listening favorites with the class. The disadvantage of this sharing is that the musical experience in class may only duplicate experiences the students can enjoy by themselves. The advantage is that the students can identify musical concepts studied in class and use their listening selections to reinforce the learning that has taken place.

After the students have played and discussed ostinatos, splendid reinforcement occurs when a student brings to class a favorite record on which the string bass player persistently repeats a pattern.

After discussion in class of polyphonic, monophonic, and homophonic music, the student brings a favorite record starting with a vocal solo, adding an instrumental accompaniment and then other voices. The student asks if the piece is monophonic, homophonic, and then polyphonic? Class listening to the record reveals that it is monophonic at first and then homophonic when the instruments enter. It remains homophonic when the other voices enter because they duplicate the chordal accompaniment rather than add melodies in a contrapuntal fashion. To include student-selected music, keep asking the students to find examples illustrating concepts learned in class. Encourage them to relate their listening outside of class to what happens in it.

A question often asked about listening lessons for children is, "What literature is appropriate?" The answer to that question is based upon the premise that the purpose of listening lessons is to give children variety in their contacts with music so they can make choices in the future from a wide spectrum rather than from a limited one. Hence, their music should be chosen from music of all periods, styles, and cultures. It should include medieval, renaissance, baroque, classical, romantic, impressionistic, modern, and contemporary selections. All styles should be included: jazz, pop, folk (worldwide), rock, country-western, swing, show, avant-garde, gospel, plainchant, rag, blues, Dixieland, background, and atonal. Both instrumental and vocal music should be heard: solo, small, and large ensemble. Secular and sacred music should be included in many forms: madrigals, oratorios, masses, motets, art songs, symphonies, suites, ballet music, overtures, concertos, program and absolute music, opera, operetta, electronic, ballads, and marches. Music of other cultures should be heard, both to emphasize common aspects of all music and to heighten the fascinating differences.

It is the teacher's responsibility to select appropriate music for the children to interact with on their own affective, cognitive, and psychomotor levels. There should be less emphasis on literature familiar to the children and more on teaching them new material. Listening lessons for young children must have obvious components for them to hear. It is especially important that the length of listening experiences be limited for the young. No matter what type of music is to be used, try to select pieces having lasting value, those that remain attractive after many repeated listenings.

To focus the children's attention, always give them something to listen for, or a related activity that will heighten their perception of what they are listening for.

LISTENING LESSONS FOR CHILDREN

The Main Event.   Recent selections of music may catch the older students' interest more readily than do pieces that are farther away in style and time than they are used to. Play Barbra Streisand's recording of "The Main Event"[1] for the class. The short version includes her singing; the longer version is instrumental only. It is not necessary to play the entire instrumental version.

Tell the children they will hear two musical selections. Ask them to describe the differences between the pieces. The obvious differences are that the vocalist sings in one piece and not in the other and that one of the selections begins slowly and softly and then gets faster and louder.

Ask the children to describe similarities between the two selections. They will find that the beat, the rhythm, the melody, the style, and the instrumentation are the same after the introduction is finished.

A follow-up lesson asking the children to do more comparative listening can use Beethoven's Symphony No. 5 in its traditional style and a contrasting contemporary interpretation.[2]

Close Encounters of the Third Kind.[3]   This has been a popular film in theaters and on television. Some of the children at all ages may recall the melody "The Conversation" from the film. Modify the activities and expectations according to the backgrounds of the various classes. The suggestions about "The Conversation" are not meant to be carried out in one lesson. Design lessons using selected activities over an appropriate period of time.

[1]P. Jabara and B. Roberts, Columbia Records.
[2]Contrast the Deutsche Grammophon recording of Beethoven's *Fifth Symphony*, Herbert Von Karajan conducting, to *Fifth of Beethoven*, Walter Murphy Bank, Millennium Records.
[3]John Williams, Arista Records.

Ask the children to listen to the music to see if it is familiar to any of them. If it is, they should try to remember what was happening when they heard it. If they have not heard it before, they should try to imagine what could be happening during the music. Caution the children who know the music not to tell anyone about it until after the music stops.

Rather than calling on the children who know the music right away, ask the children who have not heard it before to tell what was happening during the music. Because of the character of the music, many children will describe the interaction of something large and something small. They will probably mention the contrasting high and low pitches. Ask the children who have heard it before to tell where they heard it.

Name the piece ("The Conversation") and ask them to choose to be either the high sounds or the low sounds. Once they have chosen, they are to move only when they hear their sounds. As the music plays, help them to respond if necessary. Discuss the confusion that results when the high and low sounds are not heard one at a time, when they are heard together, and when they change to different registers.

Show the students charts of the main theme written in high, middle, and low registers. Ask the students to play the theme on available instruments. Show them how to play it if necessary. Ask them to describe the differences on the charts between the high, middle, and low notation. Ask the children to play the theme in the different registers of the piano. Ask three other children to hold the charts so the rest of the class can see them. The pianists will decide, unbeknownst to the other children, which of them will play the theme. The listening children will point to the chart showing what they heard. After a few tries, ask the pianists and chart holders to select their replacements. Ask the pianists to make sure that the new instrumentalists can play the theme. (For help in writing the theme, Columbia Pictures Publications recommends their big-note easy arrangement. The theme uses re, mi, do, do, so.)

Play "The Conversation" for the children. As they listen, ask them to indicate when they hear the main theme.

Ask the students to sing or play (pitched percussion, tuned water bottles, recorder) the theme. If they know the Curwen hand signals, help them to apply the signals to the theme. If the signals are new, explain the use of sol-fa syllables, their relationship to the hand signals, and how they were used in the film. Use large pictures of the hand signals for the students to flash when the corresponding note is sounded. Have the students holding the pictures line themselves up in the order in which they appear in the theme and position the pictures according to their high- or low-pitch relationship. Ask the students to flash their signs when they hear the theme in the music. Warn them that it goes very quickly. Encourage the children without the signs to use their hands to show the theme when it is played. In a future lesson, relate this musical conversation to the kind of dialogue taking place in Bach's "Two-Part Invention in F, No. 8."

Red Pony Suite.[4]   Before introducing "Circus Music" from the *Red Pony Suite,* give recorders to as many children as possible. If recorders are not available, use other pitched instruments. The preparation time for playing the recorder in this lesson will vary from class to class depending upon their recorder background.

Be sure the children know how to tongue. Check to make sure that they are holding the instrument with the left hand on top. Show them the fingering for B. Have them play the note with two sharp tongue attacks.

Divide the class into three parts and assign one note to each section. Have them practice their two sharp tongue attacks with their note. Ask them to be ready to play their notes all together as soon as you give a verbal introduction. The introduction is given: "And now, ladies and gentlemen, the president of the United States." The teacher signals the children to play their notes. Ask them if they know what they just played? The answer is a fanfare. The fanfare is used to call attention to an important announcement. Ask the children to play the fanfare again and then put their recorders down and listen to the recorded music. Without letting anyone else know, they should count the number of fanfares in the music. They may look puzzled because the piece does not begin with a fanfare. Reassure them that it is the right piece and that they will hear at least one fanfare, perhaps more. Finally, they hear four fanfares.

When the piece has finished, ask the children to show, by holding up the appropriate number of fingers, how many fanfares they heard. If they do not agree in their count with each other, use their lack of agreement as a reason to listen again, this time counting together.

After establishing the correct count by marking the number on the chalkboard, ask the children to help with the design of the music. Begin drawing a chalk line at the left edge of the board. Ask the students to tell you when to stop in order to mark the place of the first fanfare. Ask them to help locate the other ones also. What is the relationship of the second and third fanfares? How can this be shown on the board? The sketch may look like this:

Into how many parts did the fanfares divide the music? Three.

The movement response suggested in Chapter 6 would be appropriate here. The teacher should be reminded that this sequence of experiences for "Circus Music" is not to be done all at once. The teacher should plan sequential lessons using ideas appropriate for the particular class. If

[4]Aaron Copland, *Music for the Movies*, Copland conducting, Columbia Records.

the children decide to be something connected with the circus, this would be a good time to mention that the name of the piece is "Circus Music." If the children wish to label the sections of the piece according to the movements they devise, encourage this as being helpful in visualizing the form they hear: say clown, monkey, clown, or use pictures.

Have the first four measures of the main theme of the composition drawn on a large piece of posterboard. As you show it to the children, indicate that you want their help in finding the part of the composition using this theme as its main idea. Tell the students that they are going to play the theme to be sure they know what it sounds like.

"*Circus Music*" *from* The Red Pony. *©1951 by Aaron Copland; renewed 1979. Reprinted by permission of Aaron Copland, Copyright Owner, and Boosey Hawkes, Inc., Sole Publishers and Licensees.*

Review the fingerings of the notes the children used with the fanfare. Pick one student to play each of the notes. Ask them to stand next to the poster of the theme. Ask the other children to try to play low D on the recorder. Tell them it is harder than the other notes because more fingers are used to produce it. The other note needed now is high F♯. Show the fingering and play the sound before the students try it. Select one student to play the low D and one to play the high F♯. Line up the recorder players from lowest note to highest near the theme chart. Ask the students to play their note when you point to them. (This is similar to the technique using resonator bells described in Chapter 5.) By responding to your cues, the recorder players play the notated theme. Show the students the location of their notes on the chart. Now ask them to play their pitches when you point to the notes on the chart instead of pointing directly at the players. The students with the dotted note followed by the eighth note may need special help to get the rhythm right.

Bring out a chart with the next four measures of the main theme.

"Circus Music" from *The Red Pony* by *Aaron Copland.*

Ask the students to compare the two posters. They will discover that they are the same except for the last two notes. Since no one is playing those notes yet, show them to the class: low F♯and E. Ask two children to join the rest of the recorder players, each playing one of the new notes. Now have the children play the entire eight-measure theme, first with you pointing to them when it is time for their notes, then with you pointing to the notation. As soon as the players are secure, ask a student to point to the notes. To involve the rest of the class, ask the group of players to train their replacements and have the new instrumentalists play the theme.

By this time, the children should be familiar with the sound of the main theme. When they hear the piece next, they should be asked to wave a hand when they hear the theme. After listening, ask the children to help locate the main theme in the proper section of the fanfare diagram.

The main theme does not appear in the second section of the piece. Are there other differences between that section and the other two? (It is faster, the instruments play higher.) How would you describe the whole piece as far as form is concerned? (The first and third sections are the same; they are not like the center section. It is in A B A form.)

New England Triptych. [5]   Listening lessons for the children can be related to other areas of the curriculum. When the fifth- or sixth-graders study colonial America and the Revolution, for example, William Billings' "Chester," later incorporated in *New England Triptych* by William Schuman, is pertinent musical material. The children have already studied the causes of the Revolution and King George III's role in it. They have tried to realize what life was like in 1776 for a child in contrast to the present time. They have talked about living with no electricity, radio, television, supermarkets, automobiles, airplanes, refrigerators. Now, they are asked to use their recorders or other melody instruments to play a song written during the Revolutionary period.

[5]William Schuman, *New England Triptych,* Mercury.

CHESTER

William Billings

From _Making Music Your Own_, Book 7, by Lawrence Eisman, Elizabeth Jones, and Raymond J. Malone. © 1968 by Silver Burdett Company. Reprinted by permission of the publisher.

Help them clap the rhythm, learn the notes new to them, put the slurs in the right places, and work on the melody until it is accurate. Ask them to listen to the beginning only of Schuman's music and observe that it sounds like a hymn. Tell them that Billings wrote the music originally to be used in church and that later changes in tempo and dynamics occurred when soldiers sang it as a rallying song for the colonies. Ask the children to discuss the words; then sing the piece. Describe what happened to some of the men who volunteered to fight in the Revolution; how they were cold and dirty in the winter camps, how the long evenings were made bearable only by entertainment the men could devise themselves. Billings' hymn was sung by the men, but as their despair grew, the song sounded less and less like a hymn. They began to sing it faster and louder. They added instruments like the fife and drum to it. If a picture of the "Spirit of 76" is available, show it to the children.

Model by Edna Barrier. *Richard May, University of Oregon photographer.*

Ask some of the children to play the theme on the recorder to produce a sound somewhat like that of a fife. (A good follow-up activity is to listen to a recording of a fife or fife and drum corps.) Ask other children to play a street beat on a deep sounding drum.

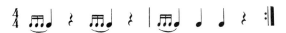

Then have the students sing "Chester" with the recorders and drum, trying to make it loud and fast as if they were intending it to be heard by King George.

Tell the students that, after the Revolution, Billings's music gradually became less popular. Musicians arrived from Europe with different ideas from those that the colonial composers had. Their European music almost obliterated the work of the Yankee tunesmiths. It was only a few years ago that contemporary musicians rediscovered the music of composers such as Billings.

William Schuman decided to use "Chester" as the theme for one part of a three-part piece he wished to write: *New England Triptych.* Have the children listen to the "Chester" section. They have heard the beginning of it. Ask them if Schuman uses Billings' music as they would have expected him to do? What happens to the melody?

After the students have listened to the composition, encourage them to comment about it. When they mention that the melody is played faster sometimes, introduce the term and the notation for diminution. When they talk about it being played slower, introduce the term augmentation.

Encourage the students to discuss the instrumentation, the variety of instruments used, and the way in which they change the original "Chester." As extra listening for students who are interested, make the entire *Triptych* available for home use, free-time use in their classrooms, or special time in the library.

Opera. Select short portions of operas. Ask the children to determine the type of major work from which they are taken. Before starting the music, be sure to tell the children when you wish them to answer. Try to prevent someone from shouting out answers before everyone has had a chance to hear the music and think about common origins of the selections. Use contrasting music such as

Part of "The Mad Scene" from *Lucia di Lammermoor,* Donizetti
"Papageno's Song" from *Magic Flute,* Mozart
"Aunt Dinah Has Blowed De Horn" from *Treemonisha,* Joplin

Since opera is not included in most students' musical vocabulary, introduce it gently, a little at a time. Older children may be interested in exploring an opera story, with musical illustrations. Don't force opera on children before they can develop sympathy for it as an interesting addition to their musical listening repertoire.

Short specials. Have tapes on hand in the classroom to illustrate musical concepts within a limited time. Use these tapes to follow up previous lessons or to introduce concepts to be treated over a long period of time. Have the students do a hand jive with "Popcorn"[6]; then ask them what kind of instrument they heard (synthesizer). Play a short part of *Switched-On Bach*[7] for instrumental recognition (more synthesizer). Ask the children to identify the group performing "The Ramayana Monkey Chant"[8] from Bali. Start the music after the introduction where it is harder to hear that all the sounds are vocal ones. Use the "Flower Dance"[9] from Japan to follow up study of the ostinatos.

Summary. The lessons described are intended to give the teacher of music ideas for listening lesson approaches with children. The teacher is urged to develop many lessons based upon a variety of lasting literature. When possible, try to weave the listening into the total musical experience, including other activities as well.

Recommended Resources

Leonard Bernstein Conducts for Young People. Columbia. Includes *Till Eulenspiegel's Merry Pranks, Afternoon of a Faun, El Salon Mexico.*

DEODATO, EUMIR. Several albums such as *2001*, CTI, and *Artistry*, MCA include piano and contemporary orchestra treatments of standard works. Provide opportunities for comparison with original versions.

Arthur Fiedler/Boston Pops: Great Children's Favorites. RCA. Includes *Peter and the Wolf, Carnival of the Animals, The Young Person's Guide to the Orchestra, Nutcracker Suite.*

Fiedler's Favorites for Children. RCA. Forty-eight dances, songs, and musical pictures including *The Sound of Music, The Flight of the Bumblebee, Chim Chim Cheree, Ritual Fire Dance.*

Burl Ives Sings Little White Duck and Other Children's Favorites, Columbia.

TIPTON, GLADYS AND ELEANOR, *Adventures in Music.* RCA. Two albums for each grade, one through six. Well-chosen music. A teacher's manual for each record includes a wealth of ideas for stimulating listening by children. One of the best sources available.

WOOD, LUCILLE, *Bowmar Orchestral Library.* Many thematic albums such as *Animals and Circus, Legends in Music, Oriental Scenes, Symphonic Styles, Overtures, U.S. History in Music.*

Suggested Projects

1. Select a piece of music that
   a. you think is appropriate for the children.
   b. has lasting value.

---

[6]Unfortunately, this record is no longer available. Perhaps your local radio station has a copy on file.

[7]Walter Carlos, Columbia Records.

[8]*The Nonesuch Explorer, Music from Distant Corners of the World,* Nonesuch.

[9]Ibid., *The Nonesuch Explorer.*

c. you like.

d. the children cannot perform.

Write a lesson plan using the selection to teach a musical concept. Be sure each time the children listen to the music that they have something to listen for.

2. Select five listening pieces for the grade level of your choice. Specify the concepts that the pieces will help teach. Be sure that each one has different instrumentation, periods, styles, keys, meters, rhythms, forms, and expressive qualities and that some include voices.

USE RECORDS AND TAPES IN MUSIC CLASS

One of the greatest boons to the teacher of music in this century has been the development of equipment to record and reproduce music with high fidelity. Not only is a host of records and tapes available for purchase in record shops, but also educational materials are widely available. Music textbooks for children come with virtually every piece of music mentioned or shown in them available on records and tapes matching the books.

One competent music educator in her first year of teaching became so enamored of recordings that she was asked by her principal if she had turned into a disc jockey. Of course, her answer was "no," but upon reflection she realized that her appreciation of the fine resources had caused her to move far away from the children's active participation in music making. Unfortunately, some other teachers are so activity oriented that they never give the children exposure to any kind of listening.

Textbook records.   The song recordings that come with the music textbooks are generally in stereo and are designed with the voices on a track separate from the accompaniment. After the children have learned a song, they can sing with the instrumental accompaniment alone, by tuning out the vocal track.

Textbook recordings offer alternatives to live experiences for use with children who are learning. The children can listen to identify the instruments playing and the voices singing (men, women, children; melody only; with harmony; etc.). They can find the form of the piece and identify expressive elements used in its interpretation. The classroom teacher who wishes to teach a new song, but who feels insecure, can help the children to learn the song through the whole-song approach by listening to the recording. The music teacher with a case of laryngitis can continue to teach using the recordings.

Having stated a positive case for using recordings to teach songs to children, it must also be stated clearly that the inherent inflexibility of recordings as opposed to the responsive behavior of the live teacher makes them a second choice for many aspects of the learning process. The teacher's ability to do all the following—to select specific phrases for the children to hear, to repeat them as necessary with motivations for listening interspersed, to help the children find mistakes in their singing and correct them, to guide the children in reading experiences, helping them only when needed, and to specify parts of the song for discussion—is reason for encouraging the teacher to work directly with the children as frequently as possible. The recordings add welcomed *extra* touches to many lessons.

Cassette tapes.   The quality of the records and tapes available for listening seems to improve continually. The copyright law of 1978 allows the owner of a record to make one legal copy. The music teacher is encouraged to do this so students can have access to the materials on tapes. The cassette copy can be handled easily by the students without fear that the needle will scratch the record. The time taken to copy the record would be well spent.

The amount of music available on cassettes is growing rapidly. The time may come when cassettes will be more readily available than are today's records. Request blank tapes in the yearly budget so as to have a regular supply. Assess the needs of the program to determine the quality of tapes to be purchased. If necessary, buy cassette tapes that can be taken apart with a screwdriver when needing repair.

Equipment.   To give the children high-quality listening experiences, good equipment must be purchased by the school. Some portable phonographs function at an acceptable level for reproducing speaking; they may be totally inadequate for reproducing music. When equipment must be shared or if the music teacher must travel from room to room, the school should purchase stereo components mounted on a special cart with high-quality speakers. If there is a music classroom, it should be equipped with a stereo system, permanently installed. The phonographs for all classrooms should be selected carefully for quality of sound, not lowest price. In addition, a good cassette tape recorder should be available wherever the children study music. If possible, a tape deck should be part of the stereo system. When music classes for older children deal with electronic music, experiments in sound, and tape composition, they will require a reel-to-reel tape recorder having the capacity to record on at least four tracks, to tape over material without erasing, to change recording and playback speeds.

The easiest equipment to handle in recording of materials and in their subsequent use is the cassette tape recorder. If the children will be doing more listening than recording, consider the purchase of relatively inexpensive nonrecording tape players. Many children will probably have their own cassette players; still the school should own as many as possible so that taped materials can be used frequently by all the children individually and in small groups. Junction boxes with earphones enable several children to use the same tape at the same time without allowing the sound to disturb the rest of the class. Try to have several tape players available to children for home use if necessary.

Use of the equipment. One of the most difficult things for a busy teacher is to take time to discover how to use the stereo system creatively. The teacher must become thoroughly conversant with both internal and external taping procedures. Some of the teacher's most frustrating moments can come with learning in front of a class proper dial setting, correct patch cord hook-ups, and proper microphone placement to avoid feedback wail when the mike is too close to the speaker.

The teacher must judge how much access the students should have to equipment without damaging it. You must develop skill in preparing instructional tapes for various purposes (both ear training and concept development) to supplement live instruction. You must be competent in taping student music making, parts of lessons for future reference, and lessons for evaluation of your own teaching.

You must become expert and fast at locating a correct place on the record, a right number on the tape. Tape recorders are now available with devices to speed the tape ahead but still emit sound to aid in finding the correct spot on the tape. Avoid continued hunting for the right place so as to prevent loss of attention on the part of the students.

Develop a systematic storage facility as soon as you begin your taped music instruction collection. As the collection grows, enter the tapes systematically under a numbering system to help you, the children, and other teachers find needed materials. A tape cabinet or shelf for easy access that allows the clearly labeled tapes to be located easily and returned efficiently would be a wise investment.

Concept development. The use of oral examples enhances concept development by having the right example at the right time.

> After the children have analyzed a song for form, play a tape illustrating the same form with a different piece of music.
> After a discussion of major and minor, play a tape with a few examples of major and minor phrases.
> After the children have sung a song from Hawaii, play some Balinese music for them.
> After an introduction to orchestral instruments, present aural and visual illustrations of the instruments discussed.
> After the children have performed a piece in class, play the tape back to them so they can hear what they sound like.

Not every tape will be used with all children, though some will. Some of the tapes will be used year after year.

Recommended Reading

Dwyer, Terence, *Composing with Tape Recorders.* London: Oxford University Press, 1976. Excellent resource on *musique concrète* for beginners. Suggestions for guiding children in sound exploration and creative organization.

Suggested Projects

1. Pretend that you are recommending a new stereo system for your school. Investigate leading brands by talking to salespeople, reading descriptive literature and consumer reports about them, listening to their quality, and comparing their abilities to meet the needs of the school.
2. List five concepts and a way in which taped instruction can help in each of their developments.

GAIN TEACHING TIME THROUGH THE USE OF CASSETTE TAPES

Whether the music teacher is a music specialist or a classroom teacher, there never seems to be enough time for music instruction. The classroom teacher feels responsible for teaching reading and mathematics; the music teacher is seldom scheduled for sufficient contact time with the students. There is no substitute for group musical experiences under the tutelage of an adult musician, so the suggestions that follow should not be construed as substitutions for that live experience. Rather, they are intended to give the children more time for music instruction than they would receive under most circumstances.

Cassette tape use outside of music class. It is possible to expand music instruction time through the use of cassette tapes. These tapes can be used by the children independently in the classroom; they can be sent home; they can be placed in the library to be checked out in the same fashion that books are. Specific assignments can be given to the children for listening. Attractive tapes can be made available for the children to use on an elective basis.

Objectives. Determine the objectives for the types of tapes you will make. Are they to be prepared carefully as permanent additions to the tape library, or are they to be spontaneous creations for short-term use? Both types of tapes are useful; determination of the objectives helps to predict the time and effort to be devoted to each particular tape.

Set some realistic goals such as one rehearsal tape for chorus by October 15, one home report for first grade by November 30, two meter discrimination tapes for fourth grade by January 1.

In addition to creating your own tapes, watch catalogues and journals for advertisements of commercially taped products to meet your children's musical needs. Offer to share your tapes with other teachers, and try their tapes to see if they are suitable for your children.

Suggestions for making tapes. The suggestions that follow are not inclusive. They are advanced as prompts for ideas you could develop to give children more music instruction time.

1. Tape the entire lesson. Start the tape recorder at the beginning of the lesson and take down everything for the absentee student or the slow student who may need review.
2. Tape portions of the lesson. Select explanations, illustrations, or group experiences as highlights of the lesson for review during the week.
3. Tape requests from the classroom teacher. Put materials on tape for the classroom teacher to use in carrying out music experiences between visits of the specialist.
4. Tape requests from the children. This can include accompaniments, game songs, or compositions—whatever may be valuable to them.
5. Make tapes in preparation for the lesson to be part of the instruction and later left with the children.
6. Make progress reports: for example, tone quality of the class in September, December, May, encouraging the children to compare and evaluate; pitch-matching efforts of the children for individual evaluation with the teacher alone; creative compositions from various lessons during the year; and so on. It is effective if each child has his or her own tape to use in judging progress. Parents should hear them too. Some children do not seem to listen to themselves; a personal tape may help the student to focus upon strengths and weaknesses previously unexplored.
7. Make tapes for home reports. These tapes are not intended to record a class concert but, rather, to summarize musical instruction as part of the children's classroom activity. Sections of the tape should include the family in musical activities. Let the class help design the tapes, being sure that the children are able to lead the family in the activities. Each child should have an opportunity to take the tape home and to borrow a tape recorder if necessary. As the children use the tape to get other people involved in music, they should be gaining more musical skills themselves.
8. Prepare instructional units on music concepts in a logical progression that will be clear to the children.
9. Prepare resource tapes. These can range from sets of songs about math concepts to descriptions of instruments and cultural characteristics of foreign countries.
10. Prepare accompaniment tapes to go with pieces learned in class and for music more advanced than all students can perform but that a highly motivated student can do with the tape.
11. Prepare illustrative material to give more background for concepts covered in class that time does not allow to be included.
12. Encourage students to make tapes of materials they wish to share with you or with the class: original music, well-practiced performances, favorite music, family music making.

13. Encourage the class to make tapes of music they have performed with the classroom teacher or the music teacher and would like to pass along to others.
14. Encourage student peer teaching. Challenge a strong student to put an example of musical competency on tape to help another student.
15. Make tapes to help chorus members improve their musicianship or their participation in group singing.

Time.   One of the scarcest commodities in most teachers' lives, time, can be eaten up by tape production. Even though the initial outlay of time seems exorbitant, it is important to note that the completed tape becomes part of a collection with potential for repeated use as needs of the students warrant. Try to have uninterrupted blocks of time for planning, writing, and taping.

Future tape use.   Taped instruction may develop to a very high level, as in this example.

> Ann moves quietly from her seat in the second-level group for mathematical interrelations and takes an empty seat at the translocation center. In response to the code she dials in the seat's operations arm, she immediately finds herself in the earth knowledge bank. She is here to do research in ancient Japanese culture. In a matter of seconds, total experience cassettes reach her study carrel. Ann activates the experience with the movement of her eyes. As she reads the information appearing on a luminescent screen, her carrel is transformed gradually into an eighteenth-century Japanese home. The interior walls of the home materialize; the fragrance of the lotus flower wafts gently through the area; koto music plays. Ann feels the texture of the clothing worn by a family of that era. She hears dishes rattling as the food for the evening is prepared that she soon will share. If Ann needs additional information or if she does not understand, the cassette goes into greater detail according to her needs. The pace of Ann's learning is adjusted to her reading level, moving at the optimum speed for her. The main point of the instruction is her koto lesson.

Is Ann's education as described a future possibility? When may it be developed? Is it just a dream?

Even today it is possible to sit in front of a computer that poses problems for students, gives answers, and reprograms learning procedures according to the responses received from the student. This same machine can produce musical sounds, assist in composition, and receive communication through a typewriterlike keyboard or by a touch on the screen itself. There are two major problems in using the computer with elementary school students:

1. Computerized instruction as it now exists is very expensive.
2. There are very few elementary music programs for school children.

Even though the cassette tape recorder lacks the sophistication of the computer, it has great potential for taped music instruction.

Research.   A research project at the University of Oregon explores taped instruction for elementary school children by asking three basic questions:

1. Can taped instruction be designed to teach specific musical concepts to elementary children?
2. Can the children use music instruction tapes independently?
3. Will the children want to use the taped music instruction?

Reports of two studies have shown generally affirmative answers to these questions.

The first study with taped instruction for sixth-graders was based on two approaches: programed instruction using small, sequential steps versus the class approach normally used by the music teacher, eliminating means of illustration inappropriate to taping. The concepts studied were major-minor discrimination and meter discrimination. Results of that study indicated a significant difference with both approaches in meter discrimination, and, with only one approach in major-minor discrimination, the programed differences were not significant.[10]

The second study was made with second-graders using two approaches: programed instruction and story-telling. The concepts included in this study were meter discrimination, melodic direction, and tempo identification. There was a significant difference in the program approach, story approach, and no instruction, with programed instruction producing the highest mean scores differences. The most effective taped instruction for the second grade children of the study dealt with melodic direction and tempo identification. Meter discrimination was consistently last.[11]

The children in both studies were able to use the materials independently. They were generally willing to use the materials. The second grade children seemed to prefer the story approach even though their score increases showed more improvement through use of the programed materials.

The Oregon taped materials include instruction in pitch, tempo, and rhythm. They are listed here as prompts for teachers wishing to create taped music materials.[12] The grades shown are only suggestions, since the materials are intended for individuals to use at the discretion of the teacher. Under special circumstances, teachers can use the taped materials in class:

[10]Lois N. Harrison, "The Development and Evaluation of Supplementary Programed Materials for Teaching Meter and Major-Minor Discrimination to Elementary School Children" (Unpublished doctoral dissertation, Columbia University, 1974).

[11]Lois N. Harrison, "Taped Music Lessons for Second Grade Children: A Comparison of Story Telling and Programed Instruction" (Research presentation session, Music Educators National Conference, Miami Beach, FL 1980).

[12]Teachers who wish to assist with research using the Oregon materials should contact Oregon Music Materials Development Project, care of Lois Harrison, School of Music, University of Oregon, Eugene, OR 97403.

1. The teacher may want to observe children responding to the taped material.
2. The teacher may be involved elsewhere and may wish the children to receive music instruction even though he or she cannot work with them.
3. A substitute who is not confident of his or her ability to teach music may be hired.

The Oregon Music Materials Development Project includes musical games, stories, and other activities for children.

I. PITCH   Grade
   A. Melodic direction: music goes up, down, stays the same.   1–2
      1. *Story:* Three sequential episodes on three tapes about the Up family, the Down family, their children, their country, and how they communicated.
      2. *Program:* Three sequential segments on three tapes   2–3
with worksheets designed to enable the child to discriminate melodic direction. The children circle ↗, ↘, or → to identify what they hear.
      3. *Pictures:* Three sequential tapes with worksheets in   1–6
which melodic direction gives clues for drawing pictures. After outlines are drawn, the children are encouraged to develop imaginative art to go with the basic structure.
      4. *Movement:* Three tapes with musical and verbal clues   1–4
to encourage children to show melodic direction with their bodies:
         a. plant growth cycle
         b. movement of water
         c. a trip with Pianita and Organika
      5. *Watch My Feet:* Three sequential tapes designed to   1–2
help the young student relate sound to notation.
   B. Pattern recognition.
      1. *MUSIC IV:* Melodic pattern recognition bingo games   2–6
using pitch with no rhythmic clues. Six games on three tapes using three-note melodic patterns.
      2. *MUSIC V:* Same as above, except four-note melodic patterns are used.
      3. *MUSIC VI:* Same as above, except five-note melodic patterns are used.
   C. Relating melodies to notation.
      1. *Melody Recognition:* Four tapes challenging the student   3–6
to identify notation matching music being played. Progression of the tapes is from very obvious to much more difficult discriminations.
      2. *Where Is the Mistake?:* Two tapes asking the student to   5–6
find the error, either printed or played incorrectly.
      3. *Music to Remember:* Three tapes challenging the student   4–6
to couple the themes of masterworks with the sight of the main thematic notation. Composers' names are matched also.

       4. *Match the Sound and Sight:* One tape similar to *Music to Remember* except only Copland's music is used.   4–6

II. RHYTHM

  A. Meter, 2 or 3.

       1. *Story:* Three sequential episodes on three tapes about the future in which a visitor from space communicates in 2's or 3's.   1–2

       2. *Program:* Three segments on three tapes with worksheets designed to increase the child's ability to discriminate between meters of 2 or 3. Immediate feedback is given; the correct answer is associated with the musical example as a reinforcer.   2–6

       3. *Game:* Four tapes and three game boards on which one to four players move two or three spaces according to the meter of musical examples. Game 1 is for one player, game 2 for two players, and games 3 and 4 are for four players. If the student moves incorrectly, certain spaces on the board are identified by the tape to send the inaccurate musician back several spaces.   3–6

  B. Patterns.

       1. *Imitation:* Two drum-playing tapes encouraging children to imitate rhythm patterns.   1–3

       2. *Recognition: MUSIC I.*[13] Twenty-five game boards for rhythm pattern recognition bingo games designed to connect the child's visual and aural experience; six games using ♩, ♩, ♪, 𝄽, and ♩.   2–6
          MUSIC II. Uses twenty-five different boards with six games adding ♪.
          MUSIC III uses twenty-five different boards with six games adding dotted notes.

III. PITCH AND RHYTHM

  A. Pattern recognition.

       1. *MUSIC VII:* Pattern recognition bingo games using pitch and rhythm. Six games on three tapes combining ♩, ♩, ♪, ♪, 𝄽 and three-note melodic patterns.   3–6

       2. *MUSIC VIII:* Same as above except that ♪'s are added and four-note melodic patterns are used.

       3. *MUSIC IX:* Same as above except that dotted notes are added and five-note melodic patterns are used.

IV. TEMPO

  A. Presto-largo, ritardando-accelerando.

       1. *Story:* Three episodes on three sequential tapes describing Presto and Largo, their baseball team adventures, and the changes that influenced their friends.   1–2

       2. *Program:* Three segments on three tapes with worksheets. Children are led to discriminate between fast-slow, presto-largo, music gets slower-music gets faster, ritardando-accelerando.   2–4

[13]These are the only tapes developed by Oregon Music Materials commercially available at the present time. More information about obtaining the rhythm pattern recognition games is available from Oregon Music Materials, 2535 Charnelton Street, Eugene, OR 97405.

Harry Houchins, University of Oregon photographer.

Prerequisites to independent taped instruction. The taped instruction just described is intended to be an extension of concept development begun in music class. It can be assigned to a child needing greater challenge than is provided consistently in class. It can be designed for a child needing more drill than can be given with the other children. It can be made available to children who enjoy the musical experiences and wish to participate in them more frequently than music classes are scheduled. The taped instruction should be used as an outgrowth of classwork.

In developing the concept of meter discrimination, deciding if music has a metrical grouping of 2 or 3, at least some of these class activities should precede the use of independent taped instruction:

1. Sing songs using meters of 2 and 3.
2. Play
   a. accompaniments to songs using strong-weak or strong-weak-weak beat sets.
   b. echo patterns in 2 or 3.
   c. improvisations in 2 or 3.
3. Listen to
   a. portions of music to determine meters such as
      (1) "Pop Corn" by Kingsley.
      (2) "Skater's Waltz" by Waldteufel.
      (3) "My Favorite Things" by Rodgers.
      (4) "William Tell Overture" by Rossini.
   b. records selected by the children. To avoid saturation with one meter only, ask each child who wishes to share music with the class to select one with a meter of 2 and one with a meter of 3.
4. Move in time to the music showing meter groupings:
   a. feet only

   b. hands and feet
   c. hands only on strong beat, feet on all the beats
   d. feet only on accented beat, hands on beats in between
   e. clap hands on beat 1, tap wrists together for other beats
   f. conduct
   g. creative movement using any body parts
5. Create
   a. four measure phrases in 2 or in 3.
   b. songs in 2 or 3,
   c. instrumental compositions in 2 or in 3.
   d. answers to musical questions asked by teacher in meter of 2 or 3.
6. Read
   a. rhythm patterns in 2 and 3.
   b. instrumental scores related to music in both meters.
   c. meter signs and relate them to notation.
7. Write
   a. missing notes in measures having two or three beats.
   b. notation of creative works.

After meter discrimination has been introduced in music class, make tapes available to the children: story tapes for the first-graders, programmed tapes for any of the children above first grade who respond to that type of instruction, and game tapes for third- through sixth-graders with a relatively higher degree of independence.

Planning for instruction extension. Teachers are encouraged to plan consistently for providing students with extensions of class instruction through listening. Some of the materials made for classwork can be sent home. In most cases, materials will be more valuable for the children if complete instructions are given on the tapes and several examples are provided to illustrate the concepts.

Recommended Resources

Games with electronic components have potential for ear training with children: *Electronic Repeat,* Tandy Co.; *Merlin,* Parker Brothers; *Simon* and *Super-Simon,* Milton Bradley.[14]
Individualized Music Program. New York: Holt, Rinehart and Winston, 1976. Activities and tapes related to *Exploring Music.*
Music I, II, III. Eugene: Oregon Music Materials, 1980. Taped rhythm bingo games.
On Your Own. Taped instruction related to Silver Burdett Music. Morristown, NJ: Silver Burdett Company, 1975.
Tap Machine. Shrader, David L., Seattle: Temporal Acuity Products, Inc., 1974. Beginning, intermediate, and professional levels of rhythmic training.

[14]See Chapter 14, footnote 1.

Suggested Projects

1. Write a plan for teaching a specified concept to a child of designated grade level through taped instruction.
2. Make the tape.
3. Observe a child using the taped instruction.
4. Evaluate the usefulness of the taped instruction. Could the child use it independently? Did the child want to use it? Did the child learn anything by using it?

8 Create

Humans create for innumerable reasons. The teacher should be greatly concerned if many of the students do not seem to create. If they do not, why not? There is generally a contrast between young children's eagerness in creativity and older children's reluctance. Primary-grade children are willing to engage in creative movement; upper-grade children often are not. Younger children will relate amazing stories; older ones are often reticent in story-telling activity.

Torrance worked with teachers, trying to change their behavior so that they break away from their usual routines to encourage more creativity on the part of the children. He focused upon the "slump in creative thinking, motivations, and activities at about the fourth grade."[1] Both this early work of Torrance and his later publications are well worth pursuing, since they show that attention to creative behavior can cause it to increase.

[1]E. Paul Torrance and Ram Gupta, *Programmed Experiences in Creative Thinking* (Minneapolis: University of Minnesota, Bureau of Educational Research, 1964). The development and evaluation of recorded programmed experiences in creative thinking in the fourth grade, a research project performed under the provisions of Title VII of the National Defense Act, U.S. Office of Education, Department of Health, Education, and Welfare (now Dept. of Education).

Perhaps children are poorly served when they hear fabulous stories like the ones about eight-year-old Mozart. As wonderful as were Mozart's talents and activities, the children may decide that they cannot measure up to him, thus perceiving themselves as uncreative since they cannot make music as well as Mozart did.

Music teachers must present opportunities for creativity to the children through very accessible means. To start, foster in the children an appreciation of their ability to present elements of music they already know in different ways, to reorganize materials. We must instill confidence in the children to help them make musical decisions without fear of criticism for errors in judgment. We must provide settings in which they can experiment. Even though printed music is a rather inflexible guide, learning to use it accurately must be viewed as a tool toward creative musical expression rather than as a rigid taskmaster.

Too much freedom, or inadequate skill, can work against the child's creativity. The teacher's assessment of the individual's capability makes it possible to set up guidelines to help the child function. Certainly, to ask a child to write a symphony when the child doesn't even know what a symphony is negates creative effort. Even asking a child to write a song may suggest an impossible task if the child has not had enough musical background.

When the teacher sings a question to the young child with the expectation that the child will sing an answer, the child is given a creative opportunity. Playing question-and-answer games, moving in response to music, chanting rhyming words or phrases, inventing music with familiar forms, combining varied timbre effects are a few natural, accessible means for encouraging children's creativity. Stories provide prompts for the children to orchestrate, move, or sing in response to the events. The child can take an idea arising from musical involvement and then expand it creatively into other unique experiences.[2]

Creating a song is a more formal act than most of the creative efforts just mentioned. It requires both words and melody. Meter, rhythm, form, and probably harmony will need attention. The children will have a much better chance of dealing with these elements creatively if they feel comfortable with them, if they have a wealth of experience using and identifying them in music.

Fluidity in working with language is a necessary component of song writing. It can be strengthened by having the children alter lyrics already set to music. Copyrighted materials should not be tampered with; consider working with traditional lyrics of folk songs, such as fun songs. After the

---

[2]Many of these creative expressions have been described elsewhere in this book. See the index for specific references under creativity.

students have sung all the verses they already know for "She'll Be Coming 'Round the Mountain," suggest that they make up other ones.

SHE'LL BE COMING 'ROUND THE MOUNTAIN

United States

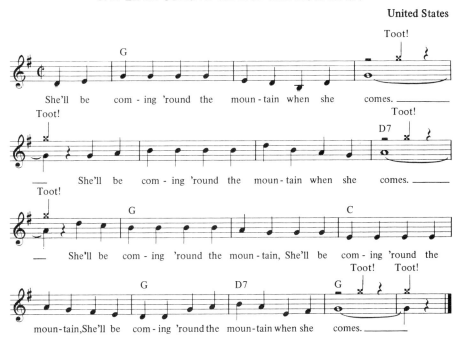

2. She'll be driving six white horses when she comes. (Whoa, back!)

3. Oh, we'll all go out to meet her when she comes. (Hi, babe!)

4. Oh, we'll kill the old red rooster when she comes. (Hack! Hack!)

5. We will all have chicken and dumplings when she comes. (Yum! Yum!)

6. We will have to sleep with grandma when she comes. (Snore, snore.)

7. She will wear her red pajamas when she comes. (Scratch, scratch.)

8. We will all blow out the candles when she comes. (Blow, blow.)

9. There'll be eighty-nine birthday candles when she comes. (Count them quickly.)

10. Etc.

At the end of each verse, accumulate the sound of the preceding verses, going backward from the newest verse; for example, at the end of verse 6 the children will add "Snore, snore." "Yum, yum." "Hack! Hack!" "Hi, babe!" "Whoa, back!" and "Toot! Toot!" Motions corresponding to these words, made up by the children, add to the fun. The new additions to the song may not be appreciated on a global scale; that is not the point. Their addition gives the children an opportunity to experiment with meter, rhythm, and imaginative language. The activity also provides them with a forum for making decisions, both musical and imaginative.

Before creating an entire new song, the children may find it easier to set a poem to music rather than writing all new components. If they begin with words already written, their entry point into the song-writing procedure discussed next is step 9. The teacher may find it appropriate for the children to create using only part of the procedure such as number 5 in one lesson, number 10 in another. The creative procedures need not be used only consecutively to write a song; they can be interpolated in lessons as desired to foster creative behavior as a regular part of music class. If children do not have the skills to do all the creative procedures suggested, the teacher can help them do what they can and fill in what they cannot do in a cooperatively creative endeavor.

CREATE A SONG[3]

When the children create both words and music, the procedure can follow these steps:

1. Select a topic. It may be chosen spontaneously by the children or related to other work whose amplification seems well served by including it in a musical framework.

2. Encourage the children to think about words or phrases related to the topic. As they tap a steady beat, have them make their contributions. They may take turns, saying their words or phrases rhythmically over the steady beat, or they can add their ideas as the teacher points to individuals who indicate their readiness. The addition of ideas can be part of a rondo in which the class chants a phrase between the individual contributions. This gives the children thinking time so they don't have to contribute their words on the next beat after their neighbor has done so. The recurring phrase can be as simple as

Sun - shine, sun - shine,

or as complicated as

Sun - shine, sun - shine,   where's the gold -en   sun - shine?

3. Ask the children to identify words or phrases most attractive to them as song lyrics. Write the preferred material on the board. Ask the group to chant the selections; then choose combinations that go together. Discuss whether or not

---

they wish the phrases to end with rhyming words. If they are to rhyme, will every line end with a rhyming word? Would they rather rhyme every second line? What other choices are there in designing the rhyming scheme?

4. Start the steady beat again. Ask the children to chant the selected phrases. Ask them to pick the one that seems most expressive of the topic. Does it have a rhythmic flow? If not, how can it be altered?

5. Exaggerate the accented words of the phrase. Draw a bar line before each accented word. Determine the meter of the phrase by counting the beats between the accented words. If the children have never done this, practice exercises such as these are useful before beginning to write the song.
    a. Say this phrase rhythmically: "Spaceship, spaceship, flashing through the sky."
    b. Say it again and accent the important words.
    c. Draw a bar line before the important words.
    d. Stamp your foot on the word following the bar line as you say it again.
    e. As you stamp the accented words and say the phrase again, tap the steady beats between the accents.
    f. Have half the class say "one" at the beginning of each accented word as the children continue to stamp and tap. How many beats are there between the "ones"?
    g. The total number of those beats plus the accented first count determine the meter of the phrase. What is it?
    h. Follow instructions a. through f. for this phrase: "Step on the skateboard before it's too late."
    i. What is the meter for that phrase?
    j. Follow instructions a. through f. for this phrase: "Put the berries in the basket just for me."
    k. What is the meter for that phrase?

The children should be encouraged to find different ways to say the phrases. Help them to devise alternate ways of chanting so that the phrases can be in either 2 or 3, and then determine which seems most appropriate. Example:

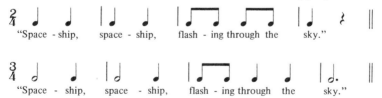

6. Add another phrase related in thought to the first phrase and with the same meter. Give the children practice in this. Use these samples plus those of your own invention with the children as preparatory experiences if necessary:
    a. Find the meter of this phrase: "Where are the salamanders from the lake?"
    b. Make up a matching phrase with the same meter as the preceding phrase and words that go with it.
    c. What is the meter of this phrase? "Two nickels are the same as one thin dime."
    d. Make up a matching phrase for it.

e. What is the meter of this phrase? "Round up the horses in Mr. Brown's field."

f. Make up a matching phrase for it.

7. Chant the two phrases for the song. Do they fit the rhyme scheme that has been selected? If not, can they be changed, or should the rhyme scheme be altered?

8. Continue to select song phrases until the lyrics seem to be completed because they say what needs to be said or because they have stated enough for at least one verse. The children should be urged to make their first efforts brief. Four phrases are sufficient for a song.

9. Ask the children to
a. Say the phrases rhythmically.
b. Clap the rhythm of the words while saying them.
c. Clap the rhythm of the words while thinking them, not saying them out loud.

10. Enlist the aid of the children in writing the rhythmic notation above the corresponding words.

11. Check the accuracy of the rhythmic notation by having part of the group chant the phrases while part claps the notation.

12. Discuss the musical form which seems best for the rhythm and the words: A A B A, A B, A B C, A B A C? Are the rhythms of the phrases similar? Should any alterations be made so a certain form can be used?

13. Discuss various styles that might be appropriate for the text. Have the children choose an appropriate style for the song.

14. Discuss the range to be used by the melody. Need there be pitch limitations, such as the lowest and highest notes the children want to sing? Will the use of instruments influence the range? If pitched instruments are to play the melody, such as recorders, include only the notes the children can play.

15. Discuss the climax of the piece. Enlist the aid of the children in identifying compositional devices to heighten the climax.

16. Decide on the key of the piece. This decision may be based in part upon the capabilities of instruments that may be used either in the composition of the melody or in its accompaniment later. Show the children how to begin and end their compositions on one of the notes of the I chord if the piece is to be in a major or minor key. Help them to deal with closure and the effects of beginning and ending on notes not in the I chord. Explore the possibilities of pentatonic composition with them.

17. Create melodies to fit the rhythmic phrases. The class members can compose the melody together. The children can sing suggestions for the teacher to notate. Since the rhythmic notation has already been written, it is only necessary to add the pitch. If it is difficult for you to notate the melodies the children sing, have them sing into a tape recorder so that later you can either use an instrument to help you write it correctly or enlist the aid of someone who is skilled at writing melodic dictation. Smaller groups of children can work together in developing melodies. This method offers opportunity for involvement by more children with less danger of stress for the students who do not respond readily to creative singing before the class. Rather than singing, the committees can use keyboard instruments, recorders, or pitched percussion instruments. Each committee should have either a composer who

will write the pitches with proper rhythmic notation on the staff above the words or a tape recorder for storing the creative efforts.

18. Encourage the committees to sing and play their songs for each other. If the class has created a song together, give the group opportunities to sing it for teachers, the principal, and other classes.

19. Ask the committees to pass their notation onto other groups to see if it is written in such a way that it can be reproduced as sung by them originally. If there are problems, the student who wrote down the piece can make corrections or give assistance to the new group.

20. Ask the class to perform some of the small committee's songs together. Add harmony. Ask the children to decide where chord changes occur or, if in pentatonic, to add ostinatos. Encourage the children to experiment with V_7 and IV chords. As they develop skill in chord discrimination, encourage them to determine why one chord sounds better than another one. Have them write chord numbers (or letters) in the appropriate places on the notation of the song. To involve the whole class, use the overhead projector or the chalkboard. After the class sings and plays some of the committee's songs with appropriate harmony, distribute the remainder of the songs to small groups or individuals for them to add chords or ostinatos to the pieces not having them.

The step-by-step procedure of creating a song is intended to be modified for the age and ability level of the children who are creating. The varied steps in the procedure are to be apportioned through a series of lessons. With primary children, most of the work will be done by the teacher, with the children offering suggestions and reactions. The most that young children can do in one lesson may be to identify a subject about which to write a song. The next lesson may find them contributing a few ideas about the topic. Older children may get as far as step 4 during the first lesson. A lot depends upon whether or not the teacher decides to concentrate only upon song writing or to intersperse some of the song writing in lessons over a long period of time that may have included many other activities.

The teacher must keep track of how far each class progresses while engaging in creative work. Guidelines can be added or subtracted as is necessary for each group. Some classes will not need the teacher to help the committees determine melodic notation; they can do it themselves. Others will require much more assistance. Time limitations may influence the teacher to eliminate some of the class discussion so as to move into musical experience.

Once they have had a taste of creating a song, some children will begin the creative process on their own from the beginning. Some will want to create independently because of impatience with the class or committee procedures that may restrict their unique creative ideas.

The procedure for creating a song is intended only to suggest a structure in which creative action for children can take place. Adherence to the procedure must be strengthened or weakened in response to the needs of the children.

For the students to keep their places in the creative process, it may help them if the teacher provides dittos of their work from lesson to lesson. For example, a ditto with their words, meter, and rhythm patterns on it will make their work more accessible when they come to class the next time ready to add pitch to their previous notation. A ditto with final copies of the songs created by the various committees will enable them to share one another's work.

Many of the song-writing procedures can be adapted to instrumental work. Even when the music begins as a response to words, they can be subtracted as the melodies begin to take shape.

Keep the songs so the children can review creative efforts of the past and be aware of the growth in creative effort from year to year.

SING ABOUT CURRENT TOPICS

Composers write to fill a void. If the topic is current and there is no song about it, why not write one? If children are studying areas with meaning for them, why not express feelings and ideas about those areas through music?

CREATING CURRENT TOPICAL SONGS

The energy question is a primary concern of our society. Our government leaders are trying to determine ways of producing fair and effective legislation to help use our energy sources wisely now and in the future. Economists are seeking ways of keeping the price of energy at levels people can afford. Manufacturers are endeavoring to use energy sources to enable them to keep their plants open without fear of temporary or permanent stoppages because of scarce resources. Scientists are trying to develop new power supplies. In our homes, we are lowering temperatures in the winter months and are turning off light switches to conserve available fuel.

What is the connection between the energy situation and music? Throughout history, music has reflected cultural concerns. Songs have detailed human dilemmas: early minstrels sang of the prowess of the knights in "Roland's Songs"; pioneers vocalized about the events of the wagon trains in "Sweet Betsy from Pike"; contemporary musicians pour their hearts into concern for the human condition in "Blowin' in the Wind" and "Where Have All the Flowers Gone?"

The songs that follow are contemporary energy songs written by children. They were initiated to involve young people in discussion of issues of our civilization and to develop their creativity through working with music concepts. They are not included to become part of standard children's repertoire. They are included to show how some children created energy songs and to suggest ways in which all children can develop means of creative musical expression. When children become concerned about issues, it is often easier for them to compose songs because they feel a need to express themselves.

CARPOOLS

Jenny Lakeman
Liesl King

Reprinted by permission of Elizabeth Muller - Lorish.

2. Take turns driving and take turns talking,
   If the car breaks down, then take turns walking.

   Chorus.

BOTTLE BILL SQUARE DANCE

Matt Kennedy
Paul Mapp

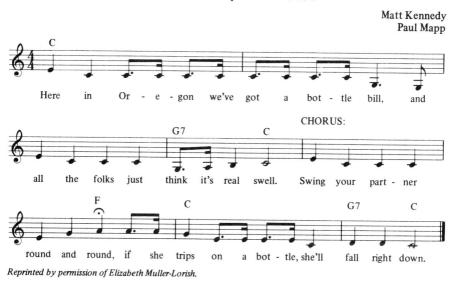

Here in Or - e - gon we've got a bot - tle bill, and all the folks just think it's real swell. Swing your part - ner round and round, if she trips on a bot - tle, she'll fall right down.

Reprinted by permission of Elizabeth Muller-Lorish.

2. Turn in a bottle, it makes a lot of sense,
   If you don't we'll all be livin' in tents.

   Chorus.

3. Stop your dancin' and please vote straight,
   For the bottle bill in your own home state.

   Chorus.

These songs and pictures were created by Condon School sixth-graders, Eugene, Oregon, with the assistance of their music teachers, Elizabeth Muller-Lorish and Connie Burden.

Summary

Although creating a song was presented in this chapter as a consecutive procedure, many of the creative steps can and should be incorporated in frequent lessons as useful activities without necessarily culminating in the creation of a song. When the children engage in these activities, the process is more important than the product. The creation of the mood, the phrase, the rhythm pattern, the choice of meter, mode, lyrics, and other features are valuable aspects of the child's creative development.

Recommended Readings

MARSH, MARY VAL, CARROLL A. RINEHART, AND EDITH J. SAVAGE, *Composing Music*. New York: Macmillan Publishing Co., Inc., 1975. Booklet with recording for older children.

PAYNTER, JOHN, AND PETER ASTON, *Sound and Silence*. London: Cambridge University Press, 1970. Classroom projects in creative music include attention to mystery, pictures, drama, movement, elements of music.

REIMER, JOYCE B., *New Music: Electronic*. Morristown, NJ: Silver Burdett Company, 1976. Booklet and record to help older students with electronic composition.

SCHAFER, R. MURRAY, *Creative Music Education*. New York: Schirmer Books, a division of Macmillan Publishing Co., Inc., 1976. A handbook for the modern music teacher including ear cleaning, the new soundscape, and the rhinoceros in the classroom.

TORRANCE, E. PAUL, *Encouraging Creativity in the Classroom*. Dubuque, IA: Wm. C. Brown Company, Publishers, 1970.

TORRANCE, E. PAUL, AND R. E. MEYERS, *Creative Learning and Teaching*, New York: Dodd, Mead, 1970.

Working with Sounds. Morristown, NJ: Silver Burdett Company, 1974. A satellite for independent study dealing with creative activity.

Suggested Projects

1. Write a lesson plan built around creative activity to teach a selected musical concept.

2. Follow the procedure for creating a song to compose a song dealing with a current topic.

3. Write a short paper explaining how the latest work of E. Paul Torrance can be applied to music.

9 *Express*

Nearly every musical activity for children becomes more interesting when expressive elements of music are added. Children moving their bodies like quarter notes or half notes find that changes in tempo make that activity more challenging. The relative rhythmic relationship of the notes remains the same, even though all of them may be either faster or slower. Adding a ritardando or an accelerando gives the young musicians still more concepts to grasp.

Singing and playing experiences become more varied when elements of dynamics are incorporated. The students who are encouraged to make decisions as to whether pieces should be loud or soft find ways to bring musical experiences closer to their own interpretations. Gradual changes such as crescendos and diminuendos help the children to become aware of subtleties in expression.

Experience with timbre (tone color) helps the children to focus upon the rich variety in tone quality that affects music. The more opportunities the children have to discriminate among various timbres, the finer their skills become in choosing appropriate tone colors for their creative work. Children, when first given instruments and asked to orchestrate music, often use their favorite instruments for everything no matter how little they fit the composition. Later, as the novelty effect diminishes, they begin to use the instruments in more appropriate ways.

The incorporation of expressive elements in music for elementary school children is dependent upon the aural perception the students have developed through listening. It is activated by applying or practicing tempo, dynamics, and timbre through making them a part of their performance of music.

Expressive elements add to the style of compositions. They help to establish musical moods. They also have direct bearing upon the aesthetic effects of music. Children should experience many combinations of the expressive elements:

> The soft, slow lullaby accompanied by a guitar.
> The slow, loud march played by a brass band.
> The lively, staccato scherzo played by a symphony orchestra.
> The spirited, heavily accented chorus in the last act of an opera.
> The dramatic, ponderous ritual dance of primitive tribes.

Children can be asked to make discriminations connected with the expressive elements in music from countries all over the world. The students may not be able to identify the tonality or sing the melodies of some of these sophisticated materials, but they usually can react to the tempo, dynamics, and timbre. Timbres outside their immediate aural vocabulary can be included in classifications of sounds. Rather than teaching children the somewhat limited timbre grouping in which instruments are identified as members of the string, woodwind, brass, or percussion families, they can be encouraged to classify in terms of

> *Aerophones:* instruments whose sound is produced by the vibration of air. Subclassifications include instruments using vibrating columns of air, such as flutes, reeds, cup mouthpieces.
> *Idiophones:* instruments made of naturally sonorous materials, such as rattles, jingles, bells, gongs, xylophones, metallophones, cymbals, sticks, slit drums.
> *Membranophones:* instruments making sound through vibration of a stretched membrane, such as drums, timpani, tambourines.
> *Chordophones:* instruments whose sound is made by vibration of strings, such as harps, guitars, violins, harpsichords, pianos.
> *Electrical instruments:* electric guitars, electric organs, synthesizers.

Memorizing the names of these groups may not be important to the elementary school child for a long time. What is important is the ability of the children to learn to classify the sounds they hear. At the primary level, the classifications are made on the broadest level: that instrument is hit; this one is blown. The older child tells whether a membrane is being hit or the sound is from the striking of a solid surface, whether the string instrument is bowed or plucked; whether the instrument is a violin or a harpsichord.

The classifications given can include instruments from all cultures, times, and places. They are inclusive rather than exclusive: children learning orchestral groupings wonder, sometimes defensively, why their favorite guitar is not part of the string family. This cultural exclusion is removed when using the broader classification.

In addition to planning lessons for children centering upon tempo, dynamics, and timbre, the teacher is encouraged to incorporate aspects of these expressive elements in all the lessons.

Recommended Resources

BOOKS

ALLEN, LARRY D., *Sounds: The Raw Materials of Music.* Morristown, NJ: Silver Burdett Company, 1976.

KRUEGER, VIRGINIA, *Do You Know?* Los Angeles: McGin Publications, 1974. Large book for young children contains twelve color photos and a cassette tape of six short lessons in timbre. Good for independent study.

MARSH, MARY VAL, CARROLL A. RINEHART, AND EDITH J. SAVAGE, *The Spectrum of Music with Related Arts: Electronic Music, Sounds of Singing Voices, Sources of Musical Sounds.* New York: Macmillan Publishing Co., Inc., 1975. Booklets with recordings and teacher's annotated editions for group and individual instruction or teacher's reference.

MIDGLEY, RUTH, ED., *Musical Instruments of the World.* New York: Paddington Press Ltd. (Grosset & Dunlap), 1976. Absorbing book for the teacher of music and older children dealing with classification of instruments. Excellent illustrations.

Musical Instruments in the Metropolitan Museum. New York: The Metropolitan Museum of Art, 1978. Beautiful color and black-and-white photographs of instruments from different times and histories. Small plastic record contains brief passages on some of the instruments.

FILMS

The Guitar: From Stone Age Through Solid Rock, 14 minutes, color, Xerox Films, 1971.

Music the Expressive Language, 11 minutes, color, Sutherland Educational Films, Inc., 1962.

New Sounds in Music (Introduction to Music Series), 22 minutes, color, Churchill Films, 1969.

Percussion Sounds (Introduction to Music Series), 16 minutes, color, Churchill Films, 1969.

The Recorder, 12 minutes, color, ACI Media, 1968.

Toot, Whistle, Plunk and Boom, 10 minutes, color, Walt Disney Productions, 1959.

The Violin, 22 minutes, color, Learning Corporation of America, 1973.

String Sounds (Introduction to Music Series), 16 minutes, color, Churchill Films, 1969.

Wind Sounds (Introduction to Music Series), 16 minutes, color, Churchill Films, 1969.

ACI Media, 35 W. 45th, New York, New York 10036

Churchill Films, 662 North Robertson Blvd., Los Angeles, CA 90069

Learning Corporation of America, 1350 Avenue of the Americas, New York, NY 10019

Sutherland Educational Films, Inc., 201 N. Occidental Blvd., Los Angeles, CA 90026

Walt Disney Educational Media Co., 500 South Buena Vista Avenue, Burbank, CA 91503

Xerox Films, 245 Long Hill Road, Middletown, CT 06457

RECORDS

The Music Makers, produced by Edward Franklin. Glendale, CA: Cypress Publishing Corp, 1973. Original release provided to schools as a public service by Standard Oil Company. Music makers play and talk about their instruments and themselves. Albums on strings, guitar, brass, woodwinds, keyboard, percussion. Pictures and teacher's guide with each album.

Suggested Projects

1. Review at least three lesson plans already written. If they do not include reference to expressive elements, devise a way for tempo, timbre, or dynamics to be an integral part of the lesson. Expressive elements need not be a major part of the lesson; their part in the lesson can be as simple as asking the children to sing the second verse softly or to play the ostinato faster and with different instruments.

2. Locate a film or filmstrip dealing with expressive musical elements. Write a lesson plan for introducing that visual aid into the development of an expressive concept.

3. Write a follow-up plan for the class after the film or filmstrip has been shown.

10 *Incorporate*

American music education incorporates ideas from many parts of the world. Dalcroze, Kodály, Orff, Suzuki, Manhattanville, and ETM (Education Through Music) are some of the strongest influences at the present time. Ideas from these sources have become such an integral part of music education that it is sometimes difficult to identify them. Summaries of these varied influences are included here so that the beginning teacher of music will have an introduction to them with encouragement to use aspects of each that will be most beneficial to the children.

DALCROZE

Emile Jaques-Dalcroze (1865–1950) was a Swiss composer interested in music education. It was while he was a professor of harmony at the Conservatory in Geneva that he began to work with movement and music. His rhythmic work gradually evolved to the point where he founded the Institut Jaques-Dalcroze in Geneva. Similar schools opened in large cities throughout Europe; in the U.S., the Dalcroze School of Music in New York trains teachers in Dalcroze pedagogy.

The work of Dalcroze is best known because of his rhythmic body movement known as eurhythmics, but his work also included improvisation, particularly with the piano, and reading music through the use of the fixed "do," where "do" is always C.

Both Kodály and Orff acknowledged their debt to Dalcroze. Even though he insisted that he was teaching music, not dance, leaders in modern dance such as Ruth St. Denis and Martha Graham were influenced by his work. Choreographers such as Nijinsky and Balanchine studied it.

It is difficult to describe the techniques of Dalcroze adequately since so much of his method was based upon improvisation. He believed firmly that every teacher of music must be skilled in playing the piano, especially in being able to create rhythmic experiences to which the students can react. The improvisation does not always emanate from the teacher; often the student begins moving to his or her own tempo. The teacher then takes the student's idea and creates music to lead the student into extensions of it.

The students who worked with Dalcroze used their bodies to show interval relationships, high and low of pitches. Even the inexperienced improviser can utilize the piano to give the children clues for these exercises. As they hear notes played on the piano, students adjust their distance from the floor according to what they are hearing. The highest notes prompt the children to stretch their arms as high as they can with their bodies in the most upright position they can manage. When children understand this activity, they not only respond accurately with their bodies, but they also volunteer to play the piano for their classmates' responses.

Recommended Readings

BLOM, ERIC, ED., *Grove's Dictionary of Music and Musicians.* New York: St. Martin's Press, Inc., 1961, pp. 593–594.
JAQUES-DALCROZE, EMILE, *Eurhythmics, Art and Education.* London: Chatto and Windus, 1930. Collection of essays by Dalcroze written between 1922 and 1925.
LANDIS, BETH, AND POLLY CARDER, *The Eclectic Curriculum in American Music Education: Contributions of Dalcroze, Kodaly, and Orff.* Reston, VA: Music Educators National Conference, 1972.
SADIE, STANLEY, ED., "Jaques-Dalcroze, Emile," *The New Grove Dictionary of Music and Musicians.* vol. 9. London: Macmillan, 1980, pp. 554–555.

KODÁLY

Zoltán Kodály (1882–1967) was a composer, conservatory teacher, collector of Hungarian folk music, and writer. All these manifestations of his talents combined to help him share a vision of having a musically literate nation that could read and write music while using those skills to perpetuate its heritage of folk song. Kodály's involvement with Belá Bartók in collecting Hungarian folk music influenced his own composition. It also provided materials to be used as he set forth to teach music literacy to Hungary. The music education that Kodály advocated was brought to the attention of his countrymen through his writing as well as through the music making he inspired.

Kodály based his work with children upon Hungarian folk songs. He perceived them as being part of the child in the same way that language is. As with language, music is first heard and then produced. It is only after a vocabulary of music is part of the child's experience that reading and writing activities can be introduced. Kodály's work was developed by Hungarian educators and used effectively in that country. As musicians in other parts of the world became aware of the development of Hungarian musical literacy, they sought to bring its positive aspects to children in their countries. Since all children do not know Hungarian folk songs, materials were sought through which Kodály's ideas could be made meaningful to non-Hungarian young people. Leaders in adapting Kodály's work for American children were Mary Helen Richards, Denise Bacon, and Lois Choksy.

The Kodály method is based upon singing. Although the recorder and some percussion instruments become a part of the child's education later, they are not the prime components of the approach. Kodály's goal was to have Hungarian adults so literate that they could read and write music as easily as words. He used *sol-fa* syllables with Curwen hand signals to represent pitch. Their function was to reinforce aural and visual experiences that would relate to printed notation.

Unlike some European practices in which *do* is always C, Kodály used the movable *do*, which means that the key name is *do* in major keys and *la* in minor ones. The advantage of using this system is that similar tonal relationships can be identified from key to key even though their note names and printed appearance will not be the same. With the movable *do*, the syllables for this phrase would be

O, HOW LOVELY

England

> Do   re   mi   do   fa   mi   mi   re   do   fa   mi   mi   re   do

The syllables remain the same even when the song is changed to another key:

> Do   re   mi   do   fa   mi   mi   re   do   fa   mi   mi   re   do

The use of *sol-fa* syllables for music reading can be traced to ancient Greek times, although contemporary use is generally attributed to Guido d'Arezzo in the eleventh century.[1] Guido took the syllables *ut, re, mi, fa, sol, la* from phrases of a Latin hymn whose starting notes were each successively one scale step higher than the previous one. *Ut* was later changed to *do; ti* was added. Guido wrote to a friend that using the syllables with his choirboys enabled them to improve their music reading.

Do   re   mi   fa   so   la   ti   do

Guido d'Arezzo also used the hand to help his students with music reading. This may have been a precursor of the hand signals as used by Kodály. He, however, acknowledged John Curwen as their originator. John Curwen was known in England as the founder of the *Tonic Sol-fa* method of music teaching.[2] He, in turn, acknowledged his debt to the works of Sarah Anna Glover who began to experiment with children's music education in 1812.[3]

HAND SIGNALS AS COMMONLY USED TODAY

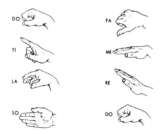

Choksy lists succinctly the prerequisites young children must master before entering the teaching sequence of the Kodály method:

> in-tune singing, feeling for beat and accent in duple meter, ability to identify rhythm patterns of familiar songs and to step and clap rhythm and beat, as well as the understanding of the concepts of high-low, loud-soft, and fast-slow. In addition, it is necessary to build a repertory of songs and singing

[1]Gustave Reese, *Music in the Middle Ages* (New York: W. W. Norton & Company, Inc., 1940), p. 149

[2]Eric Blom, editor, *Grove's Dictionary of Music and Musicians*, vol. C–E, 5th ed. (New York: St. Martin's Press, Inc., 1954), p. 563.

[3]Blom, *Grove's Dictionary*, vol. F–G, p. 673.

games of small range and easy rhythms from which to draw the later skill-teaching material.[4]

The songs used in beginning Kodály are generally limited in range and in the pentatonic mode. *Fa* and *ti* are introduced much later since their use requires the children to sing half steps which are often difficult. Many of the first songs to be used are simple ones, such as

THE COUNTING SONG

One, two, tie my shoe; Three, four, shut the door;
Five, six, pick up sticks; Seven, eight, lay them straight;
Nine, ten, big fat hen; 'Leven, twelve, dig and delve.

Lois Choksy, The Kódaly Method: Comprehensive Music Education from Infant to Adult, © 1974, p. 147. Reprinted by permission of Prentice - Hall, Inc.

RAIN, RAIN

Rain, rain, go a - way, Come a - gain some oth - er day.

From 150 American Folk Songs. © 1974 by Boosey and Hawkes, Inc. Reprinted by permission.

LITTLE SALLY WATER

Game Song

Lit - tle Sal - ly Wa - ter sitt - ing in a sau - cer, Rise Sal - ly,

rise Sal - ly, wipe a - way your tears, Sal - ly, Turn to the east, Sal - ly,

Turn to the west, Sal - ly, Turn to the one that you love the best Sal -ly.

From 150 American Folk Songs.   © 1974 by Boosey and Hawkes, Inc. Reprinted by permission.

[4]Lois Choksy, *The Kodály Method* (Englewood Cliffs, NJ: Prentice-Hall, Inc., 1974), p. 50.

GAME

> *Children join hands in a circle, with one child in the center as "Sally," covering his or her eyes with two hands. The circle moves around as they sing the song. The child in the center imitates the song all the way through, pointing to another child in the circle at the end of the song, still covering the eyes with one hand, so that the choice is accidental. The chosen child becomes "Sally," goes to the center, and the game starts again.*

The children are encouraged to sing and move to game songs such as "Little Sally Water," which uses only *la, so,* and *mi,* or "The Closet Key," which uses only *mi, re,* and *do.*

THE CLOSET KEY

Game Song

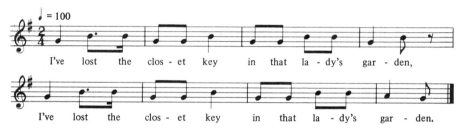

From *150 American Folk Songs.* ©*1974 by Boosey and Hawkes, Inc. Reprinted by permission.*

GAME

> *Very small children use this song for hiding and finding play. Other children play it as indicated in the folklore collection in which it was found. Children form a ring, hands behind their backs. One child walks around and places the key in someone's hand. The walker leads the singing of stanzas 1 and 2 (with all children joining in.) The child to whom the key was given then leads the singing of stanza 3 (with all the children joining in.) He then proceeds to walk around the ring himself, singing stanza 1, and the whole process is repeated.*

Later, syllables are used with the songs so that the children associate the sound of the intervals with their syllable names.

Kodály uses another type of syllable to represent rhythm: *ta* ♩ , *ti* ♪ , *ta-a* ♩ , and *ta-a-a-a* 𝅝 . When first learning to write rhythmic notation, the children use the stems without the note heads except for half and whole notes. | | ⌐¬ |

ta   ta   ti ti   ta

The child moves through sequential rhythm experiences, which include rhythmic movement, imitation of teacher-initiated patterns, question-and-answer responses, and reading and writing of patterns.

The teacher who is interested in using the Kodály method must become skilled in using the *sol-fa* syllables as applied to appropriate children's songs, to couple the hand signal with the syllables, and to use the rhythm syllables accurately.

Recommended Resources

BACON, DENISE, *Let's Sing Together.* West Newton, MA: Kodály Center of America, 1971. Songs for three-, four-, and five-year-olds.
CHOKSY, LOIS, *The Kodály Context.* Englewood Cliffs, NJ: Prentice-Hall, Inc., 1981. Includes sections on early childhood music, Kodály for older students, curriculum construction.
———, *The Kodály Method.* Englewood Cliffs, NJ: Prentice-Hall, Inc., 1974. Includes a sequence of instruction adapted for use in American schools.
ERDEI, PETER, *150 American Folk Songs to Sing, Read and Play.* New York: Boosey and Hawkes, Inc., 1974.
RICHARDS, MARY HELEN, *Threshold to Music.* Belmont, CA: Fearon Publishers, 1971. Charts and teacher's information for presenting them.
SZONYI, ERZSEBET, *Kodály's Principles in Practice.* Kecskemet, Hungary: Petofi Printing House (Corvina Press), 1974.

Suggested Projects

1. Practice the hand signals and the *sol-fa* syllables
   a. ascending and descending the major scale.
   b. with pieces included in this chapter.
2. Select three songs for a grade level of your choice. Sing them using the *sol-fa* syllables and the corresponding hand signals. Sing them using the rhythm syllables.

ORFF

Carl Orff (1895–1982), a German composer, musicologist, and educator, is probably most often heard in American concert halls through his *Carmina Burana*, a setting of thirteenth-century secular poems for soloists and chorus, orchestra, mime, and dance. His work for children is heard in schools as they sing, chant, create, move, and play instruments. Orff's educational work has grown in influence since 1924, when he joined with Dorothee Guenther in founding the Guentherschule, a school for gymnastics, music, and dance. Rather than use the piano as a source of inspiration for movement as Dalcroze had done, he turned to unsophisticated rhythm instruments that were relatively easy to learn and could be used by the students for improvisation and composition. The instruments used in the Guentherschule included xylophones, metallophones and glockenspiels, recorders, timpani, cellos and viola da gambas, guitars and lutes, and nonpitched percussion instruments. Orff's first publications for these instruments were written for the physical education teachers studying at the Guentherschule, with the assistance of Gunild Keetman who remained his lifelong colleague.

During World War II, the school was destroyed, as were the instruments, and for a time Orff turned away from his educational interests. In 1948, responding to a commission from the Bavarian Radio, Orff resumed his work, this time concentrating on music for children. He used their natural rhymes, chants, and songs to bring movement, singing, and playing together. The melodic starting point was the descending minor third, gradually increasing to the five-note pentatonic scale with no semitones. The speech patterns began with calling of names and counting out chants and elementary rhymes and songs. The Bavarian Radio broadcasts of eight- to twelve-year-old children making music brought forth an unexpected response from the schools. The subsequent demand for instruments, materials, and teacher training both in Germany and in countries throughout the world led to the establishment of the Orff Institute in Salzburg in 1963. Translations of Orff's publications, adaptations for many countries, instruments for children to use, and new materials are now readily available.

To help teachers, the American-Orff Schulwerk Association has described teacher training programs on three levels to be offered in various locations throughout the United States. Teachers involved in these programs participate in activities they will be sharing with the children. The certification program encourages the teachers to return for their next level of training after they have had an opportunity to work with children using the Orff techniques. Music teachers who become interested in Orff are urged to participate in local workshops and demonstrations as well as investigating available materials in preparation for entering Level I.

Doreen Hall and Arnold Walter translated Orff's *Das Schulwerk* into English with the title *Music for Children*. Hall's *Teachers Manual* deals with the various components of Orff with clear instructions for their use with children.

Hall describes the sequential development of a musical experience beginning with the children learning words of a simple rhyme, stressing diction and quality of vowel sounds. After the children repeat the rhyme several times, they say it again, this time clapping each syllable as they say it. The next time the children say the rhyme, they add *patschen* (German for slapping the thigh) on the strong beats and clap on the weak beats. Greater interest in the rhyme can be created by dividing the children into two groups: those with dark voices and those with light voices. The timbre of the voices will determine their assignment to specified portions of the rhyme as the children say it again with patschen and clapping. Another variation results from meter change, to triple rather than duple. An introduction of patsch-clap-clap can be used to establish the new meter. As the children develop confidence, they can patsch, clap, and say the rhythm patterns that have evolved from the rhymes in canon. Later, they can play the rhythm patterns on instruments.

Orff included song canons in his work as well as speech canons. Hall cites "Big Ben" as perhaps the simplest and most effective song canon in *Music for Children, Book I.*

BIG BEN RINGS LOUD AND LONG

Translation by Dorothy Hall   Carl Orff

©*B. Schott's Söhne, Mainz 1956. Used by permission of European American Music Distributors Corporation,   sole U.S. agent for B. Schott's Söhne.*

The teacher would be wise to do much preparatory work in triple rhythm before beginning such a project. Have the children stamp or patsch on the strong beats and clap on the weak beats to the improvisations of the teacher on the recorder. Then do speech canons in triple rhythm and follow through to the song.

(1) The teacher should sing the song musically and with expression.
(2) The teacher should repeat the words slowly and clearly, phrase by phrase, the children repeating each phrase. This should be repeated as often as necessary.
(3) Repeat the complete verse.
(4) Now add the basic movements patsch, clap, clap to the words. Only when this has been done several times can you be sure that the children

will be able to perform the canon giving each note the correct time value.

(5)   Sing the melody together three or four times.

(6)   Sing the melody together with basic movements patsch, clap, clap.

(7)   Tell the children the name of the first note and have them try to play the melody on the instruments.

(8)   If the foregoing has been prepared the children should be ready to play the accompaniment which consists of the patschen movements transferred to the notes on the instruments.

(9)   When the melody and accompaniment have been worked out successfully, sing and play the piece in unison.

(10)   Divide the singers into two groups and sing it in canon.

(11)   Add the accompaniment to the above.[5]

Orff encouraged the development of rhythm in the children with a variety of combinations of clapping, stamping, *patschen,* and finger snapping. After much echo clapping, the children are given opportunities to finish two-bar phrases given to them by the teacher with their own improvisations. They create rhythmic rondos in which all the children use body rhythms for the recurring (A) phrases alternating with individuals creating their own rhythms for the dissimilar phrases (B C D, etc.). After the children become comfortable with this type of rhythm work, the same sequence can be transferred to melodic improvisation using pitched percussion instruments from which all the notes have been removed except those that will be needed. The melodic work can start with only two notes of the pentatonic; other notes can be added as soon as the child is ready for them. Although all the pieces in Orff's Volume I are in pentatonic, Volumes II–V utilize other tonalities. The simple accompaniments for the pentatonic songs are derived from the *bordun,* the interval of a fifth.

BOBBY SHAFTO'S GONE TO SEA

Words from Mother Goose   Carl Orff

---

[5]Doreen Hall, *Music for Children, Teacher's Manual* (Mainz: B. Schott's Söhne, 1960), p. 23.

Ostinato figures are soon added.

BOBBY SHAFTO'S GONE TO SEA

Words from Mother Goose   Carl Orff

1. Bob-by Shaf-to's gone to sea,
Wood block
Soprano Xylophone
Alto Xylophone
or
Alternate Alto Xylophone

sil-ver buck-les at his knee; He'll come back and mar-ry me, bon-ny Bob-by Shaf - to!

or

Alternate Alto Xylophone

Recommended Resources

BOOKS

BURNETT, MILLIE, *Melody, Movement and Language.* San Francisco: R and E Research Associates, 1973. Games for children using four basic elements of Schulwerk.

CARLEY, ISABEL, ED., *Orff Re-Echoes.* Cleveland: American Orff-Schulwerk Association, 1977. Selections from the *Orff Echo,* the official magazine of the American Orff Schulwerk Association.

HALL, DOREEN, *Music for Children, Teacher's Manual.* Mainz: B. Schott's Söhne, 1960.

KEETMAN, GUNILD, *Elementaria,* English translation by Margaret Murray. London: Schott and Co. Ltd., 1974. A handbook for teachers first studying Orff techniques, written by his collaborator of over four decades.

LANDIS, BETH, AND POLLY CARDER, *The Eclectic Curriculum in American Music Education: Contributions of Dalcroze, Kodály, and Orff.* Reston, VA: Music Educators National Conference, 1972. Descriptions of contributions by Dalcroze, Kodály, and Orff to American music education, translations of selected writings.

ORFF, CARL, AND GUNILD KEETMAN, *Music for Children.* Mainz: B. Schott's Söhne, 1960.

_____, *Nursery Rhymes and Songs,* English adaptation by Doreen Hall. Remaining volumes, English adaptation by Doreen Hall and Arnold Walter: I. Pentatonic, II. Major: Bordun, III. Major: Triads, IV. Minor: Bordun, V. Minor: Triads.
American Edition, based on Carl Orff, Gunild Keetman, Book 2, primary, 1977; Book 3, upper elementary, 1980.

NASH, GRACE C., ET AL., *The Child's Way of Learning, Do It My Way.* Sherman Oaks, CA: Alfred Publishing Co., Inc., 1977. A handbook for building creative teaching experiences.

STRINGHAM, MARY, *Orff-Schulwerk, Background and Commentary.* St. Louis: Magnamusic-Baton, 1976. Compilation of selected articles from German and Austrian periodicals.

RECORD

ORFF, CARL, AND GUNILD KEETMAN, *Music for Children.* Angel. Children performing in English under direction of Orff, Keetman, and Walter Jelinek.

FILM

Music for Children, National Film Board of Canada, 16th floor, 1251 Avenue of the Americas, New York, NY 10020, 1968. Somewhat dated, but gives comprehensive view of Orff's ideas with children.

ORFF-SCHULWERK: American Odyssey, rental request from Edith Elliott, 3811 Richmond, Shreveport, LA 71106, 1978.

Suggested Projects

1. Practice singing, playing, and moving with the examples given in this chapter.
2. Using the materials listed in the Recommended Readings, find five more Orff activities for the grade level of your choice. Specify the concepts being developed through the activities.

SUZUKI

As soon as teachers realize that Shinichi Suzuki is a renowned teacher of string instruments, they raise the natural question: "What does he have to do with teaching general music to children?" The reason for including Suzuki in a book about elementary music is that he demonstrates successfully many appropriate techniques for working with students in general music as well as in string classes. His teaching is based upon the "Mother Tongue Approach." He feels that the prospective musician should be exposed to music from a very early age, just as the child is exposed to language. He involves older family members in learning to play string instruments even before the children begin their lessons, so when they begin, there will be someone in the home to help them play correctly. Suzuki reasons that lessons are too far apart to meet the child's need. Family members continue to attend the lessons after the child begins.

Recordings of pieces are made available to the children so they have an aural picture before they are asked to play them. The records and the adult examples present a constant concept of good tone to prevent even the suggestion of a squeaky violin sound.

Movement and games are incorporated in the lessons so learning does not seem like drudgery. The activities are used to help the student drill on basic technique as the foundation for musical progress. Playing the violin with correct intonation, good sound, and accurate rhythm are emphasized. The introduction of notation is delayed so the student can give undivided attention to accurate and pleasant music production.

Unicef photo by J. Ling

The Suzuki method does not just teach the child to play a piece and then move on to something else: the child is encouraged to continue playing the piece as part of his or her repertoire. Older students regularly play *with* younger students, both to help give them a strong perception of violin and ensemble sound and also to keep them playing their own repertoire frequently. The older students play *for* the younger ones, too, providing a live source in addition to the teacher from which the younger students can learn new repertoire.

Suzuki's concern about the quality of music to be used by his students led him to exercise great care in its selection. He encourages the beginners to develop a big, confident sound and insists that they use instruments of the right size for them; the children use progressively larger violins as they grow. Suzuki is very concerned about motivating the children and works extensively with teacher training.

Brooks summarizes the major sources of his successful motivations:

1. Praise
2. Success in small steps
3. Group work
4. Self-satisfying playing
5. Landmark literature
6. Games, many of them developed on the spot to meet a student need[6]

That the Suzuki method is not perfect is noted by teachers who are concerned about students who have difficulty with reading music or who may be slow to develop independent, expressive playing. In spite of these possible negative aspects, Suzuki's work suggests positive benefits for the music education of children.

1. Although the public school teacher meets the children for the first time in kindergarten or grade one, work such as Suzuki's with small children and research by groups such as the Pillsbury Foundation[7] direct attention to the importance of preschool learning. Rather than saving music instruction for older children, strong programs must be developed for primary-grade students.

2. A neglected area in many schools is that of involving families directly in the education of their children. If families know what the children are studying in music class, they can be involved in the music making as well. Specific tasks can be assigned for children who need remedial help and can work with family members. A repertoire of music should be developed for the children to share with different generations. Even if an intergenerational approach is not possible in school, suggestions can be advanced for family musical involvement at home. Older elementary children can share in making music with younger children, as tutors, as performers, and as co-musicians.

3. Children should hear a wide variety of well-performed music. First-class music should be selected both for listening and for performing. Independent study such as that described in Chapter 14 can correlate with class activities to give the children more time to listen to good musical models.

---

[6]Nancy Greenwood Brooks, "Toward a Deeper Understanding of Suzuki Pedagogy," *The American Music Teacher,* November–December 1980, pp. 27–28.

[7]See Recommended Resources.

4. Movement and games can help the child to achieve a high degree of musicality by not allowing music instruction to be dull.
5. Positive reinforcement should be a consistent way of life in the classroom. Even small improvement should be praised.

Recommended Resources

BOOKS AND JOURNALS

BROOKS, NANCY GREENWOOD, "Toward a Deeper Understanding of Suzuki Pedagogy," *The American Music Teacher,* November–December 1980, pp. 26–28.

MOORHEAD, GLADYS EVELYN, AND DONALD POND, *Music of Young Children.* Santa Barbara, CA: Pillsbury Foundation for Advancement of Music Education, 1978. Developmental studies of young children learning music.

SUZUKI, SHINICHI, AND OTHERS, *The Suzuki Concept.* Berkeley, CA: Diablo Press, Inc., 1973. An introduction to a successful method for early music education.

FILM

Suzuki Teaches American Children, Encyclopaedia Britannica Educational Corporation, 425 N. Michigan Ave., Chicago, IL 60611, 1967. Engaging shots of Suzuki interacting with beginning violinists.

Suggested Projects

1. Incorporate at least two aspects of the Suzuki method in an instrumental music lesson for children. Be sure that the instrument you use is one that will be readily available in the elementary music classroom.
2. List four ways in which the family can be involved in the elementary music program.

MANHATTANVILLE

Manhattanville, or the Manhattanville Music Curriculum Program (MMCP), was a research project awarded to Manhattanville College in Purchase, New York, in 1965 and supported by the Office of Education, U.S. Department of Health, Education, and Welfare. The project was directed by Ronald B. Thomas and eventually involved experimental activity from the primary grades through college. At the beginning of the project, fifteen schools at varying elementary through high school levels were selected for study because of their innovative or experimental music programs. It was found that, even though the programs varied in implementation, there were still factors that were common to many or all of them.

1. The philosophical rationale underlying the objectives of each of these innovative programs was well established.
2. In every instance the innovative program had clearly defined objectives.

3. Contemporary educational thought and new teaching techniques and curricula in other subject areas influenced most of these innovative programs.
4. There were a number of specific curricular principles that were consistent in many of the programs, such as
   a. individual or small-group learning experiences.
   b. notation being taught only in its musical context.
   c. exploratory activities rather than factually oriented presentations.
   d. flexible learning strategies.
5. In the majority of music programs, the innovative work was in a limited area of the total music curriculum.
6. With one exception, all the innovative programs were begun and have been maintained without external support.
7. Most of the programs studied were initiated by one person.
8. Seventy-eight percent of the teachers who were responsible for the innovations had active musical lives apart from their school work.
9. In each instance, the administration of the schools cooperated fully with the program.[8]

After the initial studies were completed, the project turned to the exploration and refinement of curriculum concepts and processes through a series of field centers and workshops. The objectives for the curriculum were grouped in four areas.

1. *Cognitive.* The curriculum was to be developed on a spiral of musical concepts. Although they could be identified as separate musical ideas, each of the concepts was to be explored in a variety of complete musical settings. Since the concepts were approached through a spiral, the students would grow in assimilating the concepts as they were able to understand them.
2. *Attitudinal.* The curriculum was to foster excitement in students about their own creative potential, a belief in the worth and validity of their own inventive and expressive endeavors, openness of mind, inquisitiveness, security in intuitive thinking, positive feelings toward music, and an understanding of music as a way of gaining more insight into life.
3. *Skill.* The curriculum would include dextrous, translative, and aural discrimination skills as they enhance, expand, or bring clarity to the cognitive, attitudinal, and aesthetic objectives.
4. *Aesthetic.* The ultimate achievement of musicality implies knowledge, attitudes, and skills, but it goes beyond these objectives. It includes the awakening of an aesthetic sense, the ability to comprehend beauty and to find meaning on a plane beyond analysis of mechanics, techniques, or even concepts. The capacity for such feeling involves more than the intellect and the senses. It involves the emotions and the spirit of the individual. Aesthetic insight is a condition which can exist only from one's personal affinity to the nature of the art. While the educational program can deal directly with basic information, with the mechanics of musical operation and with the development of

[8]Ronald B. Thomas, *A Study of New Concepts, Procedures and Achievements in Music Learning as Developed in Selected Music Education Programs, Final Report,* Project No. V-008, Contract No. OE-5-10-403, U.S. Department of Health, Education, and Welfare, Office of Education, Bureau of Research, September 1966, pp. 9–11.

skills, aesthetic sensitivity cannot be taught. It is, rather, an intimate response that may grow from the nature of personal experience. Many of the conditions of this experience can be basic to the educational program. Aesthetic sensitivity can be fostered by educational strategies which demand analytical, judicial and creative thinking. The search for meaning through exploratory composition, the use of available music to gain insight into one's own musical problems, the freedom to react, to accept, to reject, to personally evaluate and interpret are also learning conditions which will influence aesthetic sensitivity."[9]

The focus for the MMCP curriculum is on discovery, conceptual understanding, contemporary music, and totality of musical experience. The role of the teacher is that of a guide, stimulator, and resource. The environment becomes a music lab in which each student is involved in composing, performing, conducting, listening, enjoying, sharing, and reacting. Student and guest recitals are given, listening to recordings is implemented through individual headsets rather than one speaker, research is done followed by oral reports to the whole class, singing is encouraged, and basic skill areas are developed in piano, notation, percussion techniques, vocal pitch production, aural discrimination, and conducting.

The curriculum is intended as a flexible guide through which the teacher interacts with the students in response to their needs and directions.

MMCP Synthesis, by Thomas, gives much useful information to the student who wishes to find out more about Manhattanville. These are a *few* sample skills described in the beginning cycles:

I. Aural
    A. Identify various timbres used in the classroom and the instruments used to produce them.
    B. Identify pulse and changes in tempo.
II. Dextrous
    A. In performing
        (1) produce sounds (vocal or instrumental) at the instant they are demanded and control the ending of the sound.
        (2) produce sounds of three volume levels (f, p, mf) when allowed by the nature of the instrument.
    B. In conducting
        (1) indicate precisely when to begin and when to end.
        (2) indicate general character of music.
III. Translative—Devise graphic symbols, charts, or designs of musical ideas that allow for retention and reproduction.

In creating teaching strategies, the teacher should ensure the following:

[9]Ronald B. Thomas, *MMCP Synthesis* (Bellingham, WA: Americole, 1979), pp. 9–10.

1. Each problem should contain one new factor which demands an intuitive judgment by the student. This educated guess is most important. It is essentially the hypothesis which the student must prove. The new factor may be a new musical concept, an extension or refinement of a previously explored concept, or an organizational technique.

2. The new factor in each problem should be an outgrowth of previous experience. It cannot be imposed by the teacher simply because of the sequence of the study. It must be related to the demonstrated interest and direction of exploration of the class. To plan exploration of rhythm when the class is excited about timbre or structure is destructive. The only valid sequence is the sequence of the student's logic.

3. All other considerations in the problem must be familiar to the student. The student must have confidence that he can handle the predominant part of the problem successfully. In this way his intuitive sense can be focused on the one new concept and its relationship to and interaction with the known factors in the musical setting.

4. The problem must be well defined. The framework of the problem should be so concise that the student can concentrate his attention and creative energy. The length of the composition, the character, the style, the instrumentation, any desired techniques or concepts, any limitations, and all other considerations should be spelled out so precisely that the student can hone in on the pertinent factors. A tight framework for the problem doesn't stifle discovery, it allows it by focusing thought and creative imagination.

5. Problems should be diversified, they cannot all deal with similar ideas, activities, procedures, or solutions. Diversity may be accomplished in many ways, by varying the extent of creative demands, by using different experimental processes, by allowing the students to frame part or all of some problems, etc.

6. No strategy dealing with the same framework of operation should ever be repeated exactly. If the student was unsuccessful on the first try, the fault probably lies in problem design. If problems are designed with a sensitivity to the student's insight, he will usually succeed. However, no teacher should expect to design problems that are successful 100 percent of the time.[10]

Since the emergence of Manhattanville, many of its practices have been incorporated into more traditional programs. It has value in any program if it stimulates the teacher to examine the practices of music education for children with more perceptive insight.

Recommended Readings

BIASINI, AMERICOLE, LENORE POGONOWSKI, AND RONALD B. THOMAS, *MMCP Interaction.* Bellingham, WA: Americole, 1979. Manhattanville music curriculum for early childhood.

THOMAS, RONALD B., *MMCP Synthesis.* Bellingham, WA: Americole, 1979. Objectives, principles, and sample strategies for Manhattanville.

---

[10]Thomas, *MMCP Synthesis,* p. 33.

Suggested Projects

1. Use the six points on p. 256 to plan a Manhattanville experience. Be sure to explain the prerequisite experiences the students must have had.
2. Compare a Manhattanville based strategy with a previously written lesson plan. What factors are common to both of them?

EDUCATION THROUGH MUSIC

After years of working with the Kodály method and interpreting its use as part of American music education, Mary Helen Richards moved away from concentration upon Kodály to found the Richards Institute of Music Education and Research. The publications and workshops produced by the institute center on the child and his or her development. Richards' work has become known as Education Through Music (ETM) and makes use of song-experience-game approaches. Social interaction, language, and movement are important components of the program along with music. The materials used are English-language songs.

Richards' "Prologue" to *Aesthetic Foundations for Thinking* gives her view of "The Child in Depth."[11]

> In the beginning there is the child—
> He must discover his way.
> You lead, opening the song for his wonder—
> A wonder that grows as it is shared with others.
> The child sings, sees, hears and feels the song through movement.
> Then he sings, sees, hears and feels the song in his inner being,
> Searches for its content
> And builds his own understanding.
>
> The child can be any one of us, and each of us. In our exploration of song as a new knowledge, we all take the same pathway if we strip away pretense and ignore self consciousness and let ourselves be open. The song is made for the child, mysteriously and miraculously organized for his exploration and delight in movement and thought, a catalyst for communication with himself and others.
>
> There are many experiences hidden in the song
> Some of them exist through the whole song
> Some of them exist through the large sections of the song
> Some of them are very small—momentary sounds.

[11]Mary Helen Richards, *Aesthetic Foundations for Thinking*. (Portola Valley, CA: Richards Institute of Music Education and Research, 1977), p. 1.

The child searches through all of these for the treasure and finds that you gave him the treasure when together you opened the song.

Recommended Reading

RICHARDS, MARY HELEN, *Aesthetic Foundations for Thinking.* Portola Valley, CA: Richards Institute of Music Education and Research, 1977.

11 *Integrate*

Music lends itself readily to integration with many other subjects. It serves in a supportive way to help the child learn nonmusical concepts. The classroom teacher, particularly, will find benefits through teaching these concepts in a musical setting.

The teacher is cautioned, however, to keep perspective on music as a unique contribution to life, deserving to be part of the child's education because it has characteristics that contribute to the quality of human experience in ways that nothing else can. Music is to be studied by children to help them expand their musical experiences, gain knowledge about music, and develop skills to help them perceive the elements of music so that the aesthetic impact of music has meaning for them. Music deserves to be studied because it is a unique subject worthy of the child's attention. In addition to its independent contributions, there are many ways in which music can be integrated into other areas: the creative teacher will seek ways of including music throughout the school day as well as during time set aside specifically for its study.

IMPACT ON THE SCHOOL DAY

The day spent by a child in school has moments that can be variously exciting, worthwhile, dull, challenging, time-wasting, pleasant, or tense. The use of music in this day may help the teacher to ease some of the potentially negative times for the child. After an intense session with a difficult subject, the children may need a physical involvement such as a rhythmic activity in conjunction with music. After a wild game on the playground, the students may need a quiet moment created by well-chosen music. If the children seem depressed because of difficulties in learning, participation in a sprightly song may help them to feel more like trying to conquer the difficulty.

Use music to change a mood or provide another setting as long as the musical presence seems beneficial to the children. Although some students apparently work better with music in the background while they are studying, some members of the class cannot study when the music is playing. These students may focus so strongly on listening that they cannot concentrate on whatever else is happening. The only way in which some of these students can do their work is to ignore the music; this negates the care being taken to help them learn to listen carefully.

INTEGRATION WITH OTHER SUBJECTS

These suggestions are only a few of hundreds the creative teacher will find to integrate music with other subjects.

Music and math. Use "The Angel Band" to help first-graders with counting. The eager singers may not wish to stop. They are especially responsive to instrumental accompaniments associated with the numbers. Each time number one is sung, the triangle is played; the drum is played with 2, 22, 32, and so on. The children may be breathless when they get to 51, 52, and so on, but they beam because of their accomplishment!

THE ANGEL BAND

South Carolina

four, there were five, there were six lit - tle an - gels, There were

sev'n, there were eight, there were nine lit - tle an - gels, ___

Ten lit - tle ___ an - gels in the band. Was - n't that a band,

Sun - day morn - ing, Sun - day morn - ing, Sun - day morn - ing?

Was - n't that a band, Sun - day morn - ing, Sun - day morn - ing soon?

"The Angel Band" also lends itself to black-key improvisation on the piano. When used that way, the melody begins on D♭. Instead of singing "Sunday morning," try "Christmas morning."

Glue or tape pictures of notes on the Cuisenaire rods the children use for building mathematics concepts. Be sure to use only the rods whose combinations are in correct mathematical proportions to correspond with rhythmic note relationships. Encourage them to use the same logic for application to both math and music concepts.

The children can check many of their answers by seeing if the rods on both sides of equation take up the same space.

When studying fractions in math class, slip in a musical equation.

261

When working with simple addition and subtraction problems, have two children with different percussion instruments illustrate the problems: add 3 and 2. Child 1 plays three beats, child 2 plays two beats. The class gives the correct answer.

Music and art.   Art can both inspire music and be inspired by it. Pictures shown to children who are improvising can suggest a mood or a program of some sort to prompt their creativity. Showing another picture gives them a sense of contrast that can be depicted in change of dynamics, tempo, timbre, melodic shape, rhythmic intensity, and form.

Children listening to music can show an artistic response by using a plastic medium to demonstrate an association with the sounds they hear.

Music with letters and literature.   Traditional songs help the children learn basics such as the alphabet.

If chants or songs are not available to help learn the items under study, the teacher and children can create materials to act as study aids.

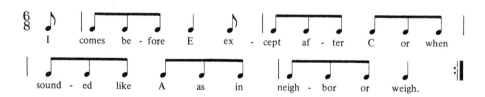

Use music as part of dramatic experience. Incorporate it into stories that have already been written. Encourage the children to include music as part of the tale when they write their own stories. Give them ideas about how music can heighten dramatic expression through singing, movement, and playing instruments when they write plays.

Let the musical elements of rhythm and meter aid them in writing poetry; explore nonmetrical poetry with the children. Challenge them to use both metrical and nonmetrical poetry as inspiration for music making.

Music and science. Couple exploration of sound with scientific inquiry. What difference is there in sound between long- and short-length bars of pitched percussion instruments? Encourage the students to saw different lengths of pieces of wood to produce a xylophone. Ask them to identify other factors responsible for resonant sound besides length.

Provide opportunities for the students to experiment with different levels of liquids in bottles or glasses. What happens when the glass is struck with more water in it? Is the effect the same in differently shaped containers? What is needed to produce a uniform scale?

Encourage the children to make observations about sound production: What happens to the sound of the triangle when it is grasped firmly by the hand? What produces the triangle sound? What is necessary for it to function properly?

How is sound produced by a stringed instrument? What happens to the pitch if the string is made shorter? How do instrumentalists make the string shorter? What causes the rattling sound when some guitars are played? Check the fingers of the guitarist to see where they are placed in relationship to the frets.

Explore the principles of sound upon which the synthesizer is built. How does the sound change as various components of the harmonic series are strengthened or weakened?

Use classroom equipment to vary sound production: What happens if a phonograph record is played at a speed different from the speed at which it was recorded? How can a reel-to-reel tape recorder be used to change sounds?

Music and social studies. When the sixth-graders study ancient Greece, recruit musical detectives to find references about music, instruments, and reconstruction of sounds that might have been created by these ancient people. Discuss and experiment with Greek modes. Take a trip to a museum where the children can see Greek works of art as well as representations of musical instruments believed to have been used at that time. Follow up the study of ancient Greek music by inviting an adult from the community to come to the school to teach the children dances he learned as a child in Greece. Teach the students songs that were part of his heritage and help them move in the $\frac{7}{8}$ meter that seems so natural to him. Encourage the children to contrast the songs with the fragments they had discovered from ancient times.

Help the fourth grade children plan and prepare a luau. Divide them into groups with responsibility for part of the festivities. One of the groups can practice an accompaniment for songs using their uli-uli, ipu, and puili. Another group can practice using both hands and feet to interpret some of the music. Although all the children should learn songs of the islands, a small group can join with the instrumentalists to learn additional songs for presentation to the entire group.

Uli-uli

Puili

Ipu

Richard May, University of Oregon photographer.

Cover the walls with maps and pictures from the islands. Borrow authentic items of dress. Study the history of the islands. Discuss the effect of the early visits of sailing vessels from Europe and the Americas. Encourage class cooks to prepare chicken long rice, poisson crue, Kalua pig, and haupia so that, after the luau begins, traditional foods can be enjoyed along with the other components of the festivities.

Music as part of a humanities approach.   The humanities approach takes different forms, often depending upon the special interests and strengths of the teacher(s) involved in it. Some humanities programs emphasize a joining together of the arts. Others include aspects of social studies. An unusual textbook series has been published by Harcourt Brace Jovanovich for elementary school children with emphasis upon art, language, drama, music, and dance. The editors felt that the incidental teaching of humanities was not enough, that random experiences do not substitute for a planned program for the exploration of values and self-expression. The six-volume text (based on grade level) for children relates to research conducted with children on stages of moral development and their effects upon the child's concept of justice. The series also focuses upon truth, beauty, love, and faith. The child's involvement is not so much with class discussion as it is on experience in the arts.[1]

Specialists and classroom teachers should consider working together on units of study. Some of the easiest units to prepare focus upon the study of a certain country. It is more difficult to develop an integrated approach to such topics as "feelings." Still, study of such concepts is undertaken regularly by the faculty of the Magnet Arts School in Eugene, Oregon. The teachers take time to consult with each other frequently concerning whatever emphasis they have chosen to have as their unifying theme. In addition to conventional studies, drama, art, music, and dance are stressed. An effort is made by the faculty to weave the arts throughout the program; the schedule is kept flexible, and the children work at their subjects in ways that are made special for each one of them.

If any single factor can prevent an integrated arts approach, it is probably rigid insistence on adherence to a schedule. Attention must be directed by administrators and teachers toward the benefits of scheduling that allows for blocks of time to be used by several teachers working with children to explore the scope of civilization rather than its isolated components.

---

[1] Paul F. Brandwein and others, *Self-Expression and Conduct, The Humanities* (New York: Harcourt Brace Jovanovich, 1974–1979). Textbooks for grades one through six. In addition to the textbooks and teacher's manuals, kits are available containing materials for dance, drama, art and music, PLAs (independent instruction cards), and filmstrips.

Recommended Resources

BOOKS

ANDERSON, WILLIAM M., AND JOY E. LAWRENCE, *Music and Related Arts for the Classroom.* Dubuque, IA: Kendall/Hunt Publishing Co., 1978.

BURNETT, MILLIE, *Dance down the Rain, Sing up the Corn.* San Francisco: R and E Research Associates, Inc., 1975. Guide for multicultural project includes songs, dances, games, art and craft ideas, literature, and cooking projects.

Corvallis District 59J Elementary Music Teachers, *North American Indian Units.* Contact Sally McBride, Adams Elementary School, 1615 S.W. 35th Street, Corvallis, OR 97330. Resources for detailed study of Indians with emphasis upon music.

CROOK, ELIZABETH, AND OTHERS, *Afro-American Music and Its Roots, Country Music and Its Roots, Music of North American Indians, Spanish-American Music and Its Roots.* Morristown, NJ: Silver Burdett Company, 1975–1976. Special-interest booklets with records.

MARSH, MARY VAL, CARROLL A. RINEHART, AND EDITH J. SAVAGE, *The Spectrum of Music with Related Arts: Afro-American Music, Music of the Orient, Music of Latin America.* New York; Macmillan Publishing Co., Inc., 1975. Booklets with recordings and teacher's annotated editions for group and individual instruction of older children or for teacher reference.

VAN RYSSELBERGHE, MARY LOU, *Experiences in Music Within the General Classroom.* Eugene, OR: School District 4J, 1977. Available from the author, 2880 Alta Vista Court, Eugene, Oregon 97403. Musical experiences based upon concepts common to those in other subjects; enrichment activities with subjects other than music.

WOLD, MILO, AND EDMUND CYKLER, *An Introduction to Music and Art in the Western World.* Dubuque, IA: Wm C. Brown Company, Publishers, 1980. Excellent resource book for teachers.

RECORDS

Free to Be You and Me, Marlo Thomas and Friends, Bell Records, Columbia Pictures Industries, Inc.

KAY, BOB, *Songs About My Feelings.* Think Stallman Productions Ltd.

Historical Anthology of Music. Orpheus and The Pleiades.

History of Music in Sound. RCA.

Masterpieces of Music Before 1750. Haydn Society.

The Musical Heritage of America. Vol. I, *From the Colonial Times to the Beginning of the Civil War.* Vol. II, *The Civil War.* Vol. III, *The Winning of the West.* CMS Records, Inc., 14 Warren Street, New York, New York 10007.

The Nonesuch Explorer: Music from Distant Corners of the World. Nonesuch.

PALMER, HAP, *Learning Basic Skills Through Music.* Educational Activities, Inc., Freeport, L.I., New York. Variety of activities and concepts introduced in musical setting.

Treasury of Early Music. Haydn Society.

WILLIAMS, PAUL, AND KENNY ASCHER, *The Muppet Movie.* Atlantic.

FILMS

Discovering Music Series: *Discovering American Folk Music, Discovering American Indian Music, Discovering Russian Folk Music, Discovering the Music of Africa, Discovering the Music of India, Discovering the Music of Japan, Discovering the*

Music of the Middle East. BFA Educational Media, CBS Educational Publishing, a Division of CBS, Inc., 2211 Michigan Ave., P.O. Box 1795, Santa Monica, CA 90406.

Miracle of Bali—A Recital of Music and Dancing.   British Broadcasting Company—TV, 630 Fifth Avenue, New York, NY 10020.

INSTRUMENTS OF HAWAII

Bishop Museum, Post Office Box 19000-A, Honolulu, HI 96819. Pictures showing authentic use.

Hula Supply Center, 2346 South King St., Honolulu, HI 96826. Instruments, clothing, accessories of the islands.

Suggested Projects

1. Develop an annotated bibliography of at least ten sources about integrating music with other subjects.

2. Write a lesson plan in which a nonmusical concept is taught through music.

3. Form a committee of at least four classmates who could be fellow teachers in a public school. Plan and execute an integrated arts experience for the rest of the class.

12 *Visualize*

Montgomery says that 85 percent of student learning takes place through the eyes and only 11 percent through the ears.[1] In light of this information, it seems particularly urgent that music instruction be coupled with visual reinforcement, to give students something they can see to help make aural abstractions more tangible.

WRITING NOTATION

"Writing notation" does not necessarily refer to creating music. That activity may or may not be related to putting notation on paper. Writing notation as used here simply refers to the student's ability to make music symbols. It is hoped that the ability to use symbols develops along with creativity so it can serve students as a means of preserving their creative efforts.

Young elementary school children learn to write. This is anticipated as part of their education. The teacher of music is encouraged to make the

[1]Robert L. Montgomery, "How to Improve Your Memory," *U.S. News and World Report,* August 27, 1979, pp. 55–56.

writing of music symbols a normal part of children's education as well. It is imperative that sound be associated consistently with what they are writing. An excessive amount of time spent in writing symbols divorced from musical meaning detracts from the value of the experience.

Writing rhythm notation. The teacher should specify music class time not being used by the students for active learning for them to make these symbols:

1. As the primary children enter the classroom, ask them to put one quarter note on the chalkboard. When they leave, ask them to put a half note on the board.
2. As the children come in the door, ask them to draw one kind of note on the board. Their movement activities will begin with whichever notes are in the majority that day.
3. When the children are moving rhythmically, have a leader draw a note on the board to show them the kind of note they represent. When the leader changes the note, the children's movement will change too.
4. Instead of having the students wait in line to play the pitched percussion instruments, ask those who are not playing to write four measures of rhythmic notation in $\frac{4}{4}$ time. Then, let them play their patterns on the instruments.
5. As the children wait for music or equipment to be passed out, ask each one to write a musical equation.

$$\quarternote + \quarternote = \halfnote$$

6. Ask older children to write a rhythm pattern in a specified meter and of a specified length. Ask them to find a partner with whom they can share their patterns. After they have performed each other's patterns, ask them to join the patterns together so they now have a pattern that has doubled in length. Next, ask the partners to find another partnership to join them. After clapping each other's patterns, have them join all the patterns together so they are now performing a rhythmic passage four times as long as the original one. As soon as the quartet is ready, ask them to present their combined patterns to the class. When this has been done successfully, ask each student in the quartet to clap one of the original patterns at the same time that the partners are clapping a different one. Give the students time to work on this. When they feel comfortable in producing the patterns accurately, encourage them to select instruments whose timbre will provide the kind of sound they wish their ensemble to have. Ask them to include dynamics in their playing. When they are ready, ask the instrumental ensemble to play for the class. If one music period is not enough for all the children to accomplish these activities, be sure they have a storage place in which to keep their written work safe until the next class time. Leaders whose groups finish a task like this swiftly can follow the teacher's example and help students who need it or be given more sophisticated tasks, such as adding sixteenth notes, dotted rhythms, or syncopation.

Writing melodic notation.   When the children begin to write pitch notation, they should have a lesson on a simple way to make a treble clef. Even after the initial lesson, some children will have difficulty in making it accurately, so the lesson can be repeated periodically for those who need it.

To save valuable time, have a supply of staff paper constantly available. Asking children to draw staff lines can be a frustrating experience. Commercially printed paper is available with staves printed in many sizes. Try to obtain wider spaced staves for the younger children. Dittos with music staff only are available. Run these off for an inexpensive supply of staff paper. Cut the paper in half or in quarters if the assignments are short, so as to save paper.

How to make the treble clef.   Show the children how to make a vertical line extending both above and below the staff.

Explore terminology to be sure that the children understand the meaning of the words "semicircle" and "target." Ask them to count from the bottom line up to the fourth line where they will put their first target mark.

Show them how to draw a semicircle from the top of the vertical line to the first target, putting the semicircle on the right side of the vertical line.

Put the next target on the bottom line.

Continue the first semicircle line to make a second semicircle to the left of the vertical line.

Put target number three on the third line.

Draw the next semicircle on the right side of the vertical line.

Finish the treble clef by drawing an incomplete semicircle that stops after cutting through the second line.

Ask the class if anyone knows another name for the treble clef. It is sometimes called the soprano clef, sometimes the G clef. The reason for calling it the G clef is that the symbol cuts through the G line four different times. It also focuses on that note by the way the semicircles are wrapped around it. If the students remember this, they will always know where the note G is in the treble clef.

After you show the class the procedure again, or as many times as they seem to need it, ask them to take their papers home so they can practice more. The children should also put G notes next to the treble clef to help them remember the location of that note.

When older children are ready, the same type of lesson should be taught for the bass or F clef. They must know that the bass clef sign starts on the F line, cuts through it again, and has dots on either side of it.

Readiness activities for pitch notation. Readiness activities help children to write pitch notation. Give each child a cookie sheet with magnets or a paper with checkers. A staff should be painted or taped onto the cookie sheet or it should be drawn on the paper. (A ditto master can be used to produce many copies.) Since cookie sheets are more expensive, perhaps only the teacher will have one. The advantage is that it can be held up so the children can see. The cookie sheet must be made of metal to which magnets will adhere. The magnets can be fanciful figures such as turtles or ladybugs available in variety stores, or they can be notes to which the teacher has attached magnetic tape (available in sewing departments).

The teacher will sing to the students: "Put your markers on the first line, second line; first space, second space; first space, third line." After giving each instruction the teacher will check to see if the students put their markers on the lines (this means the lines go through the markers rather than under them as the letters do when they print words) and in the spaces (between the lines).

ON THE LINE   **IN THE SPACE**

The teacher will show the correct placement with the cookie sheet and magnets when necessary.

Later, involve the children in melodic dictation. Add treble clefs to the papers for this. Sing the directions using the correct pitch of the notes. "Put a marker on the second line. Put another marker to show this sound." Tell the children that their markers show the beginning of a song they know. Ask them to either sing it or play it on an instrument. As soon as they know what it is, they should perform it with correct rhythm.

ETC.

As the children grow in these preparatory skills, they are moving toward taking melodic dictation when they will be asked to write the sounds they hear on staff paper with correct rhythm as well as pitch.

The music teacher should send notation back to the classroom with the children and work with the classroom teacher in providing charts related to the music the children are making. As soon as the children begin to write notation, their efforts should be displayed. The visual presence of notation is intended to be yet another musical reinforcer.

Notating creative efforts.   When the students engage in creative activity, they should be encouraged to preserve some of their efforts by notating clues to enable them to remember the composition in the next class or to allow it to be played by another student. It is not necessary for children to use conventional notation in the beginning. They can use pictures, designs, abbreviations, prose, anything to help them visualize the music. In dealing with form,

   or

may be more meaningful to them than A B A. First-graders can remember their instrumentation by noting

The communication to someone else may be limited, but the child will use it as a reminder to begin with a triangle, than shake a maraca, and finally hit the drum twice.

Melodies may be shown with curved or broken lines.

Although these early efforts are nonspecific and pose problems for adults trained to respond to notation, they do illustrate graphic representations of sound for the children. It is the teacher's task to continue to make meaningful suggestions to the children to lead them to greater specificity connected with their maturing musical skills.

Encourage the children to spend time outside of class in writing music symbols. Artistically inclined children will draw colorful and fanciful pictures using music symbols. They will use a variety of craft projects to produce objects associated with music ranging from stained glass to plastics, yarn, and clay ad infinitum. The proud music teacher will often be the beneficiary of these efforts; your bulletin boards may be full and your lapels covered with pin-on music symbols.

Jayne Cooper of the Willagillespie School, Eugene, Oregon, makes pin-on circles visualizing musical concepts that she either wears or lets the children wear. She finds these to be helpful reminders for the children through their constant and attractive presence. The cerebral palsied children with whom she works benefit from them especially. An allied arts project for the children would be to make their own pin-on buttons containing something they have worked on in music class. Schools that have invested in button makers can preserve the artistic efforts in more permanent housing, making it easier to pass the buttons from one child to another.

Caution:

1. Try always to have the symbols connected with sound.
2. Do not allow music lessons to be dominated by writing symbols; keep this activity in perspective.

Suggested Projects

1. Practice giving instructions for making treble and bass clefs.
2. Devise a means not mentioned in this section for including notation in lessons for (a) primary and (b) intermediate students.

FLASHCARDS

Flashcards are pieces of heavy paper or cardboard used to help children learn specific information. On one side they usually have a limited aspect of the subject matter, often in the form of a problem to be solved or a symbol to be identified. They are called *flash*cards because they are used to challenge the students to answer quickly after seeing the card for a very short time. They are usually designed with the answer on the back so that the person who is showing the flashcard has the correct response in front of him or her and can give feedback as to correct or incorrect replies.

Making the cards. Making the cards is not difficult. If small groups or individuals are to use them, index cards (3″ by 5″) are large enough. They are readily available in many colors and provide a uniform base upon which to put the visual material. The size of card for class use depends upon the nature of the information to be placed on them and the distance from which they are to be seen. Larger index cards (5″ by 8″) will often be appropriate. Felt-tipped markers in various widths and colors are very effective when used to prepare the visual.

If the cards are to be used a great deal, they will last longer if they can be laminated (covered with plastic, using heat to seal). Many school systems have a laminating machine or at least have access to one. The expense of lamination should be measured against the long-range saving in teacher time by cutting down the frequent necessity for replacement of the cards. An alternative to lamination is to cover the cards with transparent adhesive plastic.

Purposes of flashcards. In considering the creation of flashcards, two main questions should be asked:

1. What objective is to be met through using them?
2. Are cards already available designed to fulfill the same objective? If they are, the saving in teacher time is often well worth the purchase price.

Other questions to be raised before making or using flashcards are: What kind of a response will be generated by the card? Are the children required to give a verbal response such as naming a symbol, a note, a composer? Will the response be a cognitive one in which the child gives evidence that he or she has learned certain information about music? Will the card prompt a performance response through which the child will play, sing, move, read, or write music? Will the card act as an experiential prompt resulting in the child creating or listening to music?

The commercially manufactured flashcards that seem to be most readily available are those that elicit a verbal response from the children.

Packs of cards dealing with specific musical areas can be purchased. Some sets are designed to have the children tell only the names of notes in the treble or bass staff, key signatures, dynamic marks, tempo indicators, or instruments.

Some flashcard sets are more general and include many different kinds of musical items to be identified. Because these sets require the kind of response that can be deemed correct or incorrect by the person holding them, reading the answer from the back of the card, they are effective when used by the children or an adult who has limited background in music. Some of these cards do not require a musical response from the children; they require a verbal response made possible by memorization of information.

Use the cards to produce sound. It is highly desirable if the teacher can adapt the cards mentioned to make the responses musical ones. When the child is shown the cards with the notes written in the treble staff, rather than asking the name of the notes, ask the child to play the note on whatever instrument can be used to produce the corresponding sounds. The pitched percussion instruments are the easiest to start with because they have note names written on their bars. Even though it is easy to find the note on the instrument, the child still has to figure out which sound the notation is telling him or her to produce.

In addition to saying the name of the key signature, ask the child to show the sharps or flats indicated on the card. A keyboard instrument works well for this. The child can play or sing something illustrating the dynamic or tempo indicators shown on the cards. In implementing these musical suggestions, two conditions are altered from the use of the flashcards as first described:

1. The quick response is slowed down considerably.
2. Either the teacher or a knowledgeable student must help the child to determine if the response has been accurate.

Reading the answer on the back of the card alone is not enough; the activity now includes musical discrimination.

Unless the cards are designed to elicit some response with an aural dimension, they are not really musical, even though they may be valuable for the contribution they make to the students' knowledge about music making. In creating flashcards, keep in mind the variety of musical experiences that can be prompted by flashcards. If placed in a gamelike setting, the children will enjoy them even more.

For example, divide the class into three teams. Have a scorekeeper at the chalkboard. Provide each team with a xylophone. As the team member sees the flashcard, the youngster should play notes on the instrument showing music going up, down, or staying the same.

For every participant who plays a correct response, the scorekeeper will put a mark for that team on the board. The teacher comments positively upon correct responses and also keeps track of any students having difficulty with the game to give help to those individuals at a later date.

As the children become adept at showing general melodic directions, move into more difficult activities. The next set of flashcards will ask that they play three next-door neighbor notes going up, down, or staying the same.

The number of notes is important, the exact pitches are not, but the notes must be next-door neighbors. Variations on the game will require four notes, exact pitches, or melodic fragments.

Use similar ideas with rhythmic flashcards. Show very easy rhythm patterns to the entire class. After using them enough times that the children appear to be comfortable with them, tell them that the cards will be used next to build a long rhythmic piece. Put only one card on the chalkboard tray. After the class claps that, add a second card. Have the class clap the first and second cards. Add a third card. See how many cards the class can clap without making an error.

Let individuals earn points. Ask Sam to clap the first card. He gets a point for the card if he does it right. To get her point(s), Mary must clap both Sam's card and the new one just placed on the chalkboard. If she claps them both, she gets two points. Helen now has an opportunity to clap three cards. If she misses one, she still gets a point for each card she has clapped before producing the error. After all the children have had a chance, anyone who wants to try to clap the total number of cards on the chalkboard can do so to get a higher score. New cards are not added until someone has clapped correctly all the ones already there. If several enthusiastic players wish to keep going and are making no mistakes, but the class time is over, note the players' names and the number of cards they have used so they can resume the game at another time. Encourage the players not involved directly to help you determine the accuracy of the responses. Some of the children having difficulty with rhythm patterns will learn from the examples they are observing both aurally and visually.

Flashcards or job cards?   As flashcards become complicated, it is sometimes hard to tell the difference between them and job cards. The latter are usually used to prompt an activity involving more time and greater depth than do the flashcards. Some job cards will be summaries of flashcards.

These flashcards give the children instructions for creative responses. To implement the responses, group the class into four teams, each standing in back of a music stand. As soon as the first person in back of the stand responds to the flashcard, he or she moves to the end of the line and a new flashcard is placed on the stand. The new player will have some time to decide what his or her response will be because players from the three other teams will respond before the action comes back to his or her stand.

Day 1:   One instrument is placed by each music stand. The student is instructed to create something on the instrument to show the emotion described on the flashcard.

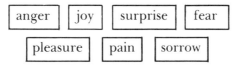

If you are not sure of words the students can use expressively, prepare for the lesson by asking the children for words to describe how they feel.

Day 2:   There are four instruments near each music stand. Use the same flashcards, but this time ask the students to select the instrumental sound that will be most helpful in showing the emotion.

Day 3:   The cards on the stands show either "2" or "3." The children are asked to demonstrate a meter of 2 or 3 with a partner chosen from the same group in which they have been working. They may each use an instrument, body sounds, movement, or whatever they want to show the meter. As soon as the class can tell the meter they are demonstrating, the group will begin to count along with them. The demonstrators may not count out loud or show their cards to the class.

Day 4:   The children will create and play four-measure melodies with either two beats in a measure or three beats in a measure. ☐2☐ ☐3☐ The same flashcards will be used. They may select the instruments that they wish to use. The class will decide if the meter is illustrated clearly.

After participating in the experiences prompted by the flashcards, job cards can then be given to the children with instructions such as these:

JOB CARD

> Create a four-measure melody
> On an instrument of your
>   choice
> In a meter of two beats per
>   measure
> Showing sorrow

JOB CARD

> Create a four-measure melody
> On an instrument of your
>   choice
> In a meter of three beats per
>   measure
> Showing excitement

Flashcards can be used too often. The creative teacher is urged to allow them to be a helpful part of music instruction without losing sight of other aspects of the children's involvement. Discretion is advised when using cards that consistently reveal that some of the children are unable to cope with the behavior necessary to respond successfully to them. Before re-exposing the entire class to those cards, give instruction to the children who need it to help them catch up to the class, or if there is a reason they cannot, give them alternative ways for musical involvement.

Recommended Resources

Flashcards and games available from Music in Motion, Box 5564, Richardson, TX 75080.
Flashcards available from Robert Pace Teaching Aids, Lee Roberts Music Publications, G. Schirmer, Inc., NY 10022.

BULLETIN BOARDS

One reason for having a bulletin board in the classroom is that it has the potential for making the room a more attractive place. The decorative bulletin board, changed frequently, can help to heighten children's anticipation in coming to school. They may be curious about the replacement for the Halloween picture or may plan their roles in helping to put up the next board.

In addition to its decorative functions, the bulletin board can add other dimensions to music instruction. It can show factual materials that the children are studying. It can couple words and illustrations to give meaning to concepts under study. It can show musical symbols not only as part of the decoration but also in ways that develop their meaning. Excellent bulletin boards can be created as prompts for musical activity. Rather than treating the children like spectators, the boards can involve them in musical activity.

A MUSICAL BULLETIN BOARD INVOLVING CHILDREN

Design a board with a border of multicolored flats, sharps, and naturals. Ask each of the children to make one of the symbols. At the top of the board, show a large flat. Under it, post the sentence: "The flat shows that the note is lower." Immediately under the sentence show the notation for B and B-flat. The instructions for hitting the resonator bells should follow: "First hit the B, then the B ♭ to hear that the B ♭ is lower. Two resonator bells and a mallet should be taped under the instructions.

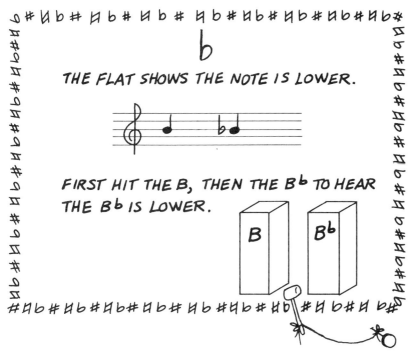

THE FLAT SHOWS THE NOTE IS LOWER.

FIRST HIT THE B, THEN THE B♭ TO HEAR THE B♭ IS LOWER.

After the children have had opportunities to observe the board, read about the flat, and play the bars, change the board so that it illustrates the sharp. Plan carefully to change as few things on the board as possible: "The sharp shows that the note is higher. First hit the F, then the F♯ to hear that the F♯ is higher." Make the new items on the board in a contrasting color so they will be readily apparent to the children.

The next transformation of the board illustrates the natural. "The natural takes away the effect of a flat or a sharp. Play the F♯ first, then the F♮ to see what happens. Play the B♭ first, then the B♮ to see what happens."

The classroom teacher should be encouraged to tailor the bulletin board to whatever aspect of music the class studies. The music teacher will have many classes coming to the music room, not all of whom will be studying the same things. You may designate bulletin boards for certain classes. You may also design traveling boards to be loaned to classes for display in their own rooms. These traveling boards may be made as folding triptychs that stand on a desk, or they may be accompanied by a tripod. The music teacher should check with the class teacher to find the best manner of display for that room. Traveling boards will be necessary if the music teacher moves from room to room with no permanent location in which to set up bulletin boards.

One of the best displays for the children to see is that of notation. Hang a song on the bulletin board. Refer to it in teaching the song and in using it to develop concepts related to that song. While it is much easier for the teacher merely to write the words, and perhaps add the chords that go with it, don't underestimate the value to the children of having notation available for them to read—or at least begin to read. At the *very* least this should help them develop an awareness of symbols.

A bulletin board especially appropriate for older children shows notation with no title or words. The board will be titled "Mystery Melody" or "Tune of the Week." The idea of this board is to have the children figure out the melody either by singing it or playing it on an instrument. Encourage all the children to try to identify it.

Many schools have bulletin board space in hallways. Take advantage of these areas for musical visuals, too. They may be general, especially if they are intended to reach adults who come into the building. A bulletin board describing the music program in unique ways will be interesting to the children too. This bulletin board will get lots of attention; the children love to see their pictures. Each sketched picture can be replaced with a photograph of the child doing the activity mentioned near it.

TIME SAVERS

Commercial products are available to save teacher and student time. Stamps can be purchased that quickly produce the staff and the grand staff. A picture of the recorder provides a handy way for the students to show a new fingering and helps them to remember it. Guitar diagrams can assist the student in discriminating where his or her fingers are to be put. Small piano keyboards illustrate graphically the location of notes and whole and half steps.

Another time saver is a white composition board marker for the room with a chalkboard that cannot have staff lines painted on it. The marker can be used with a yardstick to put a staff on the board that will not erase along with the chalk used to put notation on the staff. When the staff must be removed, it can be erased with a pencil eraser.

FILMS AND FILMSTRIPS

Films and filmstrips have a very desirable illustrative capability for demonstrating music. If these materials are to be purchased by the school, most of them can be previewed before confirming the order. The teacher should preview them to be sure that the visual materials are of high enough quality, that the concepts being taught through this medium are appropriate for the children, and that their value is sufficient to warrant the expenditure. Many school systems have access to films on either a rental or a loan basis. An advantage of having a central depository of films is that more choices are available than if only one school were purchasing the materials.

A library of filmstrips is very useful in each school. Showing a filmstrip to the entire class from beginning to end is just one way of using this type of instruction. It may be a vital component of independent instruction. It may be used in sections to illustrate musical concepts the students are studying. A return to portions of the filmstrip can be extremely beneficial to some of the students after they have had more opportunity to deal with a particular concept. In school systems having problems finding qualified music substitutes, an appropriate filmstrip can be shown by whomever has been hired for the day without sacrificing valuable music instruction time.

The use of video equipment in music class has yet to reach its full potential. When videotaping facilities are available to music classes, creative work with this equipment can include putting together a musical program, perhaps in the form of a concert, musical play, or opera, creating a musical composition that uses a process of overlaying various sounds as well as sights. The potential of videotapes is tremendous; at this point there is not much software available. A few years from now, with more equipment and greater expertise, perhaps teachers of music will be adapting the techniques described in Chapter 7 for cassette tapes to videotapes so as to include both audio and visual modes of learning.

Recommended Resources

Rubber stamps showing the keyboard, the grand staff or separate staffs, guitar tablature, and recorder fingering.   Available from Visual Aids for Music, 6665 S.W. Preslynn Drive, Portland, OR 97225.

Chalkboard white liner to use for putting staff lines on chalkboard.   Stays in place when chalk is erased or washed off; is removed easily with regular pencil eraser. Available from Eberhard Faber.

13 Research

The term "research" may conjure up an uneasy feeling, a sense of mystery, or aversive reactions on the part of the educator, particularly if the teacher has tried to read reports involving pure research whose data are treated with highly sophisticated statistical formulas. The purpose of this chapter is to highlight the value of two different aspects of research and to encourage music educators to maintain research involvement.

The first aspect of research is not necessarily carried on in the music class. It is the kind of inquiry the teacher should maintain to discover historical precedents, present practices, and future ideas. This research involves reading books and articles, consulting with experts, and observing fine teachers. It should include reading research reports in professional journals. All these activities are designed to give depth to the educator's work.

The second aspect of research is the kind the teacher initiates actively in the classroom, trying to ascertain the best educational approaches to the children's learning. This research is part of a constant effort to improve classroom processes.

While recognizing the limitations of research done with small groups, Prehm and Altman discuss the possibilities of the educator's research involvement in the classroom. They are lucid in suggesting advantages of classroom research and in identifying the problems with it. Their book is a good introductory source for the aspiring researcher.

The music teacher is urged to gain a foundation for research through study in a university setting. If the elementary music teacher does not feel qualified to undertake experimental research alone, cooperative endeavors are often fruitful and very interesting. There is need for classroom practitioners to address themselves to questions concerning children's musical maturation, the advantages and disadvantages of varying approaches to the children, attitudinal responses of the children to music instruction at different levels, and so on. The following samples of music education research illustrate some of the crucial areas for research. All of them appeared in the *Journal of Research in Music Education.*

Hufstader devised a test to measure student ability to make discriminations connected with alterations in timbre, rhythm, melodic pitch patterns, and harmony. There were 596 subjects in the study from grades one, three, six, and seven. He found that the mean test scores for timbre had reached the arbitrary criterion level by the first grade in all four school districts that were part of the investigation. The criterion level for rhythm was reached by fifth grade in all four districts. The melodic pitch pattern criterion level was reached by fifth grade in two of the districts and by seventh grade in the other two districts. The mean scores for harmony reached the criterion level in two districts by seventh grade but did not reach that level in the other districts. Hufstader acknowledged several factors that could have biased the study:

1. The selection of subjects.
2. The curriculums of the districts.
3. The test items for the musical elements may not have been equivalent.
4. Individual learning sequences varied greatly.

However, the results of the study conformed to a synthesis of studies similar to this one. Skills in timbre discrimination seem to develop by the preschool level, rhythm and melody skills develop next, harmony skills last.

Froelich investigated the relationship of classroom practices to the teaching of singing. Out of thirty-seven variables, she found that only rhythmic reading activities correlated significantly with superior singing qualities. Classes in which time was spent in extended discussions were rated average or below average in singing. This rating was also true for classes that sang the songs several times through with no instruction or correction from the teacher. "The only form of verbal instruction that correlated positively with the criteria of effective teaching occurred when the teacher talked to the students about a theoretical or formal aspect of a song and did not intend to initiate any discussion."[1]

---

[1]Hildegard Froelich, "Replication of a Study on Teaching Singing in the Elementary General Music Classroom," *Journal of Research in Music Education,* Spring 1979, p. 45.

Wassum accumulated data over a five-year period on the vocal range of the elementary school child. She found that the mean range was the interval of a ninth in first grade and that it expanded to nearly two octaves in sixth grade. She found no significant sex differences. The range levels found by Wassum were greater and extended higher than had been previously reported. The lowest tone sung by the greatest number of first graders was middle C. By third grade that lowest note had moved to G below middle C, where it stayed through sixth grade. The high note was generally C above middle C in grades one and two, moving to high G - C in the upper grades. By sixth grade more than fifty percent of the children could sing a total range of two octaves or more. The direct applications of this study to the classroom may be in the setting up of specific goals for voice development:

1. To ensure through remedial work that all children in a class can sing in a range equal to the mean for that grade level.
2. To use songs written in keys that will not exceed the lowest nor highest ranges for most children of that age.
3. To select some songs with wide ranges to stimulate vocal development of gifted students.
4. To encourage vocal development as a conscious goal of the music program, and of equivalent value to the development of other music skills.[2]

The reader is encouraged to peruse the complete reports of the articles summarized in the preceding paragraphs as well as others like them in such journals as

Journal of Research in Music Education
Bulletin of the Council for Research in Music Education
Psychology of Music
Journal of Music Therapy

Dissertation Abstracts is a good source for locating current research. It contains summaries of dissertations written by doctoral students throughout the country.

Recommended Readings

FROEHLICH, HILDEGARD, "Replication of a Study on Teaching Singing in the Elementary General Music Classroom," *Journal of Research in Music Education*, Spring 1979, pp. 35–45.
HUFSTADER, RONALD A., "An Investigation of a Learning Sequence of Music Listening Skills," *Journal of Research in Music Education*, Fall 1977, pp. 184–196.

[2]Sylvesta Wassum, "Elementary School Children's Vocal Range," *Journal of Research in Music Education*, Winter 1979, pp. 225–226.

PREHM, HERBERT J., AND REUBEN ALTMAN, *Improving Instruction Through Classroom Research*. Denver, CO: Love Publishing Company, 1976.

WASSUM, SYLVESTA, "Elementary School Children's Vocal Range," *Journal of Research in Music Education*, Winter 1979, pp. 214–226.

Suggested Projects

1. Browse through several issues of at least two research journals listed. Select one article from each journal to read thoroughly. (It may be easier to read the introduction and the summary to get an overview of the article before reading it straight through.) List briefly significant items you learned by reading the article. Also identify any problems you may have encountered in reading it.
2. Read and review Prehm and Altman's *Improving Instruction Through Classroom Research*.

14 Care

It is easy to become so caught up in making music, developing performance technique, and fulfilling teaching responsibilities that direct concern for each child is lessened. This chapter deals with various aspects of
the teacher's concern for all of the children and suggests ways of caring for
their individual variations.

INDIVIDUALIZED/INDEPENDENT INSTRUCTION

I.I., or individualized instruction, has become a regular part of some music
programs, especially in grades five and six. Teachers have developed job
cards for a variety of activities, sometimes with more than one level for the
task at hand.

Assignment of tasks. As the students enter the room, they check to see
what their assignment is for the day. The teacher's method of making these
assignments varies.

In some classes, a list of names posted on the wall is followed by empty
squares in which appear a different letter each time the students come to
class. The letters refer to the learning stations appearing around the room

that are identified by a letter hanging above it, taped to it, on the furniture, or the wall nearby. A thin piece of cardboard with all the station letters on it is moved ahead for each name in succeeding lessons.

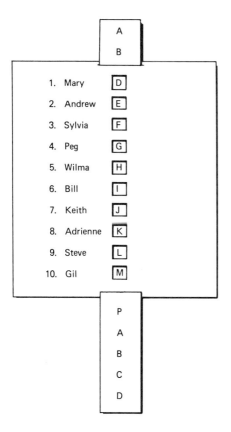

In other classes, a piece of material with index-card-sized pockets sewn on it hangs on the wall. The pockets are identified by letters corresponding to the station letters around the room. A card with each child's name is placed in the pocket to show the activity for him or her that day. As children enter the room, they find the pocket in which their name cards have been placed and proceed to the assigned stations.

Some teachers work with the students in setting up contracts. The student and teacher mutually agree on what the student will be studying for a certain period of time. When students come to class, they continue to work on the project described in their contracts.

Stations.   The learning stations set up around the room take many forms:

1. Learning how to play instruments. The materials available at these stations include commercial and/or homemade sequences guiding the students in playing recorder, guitar, percussion instruments, piano, and autoharp. There are sometimes tapes to assist the student.

2. Ear training: programs, stories, and games using tapes such as the instruction described in Chapter 7 for expanding teaching time.

3. Listening to music for the joy of hearing it, to sequential selections designed to support concept development, to music related to other areas of the curriculum.

4. Flashcards for drill in naming symbols connected with music instruction and other uses as described in Chapter 12.

5. Games for expanding vocabulary and knowledge about music.

6. Robots that hand out cards and give correct answers.

7. Electronic games such as *Simon, Super-Simon, Merlin,* and *Electronic Repeat.*[1]

8. Paperwork, including filling in the blanks, matching, and multiple choice.

9. Reading books, articles, and pamphlets connected with music.

10. Writing symbols connected with music.

11. Creating arrangements using resources available in the room, songs, stories for musical plays.

12. Improvising with a previously taped ostinato.

13. Moving in the hallway with taped music and suggestions.

During the music period, the teacher is available to answer questions, give help, and otherwise relate to the students on an individual basis.

Location. In many situations, the stations are set up for a certain part of the school year in the music room. During that time, the students work on the individualized instruction only. In other situations, a portion of the music period will be devoted to group activity, the remainder to individualized instruction.

When this type of instruction is used in a regular classroom, it can be located in its own section of the room all year. A problem can be caused by the sound generated by some of the activities. The creative teacher is challenged to find a way that music making can take place on an independent basis without bothering the rest of the class, perhaps in another location in the school.

Children can engage in the musical activities when their other assignments are completed. Better yet, the teacher can make time for each child to have a chance to work independently with music as part of his or her regular schedule.

[1]*Simon* and *Super-Simon* are available from Milton Bradley, Lincoln St., Federal Square, Springfield, Massachusetts 01105; *Merlin* from Parker Brothers, Division of General Mills Fun Group, Inc., Beverly, Massachusetts 01915; and *Electronic Repeat* from Tandy (Radio Shack), Ft. Worth, TX 76107. These are computer-controlled games that challenge the children to interact with them. Both visible and audible cues are given.

Advantages.   I.I. as described can provide many advantages:

1. Children have modes of musical activity that contrast to group work.
2. They can specialize in areas of music of greatest interest to them.
3. They can devote time to activities that may not fit into a class music lesson.
4. They can strengthen weak skills that might otherwise be neglected.

Questions.   Some questions about individualized instruction must be raised in an effort to ensure that it is of benefit to the students:

1. Is it really individualized; that is, is the instruction designed specifically for the student or, if not, is it prescribed specifically for that individual? Observation of many I.I. programs reveals that the activities are not individualized; rather, they are constructed so that they can be handled by the student independently, that is, without assistance from an adult. As independent study they still may be of great benefit to many students, but it is important for the teacher to discriminate between individualized instruction and independent study. When teachers make the distinction, they will find that they can provide experiences for students that are germane to their needs rather than assign something with only a general applicability. Rather than rotating the I.I. activities automatically with each music class, teachers should begin to make specific assignments over an adequate period of time relating to the individual's capabilities.
2. Are the activities musical? Is the students' time well spent in music class if they are engaging in learning terms, facts about music through nonaural games, or other tasks with no sound connected with them? If this activity is of value to students, are there times other than in music class where they can be done without taking time from musical experiences?
3. Is enough time allowed for students to develop depth in the area that is theirs to study? Will the students' needs be served better if this class provides a starting point? Is it possible that students can take materials home with them, return to class for follow up, and take them home again, as their involvement continues to be of benefit?
4. Is accountability built into the experience? How does the teacher know if the students are learning anything? Are behavioral objectives written for each of the activities? What system is used to ascertain if the behavior is established?
5. Is the teacher's ability to interact with the children being developed to its fullest extent? Is enough being accomplished by the students working independently to make up for the missing, or limited, group activity?

Group and individualized instruction combined.   An alternative to using stations in a classroom with little relationship to group activity is to initiate a large-group activity with the children and then give assignments related to that activity to meet the needs of children operating at different levels.

INDIVIDUALIZED INSTRUCTION EMANATING FROM GROUP ACTIVITY

These lessons follow creative song-writing activities such as those described in Chapter 8. The class has had experience in group song writing and has enjoyed performing the results of their creative efforts. The teacher uses page 52 from the Macmillan MusicCenter as a basis for assigning different tasks to the children. The observations made in creative group lessons serve as the basis for determining the various skill levels of the children. If there are children in the class whose needs are not served by the variations described in the paragraphs that follow, adaptions must be made specifically for them.

This is the card from the Macmillan MusicCenter as it was written originally. It is appropriate for some of the children.

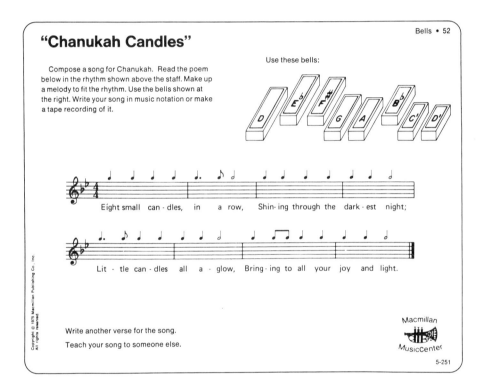

Some of the advanced musicians need more challenge than that given by the original card, so the notation to help them determine their rhythm writing has been removed. These children can do that part themselves as part of their song writing. (Adaptation I)

A few of the students have difficulty in determining key center. They are being helped by instruction about notes to use in beginning and ending their compositions. (Adaptation II)

A few of the students become confused when confronted with too many pitch choices. They are limited to using four resonator bells instead of eight. (Adaptation III)

"Chanukah Candles"

I

Section I

Bells • 52

Compose a song for Chanukah. Read the poem below in the rhythm which best suits the words. Does your rhythm fit the meter which is noted below? Will your bar lines come in the same places? If not, change the meter and the bar lines to fit the way you are saying the words. Now notate your rhythm above the staff. Let a friend clap your notation to make sure that you have written what you want to hear. Make up a melody to fit your rhythm. Use the bells shown at the right. Write your song in music notation or make a tape recording of it.

Use these bells:

Eight small can - dles, in a row, Shin- ing through the dark - est night;

Lit - tle can - dles all a - glow, Bring- ing to all your joy and light.

Write another verse for the song.

Teach your song to someone else.

Macmillan
MusicCenter

5-251

II

"Chanukah Candles"

Bells • 52

Compose a song for Chanukah. Read the poem below in the rhythm shown above the staff. Make up a melody to fit the rhythm. Use the bells shown at the right. Write your song in music notation or make a tape recording of it.

Use these bells:

Begin and end your piece on one of the notes of the g minor chord:

G B♭ or D

Eight small can - dles, in a row, Shin- ing through the dark - est night;

Lit - tle can - dles all a - glow, Bring- ing to all your joy and light.

Write another verse for the song.

Teach your song to someone else.

Macmillan
MusicCenter

5-251

III

"Chanukah Candles"

Compose a song for Chanukah. Read the poem below in the rhythm shown above the staff. Make up a melody to fit the rhythm. Use the bells shown at the right. Write your song in music notation or make a tape recording of it.

Use these bells:

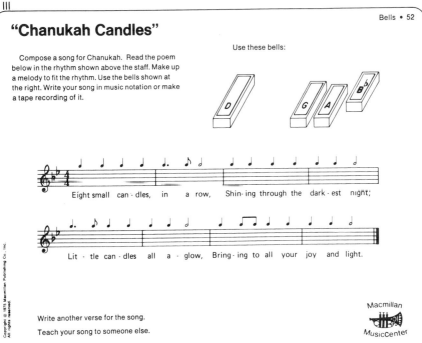

Eight small can - dles, in a row, Shin- ing through the dark - est night;

Lit - tle can - dles all a - glow, Bring- ing to all your joy and light.

Write another verse for the song.

Teach your song to someone else.

Macmillan
MusicCenter

5-251

IV

"Chanukah Candles"

Compose a song for Chanukah. Read the poem below in the rhythm shown above the staff. Make up a melody to fit the rhythm. Use the bells shown at the right. Write your song in music notation or make a tape recording of it.

Use these bells:

Eight small can - dles, in a row, Shin- ing through the dark - est night;

Lit - tle can - dles all a - glow, Bring- ing to all your joy and light.

Use a chordal instrument to help you figure out an accompaniment for your song. Can you sing your melody while playing the accompanying chords? If you want to have a friend perform the melody while you are working on the chords, that may be a big help!

Write another verse for the song.

Teach your song to someone else.

Macmillan
MusicCenter

5-251

Two of the students have shown great progress in working with chordal accompaniments. They may or may not be able to do this assignment independently, but the teacher has decided that they will probably need only minimal help if any, and the time seems ripe to give them a chance to harmonize on their own. (Adaptation IV)

To give time to the students who work more slowly than others, the children who finish first will be given additional opportunity for creative activity. These students will choose the bonus they wish to do.

HOLIDAY BONUS!

Your holiday song was well done! Could you begin another song with no help? Try making up your words first. Since we are thinking about the holidays, your topic could be Chanukah, Christmas, or anything that relates to this time of the year. If you wish to help the class get ready for events that are coming, write about Valentine's Day or one of our country's leaders like George Washington or Abraham Lincoln.

HOLIDAY BONUS!

Your holiday song was well done! Have you
thought about writing music for the holidays
using instruments only—no words? What kind of
sounds will you need to help you get into a holiday
spirit? How many sounds do you want to hear at
once? How many players will you need? As you think
of ideas, jot them down either in words or in musical notation. You may want to use pictures that
don't look like regular music notation but will
help your players know what to do. If you need
someone else to work with you, find another classmate who is ready for a holiday bonus.

Summary

One of the major contributions that individualized instruction has brought to music education is the emphasis on the child rather than on the group alone. Activities with the class enable children who cannot function successfully alone in performance activities to still be part of a musical experience. Group activities make it possible for harmony to be created by the children, with leadership coming from young people whose talent has developed more than the rest of the class. Ensemble experiences including instruments, voices, and movement are possible through groups working together. Because music flourishes in a cooperative environment, it is sometimes easy to lose sight of the specific needs of the children. Individualized instruction offers a means of providing for the individual. It has the potential of helping the gifted child toward meaningful musical learning rather than tedious repetition, of giving the slow-learning student opportunity for necessary repetition in developing concepts and skills, of broadening the horizons of children with no musical contacts outside of school, and of supplementing rather than duplicating the wealth of music-making that advantaged children have outside of school with private lessons, church choirs, and other community organizations.

The challenge to the teacher is to use I.I. in unique ways for the ultimate good of each child. Two of the most important considerations when using I.I. are diagnosis of the children and their needs and prescription of work truly suited to their special musical levels.

Recommended Resources

BOOKS AND ARTICLES

ATHEY, MARGARET, AND GWEN HOTCHKISS, *A Galaxy of Games for the Music Class.* West Nyack, NY: Parker Publishing Company, Inc., 1975.

HARRISON, LOIS N., "The Old Story: Frustrated Students, The New Ending: Independent Musicians," *Music Educators Journal,* May 1976, pp. 60–62.

HOTCHKISS, GWEN, AND MARGARET ATHEY, *Treasury of Individualized Activities for the Music Class.* West Nyack, NY: Parker Publishing Company, Inc., 1977.

LEWIS, JAMES, JR., *Administrator's Complete Guide to Individualized Instruction.* West Nyack, NY: Parker Publishing Company, Inc., 1977.

MESKE, EUNICE BOARDMAN, AND CARROLL RINEHART, *Individualized Instruction in Music.* Reston, VA: Music Educators National Conference, 1975.

MOORE, FLOY S., *Individual Studio-Stations in the General Music Class.* Portland, OR: Sumar Publications, 1974.

MATERIALS FOR CHILDREN

BURAKOFF, GERALD AND SONYA, *You Can Play the Recorder.* New York: Music Minus One, 1974. Soprano recorder, record, and book.

Conn Method of Teacher Guided Self-Instruction for Guitar. Oak Brook, IL: C. G. Conn Ltd., 1972. Cassettes of music used in text.

Guitar Class Today. Tinley Park, IL: Jerry Ackley Music, 1972. Record of songs performed as notated in lesson book.

KULBACH, JOHANNA E., AND ARTHUR NITKA, *The Recorder Guide.* New York: Oak Publications. Records and book. Instruction from first note to be played: soprano, alto, and duets.

Learning Unlimited Audio-Visual Instrumental Guides. St. Winona, MN: Hal Leonard Publishing Co. Percussion, 1972, guitar, 1971, recorder, 1973, (teacher's classroom cassette and manual; also student book and record).

LEIS, GENE, *Let Me Teach You to Play the Guitar.* New York: Music Minus One.

Mel Bay Guitar Class Method. Kirkwood, MO: Mel Bay Publications. Cassette and instruction book; moves very fast for a beginner.

Oregon Music Materials. MUSIC I, II. Eugene, OR: 2535 Charnelton Street, 1980. Bingo games for rhythm patterns, progressing in difficulty, patterns given on tape with answers, children can play without teacher.

RINEHART, CARROLL, MAX T. ERVIN, AND GEORGE DEGREGORI, *Sounds for Success.* 1201 N. Torino Ave., Tucson, AZ 85712, 1963. Variety of instruments recorded for independent instruction; record and lesson book for each instrument.

SCHRADER, DAVID, *The Tap Machine.* Seattle: Temporal Acuity Products, 1974. Booklet, tape, and machine that provides feedback on rhythm skills. Levels from beginning to advanced professional.

SILVERMAN, JERRY, *Beginning the Folk Guitar.* New York: Oak Publications.

THESE COMPANIES HAVE VARIED FORMS OF INDEPENDENT MUSIC MATERIALS FOR CHILDREN:

Harcourt Brace Jovanovich, Inc. Kits, filmstrips, and activity cards to go with *Self-Expression and Conduct, The Humanities,* 1974–1979.

Holt, Rinehart and Winston. *Individualized Music Program.* Tapes and printed materials designed to be used independently, 1976.

Macmillan. *Music Center Materials,* the *Spectrum of Music with Related Arts.* Activity cards directing independent work, 1975.

Silver Burdett. *On Your Own.* Tapes and printed material for independent study, 1975.

Suggested Projects

1. Identify a student in a music class who seems to need more help than the rest of the class. Specify one concept with which the child needs help. Design an individualized music experience for that child. Be sure to include a means by which the effectiveness of the individualized instruction can be evaluated.
2. Do the same as project 1 for a student who seems to be more advanced than the rest of the class.
3. Give the individualized instruction to the students for whom it was designed. Assess the effectiveness of the materials.
4. Make a list of independent computerized music instruction for elementary school children.

MIXING EXPERIENCED AND INEXPERIENCED OLDER CHILDREN IN MUSIC CLASS

There are times during upper-grade music classes when teachers are tempted to wring their hands in despair. Why don't these children respond like the primary-grade children do? Why don't they seem to know as much as they should? Volumes could be written in answer to these profound questions dealing with learning states of children, their physical, emotional, and social growth.

The sociological trends of the public school populations enter into the picture as well. Some of the children have attended a number of schools, so there may have been little continuity in their music education. They may have attended schools where there was no music program for the primary children. Some of the older children may have had music instruction in school every day; others may have spent a minimal amount each week. Some of the students in these upper grades have had a great deal of music training, taking private lessons, playing and singing in elective ensembles, having a musical home environment, or associating with community and church musical ventures. The results of all these factors will probably be a mixed class of musically experienced and inexperienced students.

Add to the problems the general disposition of older elementary school students wishing to gain acceptance from their peers. Lack of musical skills and understanding of concepts can turn these students into discipline problems because of the cover-up they feel is necessary. It is more prestigious to hassle the teacher than to admit they don't know how to make music. At the other extreme, the student whose musical background is more advanced than the class activities may be driven to antisocial activity through sheer boredom.

Cyclical learning.   The use of cyclical learning seems especially beneficial for older elementary school students. Mursell has spoken about introducing concepts first in a vague way, later returning to the same concept. Each return would provide an opportunity to define and experience the concept more fully. He saw the introduction of concepts not being tied to any perfect moment or to any exact sequence; rather, the concept should be highlighted "whenever any such concept has an important and significant function in music with which the children are dealing; whenever a grasp of any such concept will lead directly to a more adequate appreciation of music that is being heard or performed."[2] Using major-minor discrimination as an example, he says

---

[2]James L. Mursell, "Growth Process in Music Education," in *Basic Concepts in Music Education*, ed. Nelson B. Henry (Chicago: University of Chicago Press, 1958), p. 159.

For instance, it has been claimed that the teaching of the minor tonality should come quite late in the sequence. But an authentic feeling for the difference between major and minor can be established almost from the beginning. Then can come the contrast between the major and minor triads, the significance of the lowered third, the structure of the minor scale and its variants, the tonic and relative major. Instead of teaching the minor tonality at some one predetermined point, it is, so to speak, spread out through a number of years. So also with all other musical concepts.[3]

The cycle of music instruction allows older students who do not have basic skills or have not been exposed to concepts to enter where they are.

The use of the cycle in music education has promise only if the teacher knows his or her students and has a wealth of resources upon which to draw to meet the needs of those students. An obvious solution to meeting the needs of the advanced student is to tailor experiences especially for that child that promise interest and challenge. Care must be taken; the experienced teacher knows that other students will be quick to cry out, "Why does Sam always get to play the synthesizer?" Meeting student needs must be balanced against seeming to show favoritism. Even inexperienced older students must have the chance to use the synthesizer, but at levels that they can handle.

Manhattanville (Chapter 10) is geared to putting students in learning experiences that start where they are and encourage them to grow musically. Independent study (see Chapter 7 and first part of Chapter 14) offers hope for the older child who has missed some of the musical experiences that most of the class has had. The upper-grade student who has a one-to-one contact with the teacher, even if it is only to explore materials, may show a different kind of response in class when he realizes that the teacher is genuinely concerned with his education and is not going to place him in a position to cause him embarrassment or frustration.

Making choices. A useful approach to dealing with older children is to offer them choices. By the time students get to sixth grade, they are already exhibiting preferences for certain kinds of activities. They also may be showing varied degrees of unwillingness to be involved in some music making. This may be, in part, based upon lack of previous successful experiences in this activity. Rather than looking upon student preferences as negative factors in learning music, the teacher should harness the preferences and not put undue stress upon the avoidance behavior that some of the students seem to have mastered. The preferences may be connected directly with skills and will change as the skills develop.

[3]Mursell, ibid.

Large-group activities can be planned in which the children who wish to sing can sing, the instrumentalists can play, and the composers and conductors can be involved as they wish. Students who do not want to be active are a special challenge for the teacher. Many adults have contact with music only through listening. For children who may already be exhibiting that kind of preference, it would not seem to be in their best interests to have them just sit in class. That would have a demoralizing effect upon others! Guided listening experiences to help the nonactive child may be of more ultimate good to that child than forcing him or her to join in class activities. Have a listening station in the room where children can use independent listening materials. Use music for the listening experiences that is familiar to these students but also include enough other pieces that they develop a more eclectic listening capability. Design the listening experience to focus on concepts; give them something to listen for.

Even while listening, children may observe something else they want to try and may voluntarily choose to broaden their involvement. When this occurs, the teacher must be available to help students with whatever entry behavior they need. It can be as simple as a quick lesson on how to handle a percussion instrument or as complicated as how to read rhythm patterns.

Peer teaching.   When the teacher cannot be available to help the student, an alternative to his or her immediate attention is peer tutoring. Although it is undesirable to ask the advanced child to teach continually, he or she can make a positive contribution by occasionally helping other students. A distinct advantage of peer tutoring is that children who have only recently learned something may have a much fresher perception of the process required for that particular learning to take place. It is sometimes amazing to observe how clearly a young person communicates exactly what is necessary to help a classmate understand. Some peer tutors also have a strong "take-charge attitude." On the other hand, if it is evident that the students are fooling around instead of working, the combination of students may be wrong. Recombine peers with the hope that a different match may work. Often peer tutoring is successful because the students develop respect for the accomplishments of their classmates.

Suitable literature.   Older students who have not experienced even the most basic concepts respond better if the music used to introduce them is different from that used in the primary grades. Some of the children in the class may have dealt with the concept of melodic direction many times. Reintroducing the concept again, but with more sophisticated words, music, instrumentation, and style keeps the experienced children interested in the literature while the inexperienced musician concentrates on the basic elements.

Questioning strategies.   Plan questioning strategies carefully. Save the difficult questions for the experienced children. Include more obvious responses for inexperienced children so they can participate rather than just listen to other children making observations.

Sequential planning.   Another way of recycling concepts is through new experiences. As you look at the musical activities the children have had before coming to your class, identify activities for them that they have not had previously. As you plan for six years of lessons, you should deliberately save special things for the older children so they don't feel as if they have done it all before. If the children have not studied recorders, introduce them in one of the upper grades and use the instrument as a vehicle for reviewing concepts or, in the case of the inexperienced student, introducing them. If the children have had no access to a synthesizer, save work with it for the upper grades. If the elementary school cannot purchase a synthesizer, borrow one from the high school or a friendly music store. The latter may have a rental plan for using the instrument for a short period of time. If the students' compositional activity has never included work with tape recorders, use that fascinating way to interest them anew in creativity.

Modular approach.   Change the style of class presentation for the upper grades. Consider using a modular approach through which certain emphases are offered to the class for a designated amount of time. If the emphasis is on instrumental work, divide the class according to instrumental interest, give them materials to work on in groups, and circulate to help where needed. A practical advantage of this approach is that the students will be more likely to have an instrument to try than they will if the whole class studies the same instrument at the same time. Schools with small budgets may not be able to equip an entire class with the same instrument.[4]

Develop a class project in which the children take different responsibilities. If they plan a school assembly, some of them can select the music to be used; others can be responsible for the movement, accompaniments, staging, costuming, audience participation; and so on.

Pose a specific musical problem for them to solve. A study of the beat in contemporary music will show them the use of duple meter in rock music. Ask them to bring examples of contemporary music to class that use triple meter. Analyze a piece of music for its form; ask them to find another example with the same form.

---

[4]For a description of a plan like this that worked, see Lois N. Harrison, "The Old Story: Frustrated Students, The New Ending: Independent Musicians," *Music Educators Journal,* May 1976, pp. 60–62.

Summary

No matter which of these varying approaches for the older elementary school children is used, the teacher must keep in mind the opportunities being made available for the contrasting ability levels of the children. The music program is succeeding if the talented children continue to grow, if previously inexperienced children are beginning to have musical success, and if children between these extremes are able to participate in a way that meets their needs also.

Recommended Resources

See recommended resources in the individualized/independent instruction section.

Macmillan publishing Co., Inc., and Silver Burdett Company have published attractive modules intended for upper-grade use.

Suggested Projects

1. Identify certain observable characteristics such as attitude, class participation, discipline, willingness to volunteer, and distribution of children answering questions. Make written observations of a primary class and an upper-grade class. Compare the observations.
2. Select one upper-grade class. Discuss the types of musical activities these children have experienced within the last two years with their teachers. Plan a musical activity for them different from any they have had in these last two years that deals with a basic concept on levels suitable for both experienced and inexperienced students.

MAINSTREAMING

Since the passage of Public Law 94-142 in 1975, educators have increased their efforts to make instruction available to every child in the least restrictive environment. Much time and energy has been spent in diagnosing the children's needs properly so that recommendations can be made for their best instruction. In spite of expert diagnosis, music class often shows contradictions in otherwise accurate information about the children. Handicapped students may not be handicapped as far as music is concerned. The study of music may be one of the most potent reinforcers the child has, especially if the child is limited in other subject areas. On the other hand, very capable students who show no reason to be called handicapped in any other area may have musical handicaps such as limited pitch perception, poor rhythmic response, and so on.

Whatever the nature of the musical handicap, the teacher must maintain a positive attitude toward prospective improvement. Many adults with no involvement in music can trace their dislike, or their incapability, back to specific situations in which an adult not only said that the child couldn't do something but made no effort to help the child learn to do it. After consistently being put with the *crows* instead of with the *canaries*, being turned away from membership in the chorus, overhearing a cruel remark about "that unmusical child," skill development in that area became psychologically impossible and eventually a handicap resulted, which persisted into adulthood. A consistently positive attitude toward children's progress and a sense of expectation emanating from the teacher are immeasurable in terms of value to the child's achievement at the highest level of which he or she is capable.

I. E. P. The Individualized Educational Program is a plan for the handicapped child's education. It is written by a team of teachers, administrators, parents, and specialists. They plan the child's school year based upon their concerns, knowledge of his or her capabilities, and judgment about what he or she can learn. Unfortunately, the music specialist is rarely included in the I.E.P. conference. The classroom teacher, who is normally included, is urged to consider, consistently, the benefits music can offer to most children and to include plans for musical development in each I.E.P. Whether or not you as the music specialist attend the I.E.P. conferences, you can discuss aspects of the handicapped child's musical education with members of the I.E.P. team and submit written recommendations for it. Information and advice from the I.E.P. team is also valuable for the specialist.

Each school has developed certain formats for writing I.E.P.s. They usually include long-range goals, short-range goals, identification of areas in which the child will have a normal program, specification of areas needing different kinds of treatment, special equipment or materials that may be needed, a timetable for accomplishing certain goals, the methods by which the goals will be accomplished, and means of evaluating progress toward the goals. The music teacher should use the school's format to help consider the handicapped child's musical education as thoroughly as other specialists are scrutinizing their areas of study. Even though musically handicapped children may not have general I.E.P.s written for them if music is their only handicapped area, it is beneficial for the teacher of music to write an I.E.P. for them, too.

When P.L. 94-142 was first passed and "mainstreaming" became mandatory, educators were apprehensive about putting handicapped children into environments that had not been open to them before. The reservations that teachers shared have resulted in their concern being translated into caring action for these children. Although a staggering amount of work would result, the demonstrated value of the I.E.P. probably indicates that one should be written for every child.

Identifying handicaps.   All teachers have a responsibility for identifying the child's handicaps, especially if they have not been found before the child enters school. Once the handicaps have been identified, it is important that teachers share as much information as they can to help the student. The classroom teacher can be invaluable in helping the specialist know the child's needs, problems, and plans for helping him or her.

Before the first music classes are held, the music teacher should meet the handicapped children, talk to them about the things they most like to do in music class, what they wish they could do, and adjustments they would like to have made in some aspects of the music program. This personal contact will enable the teacher to judge if the child can communicate effectively about his or her musical needs, or if the bulk of the diagnosis will have to come either from teacher observation or from other teachers and special education advisors.

The earlier the teacher can learn about the handicapped student, the better. Special equipment and/or textbooks may take longer to get than regular equipment. They should be ordered only after the teacher has had a chance to assess the needs of the student and talk to members of the special education team about the suitability of music plans for that particular child.

Teacher aides.   If teacher aides are available, their attention should be directed toward helping the handicapped child in areas of music that benefit from one-to-one instruction. The music teacher can train the aides in techniques related to pitch matching, ear training, and so on. The availability of a music teacher aide, or time built into the schedule for the music teacher to work with children in small groups or independently, should be considered when writing the I.E.P.

Advance planning.   If the class requires the student to be involved in an activity that he or she can do but that takes the student longer than anyone else, try to give the project to the handicapped student in advance. Think of alternatives to activities that may cause difficulty; for example, if the child can't write, can he or she respond by speaking or singing into a tape recorder?

General groups of handicaps.   The generalizations that follow about possible aids for handicapped children must be tempered with specific knowledge about the child and the exact nature of the handicap related to that individual and music.

Limited mobility. A primary consideration for the children with limited mobility is accessibility. Is it possible for them to get to the music room? Can they get on the stage where programs are held? Is the room designed so they can reach the equipment to be used in class? Once arrangements are made for the child to get to the music room, on stage, and to the necessary equipment, and if mobility is the only handicap, the child probably can participate in the regular music program except for activities involving movement.

If the child can move his or her arms, devise adaptations accordingly. When it is necessary to change locations with movement, such as in dancing, consider pairing the child with a mobile youngster who can push the wheelchair through the main parts of the dance. If the handicapped child clearly doesn't like this, it shouldn't be forced.

Equipment for activities in which this child will be involved should be placed within the child's reach to avoid a situation of dependency. The child may even have an individualized spot in which his or her musical equipment is kept to make it unnecessary to try to circumvent the various bottlenecks that sometimes appear in the music class. There should always be a route kept open for the child to get to the area in which he or she is to function.

Efforts must be made, too, to keep the sight lines open for the child in a wheelchair. If the children are standing and must see the chalkboard, find a place for the student who cannot stand so he or she has a view to the front.

Hearing impaired. There are many different forms of hearing impairment ranging from volume loss to various types of auditory perception problems. Before the teacher decides on musical recommendations for the child, it is necessary to know what the child cannot hear or has difficulty in hearing. If the loss is severe, the child will need to be put in a location where he or she can feel musical vibrations: touching an instrument, sitting on a piano (not recommended for upright pianos), being in contact with speakers of the stereo system. A wooden floor transmits music well. Put the speakers on the floor and let the children sit on the floor or feel the vibrations through bare feet.

If the child has difficulty in understanding words, particularly the words of a song, and is able to read, be sure the child has them in writing. If the child has difficulty in understanding the spoken word, give directions slowly and clearly, write key phrases and important words on the chalkboard. This may help the slow learner, too.

If the child has trouble with pitch, work individually to see if you can help the child to associate certain physical sensations with the pitches you produce vocally. Let the child feel your larynx as you sing; help the child to feel his or hers. Show the child what happens with high and low notes as you both sing.

Speech impaired. Therapists who work with the speech impaired child are a valuable resource. They can communicate with the teacher of music about the specific techniques they are using with the child. The music teacher can help by creating chants or songs to make the learning tasks more pleasurable.

Retarded. Just as the degrees of retardation vary, so do the musical capabilities of these children. Depending upon their degree of retardation, many of these children will eventually gain some skills that are expected of an adult, but it will take them much longer than the child who is not retarded. The teacher of music must provide experiences for retarded children that allow them to have many repetitions of the materials to be learned. Because these children have few verbal skills, direct involvement in making music is more valuable to them than talking about it. The music teacher must plan to meet the needs of many children in class: a complicated descant can challenge the musically gifted child, an appropriate song can be sung by the majority of the class, an attractive ostinato can be contributed by retarded children who need that kind of repetition.

Learning disabled. This category includes children with dyslexia, brain injury or dysfunction, perceptual problems, and developmental aphasia. The reader is urged to consult some of the fine resources available to derive musical insights on the best ways to help children with these forms of handicap. The same is true of children with specific *physical disabilities* including conditions such as missing limbs, rheumatoid arthritis, muscular dystrophy, cerebral palsy, spina bifida, and chronic health conditions; those with *psychological handicaps;* and the children who have *multiple handicaps.*

Visually impaired or blind. These children may have problems with mobility, so the considerations of accessibility must be explored with them as well. Reading is one of the blind child's greatest problems. If the child is partially sighted, large-print music may be used. Stands are available to keep the printed material close to the student's eyes and hold it there conveniently. An advantage of using large-print music is that the student's hands are free to manipulate an instrument.

Some children with impaired vision respond well to learning music aurally and add new pieces to their repertoire through using cassette tapes that help them to establish correct aural images. The teacher's responsibility is to make quality tapes for the student if they are not otherwise available.

The Optacon is an expensive device that scans regular print and then converts it into tactile stimuli that can be read by touch. This instrument is valuable for materials not accessible through any other means, but it involves a slow process.

If none of these alternatives is appropriate for the student, or if the student needs to use more than one technique, the blind student should consider learning to read music braille. The musician's involvement in the process is important because a braille specialist may not know music braille notation. It is different from regular braille. This is the musical alphabet:

Contrast it to the same letters of literary braille:

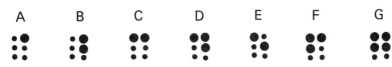

Six dots can be used in each braille unit or cell.

Rhythmic differentiation is accomplished by the placement of dots under the letter configuration. The C note shown is an eighth note.

To make a quarter-note C, a dot is added under the right side.

The dot is shifted to the left to represent a half note. When both dots appear under the note, it may be either a whole note or a sixteenth note depending on what else appears in the measure.

If one of the following symbols appears before a note, it represents the octave in which the note is to be played, counting from the lowest C on the piano. If it appears after the note, it represents the finger that is to play that note.

When accidentals are needed, they appear before the notes. flat ⠣ , sharp ⠩ , and natural ⠡ . The key and time signatures are shown before the notation begins.

These are rests: eighth ⠦ , quarter ⠧ , half ⠥ , and whole or sixteenth ⠴ . A bar line is shown by a space between the measures.

This limited introduction to music braille is enough to help the music teacher realize the different information needed by the blind student in contrast to the sighted student reading music. The National Library Service for the Blind and Physically Handicapped, Library of Congress, is a major source for braille, large-print, and recorded materials for the blind. A teacher working with a blind student for the first time should contact that institution immediately for help.[5]

If the music best suited for the student is not available in braille, the music teacher should gain access to either a braillewriter or a braille slate to produce it for the student.

Since mainstreaming was legislated, there has been much consideration of possible benefits to children *without* handicaps. These young people can learn to help others in need, to accept differences, to be creative in devising ways of overcoming obstacles, and to develop patience. Mainstreamed classes should benefit all their members.

Recommended Readings

ALVIN, JULIETTE, *Music for the Handicapped child.* London: Oxford University Press, 1976. Good insights on suitability of musical activities for child's process of musical maturation.

BESSOM, MALCOLM E., "Music in Special Education," *Music Educators Journal,* April 1972. An entire issue devoted to music and many special children.

DOBBS, J. P. B., "Teaching Music to Handicapped Children," in *Handbook for Music Teachers,* ed. B. Rainbow. London: Novello, 1968, pp. 131–138. Descriptions of various types of handicapped children with suggestions for their music education.

DYKMAN, RUTH ANNE, "In Step with 94-142, Two by Two," *Music Educators Journal,* January 1979, pp. 58–63. Article and pictures showing how regular-class children assist handicapped students.

FROEMKE, MARCIA STEWARD, "Supercalifragalistic," *Teaching Exceptional Children.* Reston, VA: Council for Exceptional Children, Fall 1976. Discussion of and examples to teach children nonmusical skills through song.

[5]Music Section, National Library Service for the Blind and Physically Handicapped, Library of Congress, Washington, D.C. 20542. Telephone via toll-free number 800-424-8567.
Another source of music and equipment is the American Printing House for the Blind, 1829 Frankfort Avenue, Louisville, KY 40206.

GILBERT, JANET PERKINS, "Mainstreaming in Your Classroom," *Music Educators Journal,* February 1977, pp. 64–68. Elaboration of limitations of retarded children with suggestions for coping with them in the mainstreamed music class.

GINGLEND, DAVID R., AND WINIFRED E. STILES, *Music Activities for Retarded Children.* Nashville, TN: Abingdon Press, 1965. Songs, dances, and other musical activities plus music that goes with them.

GRAHAM, RICHARD M., COMPILER, *Music for the Exceptional Child.* Reston, VA: Music Educators National Conference, 1975. Collection of chapters, each dealing with a specific handicap. Contributions are from music educators who have worked directly with the children whom they describe.

GRAHAM, RICHARD, AND ALICE BEER, *Teaching Music to the Exceptional Child.* Englewood Cliffs, NJ: Prentice-Hall, Inc., 1980.

GREER, R. DOUGLAS, AND LAURA G. DOROW, *Specializing Education Behaviorally.* Dubuque, IA: Kendall/Hunt Publishing Co., 1976. A behavioral approach to special education. Includes values, principles, and techniques.

HARDESTY, KAY W., *Silver Burdett Music for Special Education.* Morristown, NJ: Silver Burdett Company, 1979. Well-structured ways of adding music to experiences of handicapped children.

HARRISON, LOIS N., "Modifying Programs in Music Education," in *Impact of Mainstreaming on Educational Role Groups,* eds. Fay B. Haisley and Greg Weisenstein. New York: Allyn & Bacon, Inc., 1983. Deals with impact of mainsteaming on educational role groups. Main focus on deviations in materials and management necessary to accommodate various exceptionalities in regular educational settings.

HOUSEHOLD, NICKI, "An Ear for the Future," *North Dakota Music Educator,* March 1979, p. 16. Reprinted from the *London Daily Mail.* An account of Audrey Wishey's work with literacy problems and their relationship to hearing losses in infancy. She treats children whose problems have been related to dyslexia through regular pitch discrimination training.

KROLICK, BETTYE, *Dictionary of Braille Music Signs.* Washington, D.C.: National Library Service for the Blind and Physically Handicapped, Library of Congress, 1979.

KROLICK, BETTYE, *How to Read Braille Music.* Champaign, IL: Stipes Publishing Company, 1975.

LAMENT, MARYLEE MCMURRAY, *Music in Elementary Education.* New York: Macmillan Publishing Co., Inc., 1976. Chapter on special education in the regular classroom, pp. 275–316.

MADSEN, CLIFFORD K., R. DOUGLAS GREER, AND CHARLES H. MADSEN, JR., EDS., *Research in Music Behavior.* New York: Teachers College Press, 1975. The three parts of this book deal with (1) behavior modification relevant to music instruction and research methodology, (2) models for researchers and educators, and (3) an annotated bibliography.

NOCERA, SONA D., *Reaching the Special Learner Through Music.* Morristown, NJ: Silver Burdett Company, 1979. Includes many activities for special learners.

Project Beacon. Falls Church, VA: Fairfax County Public Schools, 1978. Music supplement to perceptual-motor activities developed by Department of Instructional Services, 6131 Willston Drive, Falls Church, VA 22044.

SHERIDAN, WILMA, *Oregon Plan for Mainstreaming in Music.* Salem, OR: Department of Education, 1977. A handbook for music teachers who are developing their understanding of the implications of mainstreaming. Examples of individual educational programs.

SLYOFF, MARTHA, *Music for Special Education.* Fort Worth, TX: Harris Music Publications, 1979. Sample lessons for children with various handicaps.

STUART, MELANIE, AND JANET GILBERT, "Mainstreaming: Needs Assessment Through a Videotape Visual Scale," *Journal of Research in Music Education,* Winter 1977, pp. 283–289. Videotape excerpts of atypical students were used to develop a scale measuring attitudes toward them and their behavior; the scale was then used to investigate reactions of music education and music therapy majors.

WARD, DAVID, *Hearts and Hands and Voices.* London: Oxford University Press, 1976. A warm description of music in the education of slow learners. Although these children were not in mainstreamed situations, many techniques are applicable.

ZANATTI, ARLETTE, "Melodic Memory Tests: A Comparison of Normal Children and Mental Defectives," *Journal of Research in Music Education,* Spring 1975, pp. 41–52. The performances of normal children and mental defectives were measured in a melodic memory test.

Suggested Projects

1. Volunteer to help with music needs for special eduation students in your local school system.
2. Describe a handicapped student. Write a music I.E.P. for that child.

AVOID DISCRIMINATORY PRACTICES

Since the 1960s, laws have been passed in the United States designed to lessen discriminatory practices. PL 94-142 was one of these laws. Others have dealt with rights and opportunities regardless of color, sex, age, national origin, or religion. The intent of the laws is clear; they are designed to give all people equal opportunities. Certainly they have increased sensitivity to the issues. Unfortunately, progress in dealing with discriminatory practices does not always keep pace with the law. Part of the problem is that common practices are so much a part of life that it is difficult to look at equal treatment of all segments of the population with clear vision. The musical life of the United States shows a pattern of discrimination that public school teachers must address.

Sex. The rock bands seen on television and heard from records nearly always have a stereotypical group of male instrumentalists, some of whom may be either backup or lead singers. If women are part of the group, they may be backup or lead singers; they are rarely part of the instrumental ensemble unless the group is all female. Even this is rare. The same patterns apply generally to country-western groups.

Symphony orchestras have begun to allow women to join their ranks. The more prominent the group's reputation, the lower the ratio of women members who appear in it. Women conductors are so rare that it is difficult to compile a list of them who are responsible for conducting major professional groups. Sarah Caldwell, frequent guest conductor, impresario, and founder of the Opera Company of Boston, is a brilliant exception.

Women singers seem to fare generally better than instrumentalists; their voices are heard especially in opera, oratorio, and in Broadway musical productions to provide the contrasts of range and timbre needed in those works. Although there are boy choirs of national and international fame, girl choirs have not been sponsored in an attempt to achieve that same stature.

Few women composers are included in music history books, on concert programs, or as teachers of composition in conservatories or universities.

Music teachers of young children are most often women; secondary school ensemble conductors are generally men; higher-education professors are overwhelmingly male.

Age.   Like elder statesmen, conductors seem to become more appreciated as they grow in musical understanding. Notable examples are Eugene Ormandy of the Philadelphia Orchestra who retired in 1980 at the age of 81, and Arthur Fiedler who led the Boston Pops up until the time of his death at the age of 85.

Although it is not legal to discriminate against persons because of age, some music schools are reluctant to allow performers past a certain age to enter their programs; when hiring professors, the person's age is invariably discussed.

Color.   When listening to a major symphony orchestra from a city whose population is predominantly black, it is distracting to realize that the low percentage of black musicians does not approach the percentage of the black population in that city.

Handicapped.   Some of the best reasons for listening to handicapped performers are furnished by the performers themselves: Stevie Wonder and Itzhak Perlman on any terms are superior musicians.

Textbooks.   Children's music textbooks seem to be improving in regard to picturing children of various colors. The current textbooks also tend to present more music reflecting other cultures. In reviewing third grade books from four major music textbook publishers[6] it was revealed that

> One book had ten pictures of black children; the other books included three, six, and seven pictures of black children.
> Four to seven pictures of Oriental children were included in each of the four textbooks.

[6]They were American Book Company 1976,; Holt, Rinehart and Winston, Publishers 1975; Macmillan Publishing Company, Inc., 1978 and Silver Burdett Company, 1978.

American Indians were identified in two pictures in two of the books, one in the third, and none in the fourth.

Two books showed one picture each of an Eskimo child.

In the same survey, no one in any of the four books was pictured with a handicap. Two books showed one picture each of a person wearing eyeglasses. One book showed two pictures of children with imperfect teeth.

Only three pictures showed anyone who looked elderly: one was a composer, one was George Washington, and the other was a witch. A bald person appeared in two pictures.

The total number of boys pictured in all four books was 207 (52 percent); 191 (48 percent) girls were shown. Some 69 (65 percent) men were included in pictures; 37 (35 percent) women were shown. In only one book were there more female pictures than male. The five conductors who appeared were all men.

It appears from this limited survey that people who participate in music, or in activities associated with music as shown in these textbooks, do not reflect society as it actually is, insofar as the aged and handicapped are concerned. Nor do they present nondiscriminatory sex-role models as effectively as they might.

Research.   Abeles and Porter[7] have substantiated discriminatory practices in four studies related to the sex stereotyping of musical instruments. Their findings suggest that in

Study 1:   The association of gender with musical instruments exists in the general population. The adults in the study preferred clarinet, flute, and violin for their daughters, while drum, trombone, and trumpet were preferred for their sons.

Study 2:   Both musicians and nonmusicians were similar in their instrument gender associations; the same general masculine-feminine association with instruments appeared as in Study 1.

Study 3:   The maximum difference between the sexes in instrument gender associations occurs around third and fourth grade. Selections by boys remain relatively stable at the masculine end of the scale developed in the first two studies; selections by girls from kindergarten until they selected an instrument moved toward the so-called "feminine" instruments. The girls regularly chose a wider variety of instruments.

Study 4:   Young boys responded differently to an unbiased presentation of the instruments than to the two other conditions; girls were generally not affected by the mode of presentation.

Abeles and Porter suggested that, even though gender association is widespread throughout all age groups, its impact may be diminished by

[7]Abeles, Hal and Susan Porter, "The Sex-Stereotyping of Musical Instruments," *Journal of Research in Music Education*, Summer 1978, pp. 65–75.

careful initial presentation of the instruments, with consistent reinforcement of nonstereotyped instrumental selection.

Religious.   A number of court cases have been tried in recent years dealing with the possibility of religious discrimination on the part of music educators. The cases seem most often connected with the performance of religious music, especially at Christmas time. The ruling of the Supreme Court in November 1980 upheld "a lower court ruling upholding school district guidelines that allow some religious music and materials to be used in programs marking holidays such as Christmas."[8] The interpretation indicated that, as long as the music demonstrates a significance no longer confined to the religious sphere and is part of our national culture and heritage, it can be used with public school groups. The main concern is that the music not be used in a way that will be offensive to students having beliefs differing from those expressed in the Christmas music.

In an effort to avert problems, many schools now have winter vacations and holiday concerts instead of Christmas vacations and concerts. The teacher of music is urged to be sensitive to the community in dealing with this issue. If you are unsure as to when to include religious music in concert programs, consult with your administrators.

Suggested Projects

1. Plan and execute a research project dealing with discriminatory practices in music. Possible components of the project may be textbooks, concerts, performing group members, and identification of people holding certain jobs or salaries.
2. Write a lesson plan for a grade level of your choice based upon a concept of equal opportunity in music.

KEEP IN TOUCH WITH FAMILIES

Try to make frequent contacts with families. Involve family members in the music program as much as possible so they can help the children make music and participate in it themselves.

Report cards and conferences.   These approaches have traditionally been the most common ways of keeping in touch with families about their children. The report card sometimes is simply a listing of subjects and grades, but more often, especially in the primary grades, it takes the form of commentary about the child's progress. These contacts are made with

[8]"Christmas Ruled Legal for Schools," *Eugene Register-Guard,* November 10, 1980, p. 1.

families periodically throughout the year to let families know how their children are doing in school.

Unfortunately, in many schools, music does not become part of the parental reports until the end of the school year when an "S" for satisfactory is placed on the card next to the word "Music." An alternative is to put a "U" for unsatisfactory, but in elementary school the "U" is rarely used for music. Putting an "S" on a report card once a year does not seem to give parents much information about their children's musical progress.

In getting ready for parent conferences and in writing commentaries, the classroom teacher has a tremendous responsibility for many subjects. Music teachers may have hundreds of students and are fortunate if they know who all the children are by the time the first report to the parents takes place. These factors work against communication. The classroom teacher and the music teacher must combine their knowledge about each child and try to concentrate on specific items related to him or her during the report period so that not only do they give feedback of musical information to the parents, but at the same time they can determine the child's needs and help him or her grow musically.

During the first marking period, the music teacher should determine at least one specific objective for each of the grades and use that objective as a guide in determining each child's progress. For example, in first grade during the first report period, the objective can be to improve the child's capability in pitch matching. The information sent to the parent can be

> "Jo needs to work on pitch matching."
> "Susan shows great progress in matching pitches with her voice."
> "Jim sings very accurately."

Parents may respond to these comments: Jo's musical parents, concerned about her pitch-matching problem, may request a conference to discuss it further. The teacher will then have an opportunity to discuss the work she is doing with Jo and can suggest ways in which her parents can do additional work with her at home.

Jim's parents may be delighted to hear about his accurate singing because there has been little else to celebrate in the rest of his first report.

Even though the teachers are concentrating on only one main objective in reporting to parents during the first marking period, other pertinent comments should be added if possible. For many of the more than four hundred children in his or her care, the music teacher may not have much to report. The children who are especially talented will have been identified, as will those who need extra help, and those who tend to upset the class. These observations should be shared with the classroom teacher who can pass them on to the parents in their conferences. The classroom teacher should know about children having problems in music class so that parents and teachers working together can develop plans to help.

Since the music teacher can't schedule conferences with all the parents, it will be helpful if music and classroom teachers work together in selecting parents for music conferences. The music teacher can add to the information that the classroom teacher has shared and make specific musical recommendations for the child. The music teacher should strive to schedule appointments with parents whose children are doing well in music, not only those who have difficulty.

Frequent home tasks.   There are more immediate ways to let families know what is happening in music class other than by the report card or the conference. Be creative about sending musical tasks home with the children. Here are just a few suggestions for having the children take music home. Ask the children to

1. Sing a well-known song for the people they eat dinner with that night.
2. Teach a person younger than they are to sing a favorite song. If they cannot find someone younger, let them choose the person they wish to teach.
3. Take home the paper they completed in music class.
4. Finish their incomplete paper at home.
5. Show someone else how to make _____ (whatever symbol they learned to make in class).
6. Bring to class on Tuesday a rhythm pattern they have written themselves.
7. Bring to class an art project associated with music.
8. Take some independent study tapes home.
9. Take some instruments and job cards home to use over the weekend.
10. Bring a plan for playing A B A C A form with nonpitched instruments to class on Wednesday. Talk to friends about the plan in advance so they know who will be in their group and what they will be expected to do.
11. Take a job card home with instructions for creating music using materials available at home (kitchen utensils, food containers, bottles or glasses, etc.).
12. Collect materials at home to be used in exploring sound and bring them to school. The teacher may send a list home so the parents can help the student gather materials. If they are for a certain class, the note should give information about the date on which they are needed.
13. Ask the parents to write on a piece of paper the name of the song they liked best when they were in school. Ask them to write the name of their favorite song now.
14. Listen to music tonight with someone else at home. Write the name of the piece(s) they listened to.

Follow-up of home tasks.   These tasks cannot be given to the children with no follow-up. Devise ways in which to show the children you care about whether or not they do what you have asked.

1. Ask for general feedback such as, "Raise your hand if you sang at dinner last night." Then, ask specific questions: "What song did you sing, Sally?" or "Did you teach your song to your family, James?" Allow the children a chance to

volunteer information about their experiences with family singing, but limit it in a way that will not hurt feelings. Young children, especially, want to share tales of their adventures. While their stories can be very interesting, they may take all the instruction time. Limiting statements should be used: "Let's take two minutes to hear about some of your adventures" or "We have time to hear special stories from three people now."

2. Ask the children for specific written work as they enter class. Be prepared to collect forgotten papers during the next music class if necessary; it is a rare class when everyone remembers!

3. Ask the first people bringing in their rhythm papers to put their patterns on the board for the whole class to clap.

4. Check on the papers (if any) that were done with the independent study tapes.

5. Have the children play what they learned on the instrument they took home over the weekend. Be sure the instruments come back when they are supposed to.

6. Let the children who planned their A B A C A form get out the instruments they will need and prepare their group to play the example they created.

7. Loan a tape recorder or ask the child to use his or her machine to tape the results of the job card assignment done at home. Play the tape for the class.

8. Let the students know how pleased you are when the collected sound exploration materials begin arriving in class.

9. Have a conspicuous place to display the songs and listening music the children had their families write down for them (after you have added the names to your master list). Try putting a listening tree next to the music room listening center on which the home returns can be taped.

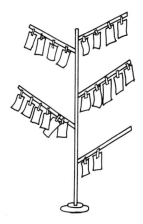

Use a song string in front of the room. The children will be happy to watch it grow. Ask the janitor to help put up a string or wire so the song titles can be attached to it as they come in.

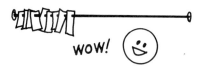

WOW!

Family description.   In talking about work to be done at home, or other family involvement, be careful not to imply that all family groups fit a two-parent model. An assignment directing the child to do something with his father can have a negative effect on the child who does not have a father or who does not see him often. General terms may save the feelings of the child whose family may not conform to a stereotyped expectation. Descriptions of work to be done at home with somebody may include family members, friends, someone older than you are, someone you like to make music with, someone who would like to make music with you.

Record keeping.   Charts or a grade book will help the music teacher to keep track of the individual's progress. The teacher who works with over four hundred students must think in terms of efficiency. A simple check after the child's name may indicate that he or she can show melodic direction with body movement. A question mark after another student's name may simply indicate that the teacher should observe that child during the next few classes to see how the child is doing. A dash indicates to the teacher that this child needs help in perceiving melodic direction. Save space next to these marks. A few weeks later, the teacher should make additional observations to see if progress in this skill has taken place.

Invitations.   Some parents are aware of the school's music program only when they are invited to come to the REALLY BIG CONCERT before the holidays or at the end of the school year. As enjoyable as these programs are, they often do not communicate the depth or the spectrum of the curriculum. More frequent invitations to the parents to enter into the musical lives of the children can be designed effectively. Parents with flexible daytime schedules should be invited to come to certain music classes and then be made welcome to come anytime they wish. Involving the parents in the musical activities is desirable so the lesson does not become a concert. Some evening events can be arranged for parents who work during the school day, perhaps in conjunction with the Parent Teachers Association or Back-to-School Night.

The intergenerational contact need not be based on the music making of the children alone. The song string came from songs sung by parents, perhaps grandparents, too, and can be the basis for a community sing. If you have noted the songs and tabulated them, you will have an idea of the parents' repertoire. The most popular songs on the list should be taught to the children, used in concept development, developed instrumentally, and be associated with movement. The invitation to the parents should mention the results of the poll and tell them that the children are preparing to join with them in some of the good old favorites. Teacher discretion will be exercised in selecting the final list of songs to be sure they are appropriate for the children as well as the parents.

Other ways of sharing with families will be suggested by the talents of the parents themselves. Guitar players, other instrumentalists, dancers, and singers can be invited to come to perform for the children. Instrument makers and music store owners may generously invite the children to come to their stores for demonstrations. Church musicians will be happy to show the children their pipe organs; some churches with harpsichords will add them to the musical tour. Managers of theaters and concert halls are often generous hosts, as are the music teachers in middle, junior, and senior high schools who will demonstrate instruments, give concerts with their performing groups, and even come to the elementary school with special programs. Composers are sometimes willing to talk to the children about their ways of working with the raw materials of music, presenting their compositions to the children and even giving the young musicians a chance to be involved in their creative process. Older musicians will be willing to form backup groups when the elementary school children perform their musical plays. As these children become adept at playing instruments, they benefit from playing in ensembles with musicians more skilled than they. Once the musical door is open for sharing, remarkable benefits for the students can accrue.

Suggested Projects

1. Describe three musical tasks children can take home.
2. Plan an activity in which families can be involved with the school music classes.

15 Nurture

Nurture music through the school. Provide opportunities for the children to make music spontaneously and creatively. Encourage them to weave music into the total pattern of their lives.

Teacher cooperation. The school with a music specialist and classroom teachers making music with the children is on its way to adequate nurturing of music. The roles of the teachers can be defined clearly, or they can be flexible, with each teacher having responsibility for leadership as the occasion demands. A highly desirable partnership exists when the music program is carried on daily by the classroom teacher, with the music specialist acting as a resource person for materials, strategies, ideas, musical problem solving, and in direct contact with the children several times a week. All teachers working with the musical education of the children establishes continuity and provides adequate musical involvement.

At a school in which the music teacher alone provides music instruction, lapses between lessons are woefully long; concepts being taught are left without teacher reinforcement. If the classroom teacher cannot be involved in music instruction, sufficient time should be allotted to the music teacher to meet with the children on a daily basis.

Some schools do not have music specialists. The classroom teacher is expected to be the sole provider of the instruction or, in unfortunate situations, is *not* expected to provide music instruction, which means that the children do not engage in any music activities.

It is rare that an elementary teacher does not have the capability to share music in some way with children. If all elementary educators could develop a sense of confidence in their own abilities to contribute to the musical life of the child, and keep working to bolster their skills in making music, vast numbers of children would be the beneficiaries. Classroom teachers are encouraged to observe the highly capable people who are not specialists but who carry on excellent music programs with the children. The advantage of the classroom teacher in music instruction is that he or she can weave it appropriately through the entire day.

New music teachers will find that experienced classroom teachers will help them in many ways, not the least of which will be in techniques that work with the children, especially in classroom management. These same teachers will be grateful to the music specialist for help in finding music needed for specific purposes, for working with the children on advanced musical skills, for planning concept development, and for providing alternative ways of instruction.

Constraints.   Classroom and music teachers cannot always provide the ideal music program because of circumstances beyond their control. Contracts are sometimes negotiated carefully to provide the teachers with preparation time during the periods the music teacher comes to the classroom. Budgetary considerations control the number of music teachers for a school system and the time they devote to each class. When the contracts are negotiated and the budgets are set up, other areas may have a higher priority than the music program. Teachers are urged to become eloquent in speaking for adequate time to be spent with the children in music.

The principal.   A most influential person in setting district policy is the principal, who can be a powerful advocate for a good music program with other members of the administration and the board of education. Teachers and principal working together may be able to devise alternative ways of scheduling to provide more music instruction. They may utilize instructional resources in ways that will concentrate the teacher's greatest capabilities most effectively with the children.

The principal should be included in the music program as much as possible, both in making music with the children and in planning for various aspects of its implementation. The principal's interest, leadership, and commitment to the music program can be the largest single factor in nurturing music throughout the school.

All-school involvement.   Some of these ideas have worked very well with administrative support.

1. Rather than scheduling the music teacher's time straight through the day, time is left for consultant work and individual and small-group instruction.
2. The classroom teacher and music specialist agree on a project in which they will both work with the children. They arrange for large blocks of time in which to concentrate on the project rather than short, irregularly spaced periods.
3. Classroom and music teachers develop a theme to include the entire school. One result is classes sharing with each other.
4. The music teacher develops a musical unit, such as recorder playing. The classroom teachers implement it; the specialist visits the classes periodically to give extra help.
5. Time is made available in which the music teacher gives the classroom teachers workshops on new techniques.
6. Some classes are scheduled so that children of the same ability level rather than just grade level have music instruction together.
7. Special-interest groups are formed in the school with teachers having a particular specialty meeting with students interested in that specialty (e.g., guitar, modern dance, musical drama, contemporary music).

Judicious rehearsal time. Much concern is expressed today about tumbling test scores. The reasons for the depressed scores have been debated elsewhere. This concern is interjected in this discussion to help the music teacher keep rehearsal time, especially for shows involving children, in perspective with regard to the responsibilities of the rest of the school program. The musical show or concert that forces the entire school to shut down for endless practice does little to dispel the notion that the music program can work against the children learning the "basics." (Adults expressing that notion lose sight of the fact that music is basic, also.) Probably any production by the children that requires an inordinate amount of extra time indicates that someone has lost perspective. Adequate time spent on music instruction as a regular part of the curriculum can result in performances demonstrating learning as well as being enjoyed thoroughly by the spectators without demolishing other parts of the school program.

Mountaintop experiences, such as shows put on by the children, may be the best remembered highlight of the year. They can be most important for children who achieve in music and, perhaps, not in much else. They can provide opportunities for children to be creative in a wide variety of ways. But the time spent must be kept in perspective along with the rest of the school's program.

AN EXPERIENCE THAT NURTURED MUSIC THROUGHOUT THE SCHOOL WITHOUT JEOPARDIZING THE REST OF THE PROGRAM[1]

About eight weeks before the December vacation, some of the teachers met in the faculty lounge to talk about a school celebration to be held

---

[1]Hilltop School, Mendham, NJ, Ralph Scheffert, principal.

just before vacation time. They were interested in providing creative musical experiences for the children, along with drama and dancing. They also wanted to foster a strong sense of respect on the part of the children for both older and younger students who were in the same building (kindergarten through grade four). Within each class, they wished to encourage the students to grow in cooperative endeavor.

The productive conversation resulted in a plan to take the entire school to *Christmas on the Moon*. Each grade level was to devise a short exposition of its perception of what it would be like to celebrate on that distant satellite and share their imaginings with the rest of the school. Time was rationed equally among the groups so the program would be less than an hour. To use every precious moment, the children went into action as they left their seats to ascend the stairs on stage right.

The children were involved with the classroom teacher and the music specialist in deciding how their presentation time would be spent. Once the groups had created their material, they rehearsed with both the music and classroom teachers. From the time the first-graders headed for the stage lustily singing, "Don't throw that moonball, safety first," set to an original melody, through the third-graders' brilliant rhythm routine in which they swirled flashlights on the darkened stage, until finally the fourth-graders helped Santa Claus arrive on the moon via a rocket ship that flew across the auditorium to explode center stage and reveal Santa happily greeting the children, the sharing program was a productive and enjoyable experience. The same was true of the preparation for it. The teachers and the children wrote some poetry for the lyrics they wanted to sing. Some of the music was original; some was already written. The instrumentation was mostly created by the children. Much of the inspiration for the class acts came from the students. The children planned costumes, stage decorations, and lighting—all simple and inexpensive. The second-graders decorated a moon tree: a maple branch sprayed with silver paint and dusted with glitter. The ornaments were recycled orjects altered for the moon celebration. The second graders put bows on tin cans, decorated paper towel rolls to give them an icicle (or candle?) appearance, and crumpled aluminum foil in a variety of ways.

Every child in the school was part of the program. Every child was part of the audience. The teachers carefully monitored the time spent so that studies in other areas were not neglected even in the days just before the holiday. Students, teachers, and administrators put their best efforts into the program so that it would be a pleasant experience for all.

The advantages of *Christmas on the Moon* clearly included strengthening music instruction for the children. The motivation was very high. The students spent time outside of school thinking about creative contributions; this was evidenced by children bursting into school with new ideas. Enough time was allowed before the program was presented so that creative alternatives could be explored. The program wasn't set until a few hours before the second (and last) rehearsal that each grade level had on the stage. (There was no dress rehearsal; the entire school shared the program only once.) In the decision-making process, the students had ample opportunity to try different timbres in accompaniments, to change song lyrics, and to respond rhythmically to music in a variety of fashions.

The music program provided a vehicle to enable the children and teachers to work cooperatively on a common venture. The spirit of that endeavor carried on long after the holidays. The classroom and music teachers renewed efforts to plan music classes jointly They discussed the scope of the music learning from grade to grade and the expectation for each class with heightened interest. Probably the most significant nonmusical achievement of the program was the spirit of the school. It is not easy to define, but the inhabitants of the school seemed happier to be there, more friendly with each other, and certainly more aware of the other people who studied there.

For many years afterward, similar creative efforts were put together by teachers and students of that school. The faculty wisely did not try to duplicate *Christmas on the Moon;* each year brought a different kind of joint effort. One of the strongest reasons for the survival of the programs was the balance that was always evident in creative activity and the concentration upon the other aspects of the curriculum.

One mildly negative factor in the programs stemmed from the fact that, since the shows were for the children, and the auditorium would hold only the student body, parents were not invited. Every year, some parents would come, taking the few empty seats and standing where they could. Ideas were advanced on how to include the community, but each year, the faculty decided that the spontaneity of the effort would be jeopardized by making it into a public performance or by doing the program more than once. Decisions such as this are not easy to make; the educators hoped in this case that the educational benefits to the children would outweigh the disadvantages to the parental outreach.

Strategic placement of equipment. Besides the involvement of people working together to nurture music throughout the school, equipment made available to the students at strategic places in the building can help, too.

Every classroom should have a listening center where records, tapes, independent instruction, and filmstrips can be used by the students. Tape recorders, a phonograph, earphones, patch cords, and junction boxes should be readily available to provide the flexibility necessary to make these listening areas function properly.

Areas should be set aside where the children can use instruments, experiment with sound, and engage in creative musical experiences without inflicting unwanted sound on students who are studying. When a new

school is planned, dialogue should be initiated with the planning committees and the architect to see if soundproof areas near or in classrooms are
possible.

The library should be considered a media center. When children go
to the library to check out textbooks, they should have tapes, records, and
books with floppy discs available to check out also. Children with no resources at home should be able to borrow tape players. Listening stations
should be part of every library so children can choose their materials selec-
tively by listening to them as well as looking at them. There should be times
when the child can go to the library to listen to materials as well as in the
classroom and at home.

Music in the environment.   Just as art works should be part of the
human environment, so should musical objects. Paul Bodin and his children installed a pitched percussion instrument made of pipes on the playground near the school office of the Edgewood School (Eugene, Oregon)
in 1975. As children go past it, they knock the pipes together or strike them
with anything that happens to be available. One of the first things visitors to
the school do is experiment with the instrument. (In the years it has been
hanging there, it's been left unharmed, while nearby recreational equipment has been subject to vandalism.) The pipes adorn the playground both
as a center of musical activity and as a work of art.

Paul Bodin's latest installation is at the Howard School (Eugene,
Oregon), where the pitched percussion instrument hangs in the hallway
near the principal's office. It extends an attractive invitation for musical
involvement.

Summary

Nurturing music throughout the school with an abundance of creative effort by the children, teachers, and administrators is part of a plan
for life in which music will continue to be an integral component of the
child's artistic involvement.

Suggested Projects

1. Describe a means for nurturing music throughout the school not mentioned
   in this chapter.
2. If you plan to be a classroom teacher, list five ways in which you can be
   involved effectively in the music program. List five ways in which the music
   teacher can help you.
3. If you plan to be a music teacher, list five ways in which you and the classroom
   teacher can work together with the children. List five ways in which the
   classroom teacher can help you. List five ways in which you can make the
   classroom teacher's work in music easier because of the help or resources that
   you can provide.

16 Grow

Graduation from college is just the beginning. Even as an experienced teacher you are always responsible for continuing your musical education.

Read. Research has been mentioned in Chapter 13 as a way of continuing your development, specifically by reading professional materials. However, reading should not be confined to those resources only. Both music and education operate in a larger framework of human existence. While newspapers, magazines, and novels do not require the depth of concentration required by professional reading, they do give the teacher further insight into the world. Historical, scientific, and psychological materials, while not obviously related to music education, help the teacher to cultivate a broad view of civilization. In fact, this paragraph is meant to encourage you to maintain a lifelong receptivity to scholarship. Even seemingly unrelated areas may ultimately contribute a great deal to the quality of music education through the creative insights they foster that can be integrated and applied to the subject. Browsing in libraries and music and book stores is a highly recommended activity.

Make music. Keep yourself involved in music on an adult level as well as with the children. Find an orchestra, choir, band, opera group, or small ensemble with which to meet regularly. If you are a soloist, continue to work with an accompanist either for your own pleasure or to present your music to others. Some of your adult music making may be shared directly with the children by having your group give concerts for the schools. Other effects on your professional life will be the continuation of your growth in musicianship and the nurturing of your enthusiasm for creating and re-creating music.

The encouragement of your participation in musical groups is not intended to be a political move, but it is realistic to note that your involvement with community musicians, your interpretation of what is happening with the children's music, and your encouragement of their efforts on behalf of the children can be very beneficial to the school music program.

Lead. If you teach in an area with few organizations of the type just mentioned, you will be a valuable resource to the community. Find kindred spirits and take the initiative to start adult musical organizations. This interest in adults will help you to discover musical resources that may have been unidentified previously.

1. People who have had professional training but for a variety of reasons have not pursued their music making.
2. Talented musicians from high school and college days whose busy lives have settled down now so they can return to music making.
3. Fellow teachers who enjoy performing together.
4. Composers who live in the area but who previously have had no opportunity to have their works performed.
5. Material resources, including instruments stored in the attic and unplayed for years.
6. Money donated by businesses willing to sponsor arts activities.
7. Individuals who are happy to attend musical events and support them even though they do not wish to be active in their production.
8. Space for rehearsals to be loaned in support of the new groups.

Locate as many local musicians and musical resources in the area as you can. Even if you are not immediately associated with some of the local musicians, learn about them as potential resources. Instrumental craftspeople, whether they are making slit drums or violins, can teach you and the children about their craft. The bagpipe player will not fit into a conventional orchestra, but his expertise may willingly be shared with you and the children.

Study. Maintain your association with colleges and universities in your area, taking courses even when you don't have to. Explore the resources of special music education collections and laboratories if they are available. In the summer, plan to spend some time in another area of the country or in other countries, taking courses that are the specialty of a particular institution. Seek a variety of viewpoints on varying processes in making music with children to find the best synthesis for your children and you that is possible. A summer vacation combined with study and a living experience away from your immediate vicinity can be a vitalizing experience.

Professional organizations and conferences. Join professional organizations and be active in them. The Music Educators National Conference is the organization that speaks for public school music throughout the United States. Its *Music Educators Journal* comes to members throughout the year with a wealth of interesting articles. The MENC sponsors national conferences in various parts of the country so that talented musicians, music educators, and leaders in other fields concerned with music education can share their expertise.

The MENC has six divisions throughout the United States. At the present time, the eastern and northwest divisions continue to hold biennial conferences for members who cannot travel to the MENC national meetings. Each state has its own music educators organization. The state groups have developed patterns of conferences and workshops to meet the needs and professional patterns of their own constituencies. The value of these national, divisional, and state MENC groups is that they include music educators with different kinds of specialties. Associated groups include band directors, string teachers, jazz educators, and choral directors. A proposal to begin a general music association as part of MENC was passed by an overwhelming majority in 1981. Elementary music teachers are urged to take an active part in helping this organization to get started and shape its direction to their needs.

Classroom teachers should also explore the benefits to be derived from these professional music educators' organizations. Almost all the MENC-sponsored activities have sessions to help the elementary classroom teacher in bringing music to children. Some of the conferences have a special fee to encourage participation by classroom teachers as well as the music specialist. Local in-service days are often designed to be of benefit to both the music specialist and the classroom teacher.

In the beginning of your professional career, you will be the beneficiary of the presentations at these conferences by experienced educators. As you develop professionally, you will find yourself involved increasingly in planning the conferences, identifying needs to be met by in-service education, and perhaps presenting sessions. Throughout the music educators' organizations there exists a high level of generous sharing, which is part of a profession seeking to give students the best music education possible.

Evaluate. One of the most important aspects of your continued professional growth will be your attention to improving the process through which you teach the children.

During the student teaching experience, help with lesson evaluation can be obtained from the public school cooperating teacher and the supervising college teacher. After student teaching is completed, beginning teachers must continue to improve their teaching. At the outset the children will help with this. Their immediate reactions in class give many clues as to the effectiveness of the style of presentation. Confusion in answering questions, bedlam in executing a change of activity, and so on, will indicate the need for improving questioning strategies and direction giving. Evaluation of lessons based upon the writing of the behavioral objectives will point to techniques in need of strengthening if the musical behaviors are not established.

The principal will probably observe the beginning teacher and may or may not be able to help with musical techniques. The principal will probably be very helpful in making suggestions related to classroom management and treatment of individual children. If there is a music supervisor, that person can be most helpful in suggesting techniques related specifically to teaching music.

Whether or not this kind of supervision is available to the beginning teacher, there will still be the need for a great deal of self-evaluation. The use of the cassette tape recorder is very helpful for this. It should be turned on at the beginning of a lesson to run without stopping. The lesson can be analyzed later in solitude. Specific items should be identified:

1. Determine the ratio of positive to negative comments. If the negatives are high, how can you communicate in that particular situation with a more positive approach?

2. Tabulate the time spent in nonmusical activity such as passing out materials, finding equipment, and getting the attention of the class. Devise alternatives for the procedures that are wasting the time.

3. Listen to the questions you ask the children. Are they clear? Does the student response indicate comprehension? Is the response dependent upon subject matter knowledge or ability to decipher the reply the teacher is looking for? How can you restate the questions for greater clarity? Are they useful questions?

4. Determine the students' responses to the directions given. Do the directions contain enough information? Do the students follow them? If not, what is missing?

5. Check the behavioral objectives in the lesson against what is heard on the tape. It is important to concentrate upon the musical behaviors to see if what you hear on the tape corresponds to what you thought you heard in class.

The videotape is even better than the audio cassette tape for teaching evaluation. With that tool, you can observe body language, facial expression, movement, and reactions. If the school owns that type of equipment, it may be readily available.

Summary

The suggestions for continuing your musical education will leave you with no sleep if you try to follow them all. Relax! Especially after your first year, when you have a grasp of the scope of the year's work, when you have accumulated necessary materials, and when you know what you must add to the program, your life will become less hectic. When this happens, it becomes easier to develop your professional life from the perspective of your deepest desires and most important goals. Teaching music to elementary school children is an enjoyable vocation as well as a responsible one. Because the children are forming habits, attitudes, and skills for the rest of their lives, you must be one of the finest musical influences they will have.

Although they may lose sight of exactly what happened to them musically in elementary school, you may be directly responsible for the vocational and avocational choices they make in the future. The expertise and the joy you bring to the children's musical experiences are part of their aesthetic response now! They are part of the foundation upon which they will build their musical lives. All people who teach music should be working toward the day when every child is able to function independently as a musician. Whether the young musicians choose to be involved as singers, instrumentalists, creators, dancers, or listeners, teachers of music are responsible for giving them enough skills and positive affective input so that each child is able to make, interpret, and enjoy music.

Suggested Projects

1. Compare a videotape, audiotape, and live observation of the same lesson. What are the advantages and disadvantages of each?
2. Make a list of books you want to read in the near future. Check the list in one year to see how much you have been able to read.
3. Contact one of your state music educators association officers. Volunteer to help the state general music organization plan its next conference.
4. List articles of interest to the general music teacher in the last four issues of the *Music Educators Journal*.

Index

Religious, 313
Repeated phrases approach, 83
Report cards, 313–315
Research, 217–219, 283–286,
    312–313, 325
Resources, 12
Recommended Resources, 68,
    155–156, 160, 164–165,
    181, 187, 199, 210,
    221–222, 237–238, 245,
    250, 253, 266–267, 278,
    282, 296–297, 302
Responsibility, divided, 141
Retarded, 306
Retuning, guitar, 161
Rhythm, 16–17, 21, 104, 182, 219
    syllables, 244
Richards, 257–258
"Ringing Bells," 176
"Rock Row," 57–59
Rote teaching, 88
Rounds, 114
"Row and Waltz," 56
"Row as You March," 56
"Row, Row, Row Your Boat,"
    55–57, 114, 141, 170

"Save Electricity," 140
School day, 260
"School Song," 58
Schuman, 206–209
Science, 263
Score, 33
"Scotland's Burning," 63
Sequence, 12, 17
Sequencing, 36
Sequential planning, 301
"Seven Joys of Christmas," 94
Sex, 310–313
"She'll Be Coming 'Round the
    Mountain," 225–226
Short specials, 210
Simplifying chords, 161
Singing, 15, 21, 25, 28, 53–129
    conversations, 73
    exercises, 73
Sirens, 72
Social studies, 263–265
"Solar Energy," 84–85, 88
Sol-fa, 241, 245
Song:
    pentatonic, 178

presentation, 78–79
teaching, 77–87
writing, 223–234
Sound effects with stories, 72–73
Speech impaired, 306
Stations, 288–289
Steady beat, 182, 190
Stories, 224
Streisand, 202
Strums
    autoharp, 157
    guitar, 160–161
Student leaders, 70
Studio upright, 167
Study, 326–327
Substitute teacher, 35
Suggested Projects, viii, 10, 22, 32,
    41, 52, 59, 68, 70, 77, 87,
    102, 106, 129, 156, 160,
    165–166, 172, 181, 187,
    199, 210–211, 214, 222,
    234, 238, 245, 250, 253,
    257, 267, 273, 286, 297,
    302, 310, 313, 318, 324,
    329
Suitability, 42
Supervisor, 328
Suzuki, 77, 239, 251–253
"Swinging Along," 114–115
"Switched-On Bach," 210
Syllables, 73
Symphony No. 5 of Beethoven,
    202
Syncopation, 105

Take-home, 136–137
Tanglewood, 41
Tapes, 211–222
    making, 215–216
    outside of music class, 214–222
    time, 216
Teaching skill, 21
Teaching technique, 21
Teacher
    aids, 304
    cooperation, 319–320
    performance, 325–326
Tempo, 16, 19, 21, 54–56, 67, 69,
    82, 178, 189–190, 197, 219,
    235–237
Tests, 20
Textbook records, 211–212